100.00

2013

Passivity Generation

Studies in the Psychosocial

Titles include:

Stephen Frosh
HAUNTINGS
Psychoanalysis and Ghostly Transmissions

Uri Hadar
PSYCHOANALYSIS AND SOCIAL INVOLVEMENT

Derek Hook
(POST)APARTHEID CONDITIONS
Psychoanalysis and Social Formation

Margarita Palacios
RADICAL SOCIALITY
Studies on Violence, Disobedience and the Vicissitudes of Belonging

Garth Stevens, Norman Duncan and Derek Hook
RACE, MEMORY AND THE APARTHEID ARCHIVE
Towards a Transformative Psychosocial Praxis

Also by Irene Bruna Seu

WHO AM I?
The Self and Ego in Psychoanalysis (*editor*)

FEMINISM AND PSYCHOTHERAPY
Reflections on Contemporary Theories and Practices (*co-editor*)

Passivity Generation
Human Rights and Everyday Morality

Irene Bruna Seu
Department of Psychosocial Studies, Birkbeck, University of London, UK

First published 2013 by
PALGRAVE MACMILLAN

Palgrave Macmillan in the UK is an imprint of Macmillan Publishers Limited, registered in England, company number 785998, of Houndmills, Basingstoke, Hampshire RG21 6XS.

Palgrave Macmillan in the US is a division of St Martin's Press LLC, 175 Fifth Avenue, New York, NY 10010.

Palgrave Macmillan is the global academic imprint of the above companies and has companies and representatives throughout the world.

Palgrave® and Macmillan® are registered trademarks in the United States, the United Kingdom, Europe and other countries.

ISBN 978–1–137–30502–2

This book is printed on paper suitable for recycling and made from fully managed and sustained forest sources. Logging, pulping and manufacturing processes are expected to conform to the environmental regulations of the country of origin.

A catalogue record for this book is available from the British Library.

A catalog record for this book is available from the Library of Congress.

This book is dedicated to my daughter Lia Marta
And in memory of Stan Cohen

Contents

Figures

Acknowledgements

This book is based on a research project funded through a one-year fellowship from the Leverhulme Trust (RF&G/11158). Besides my gratitude to the Leverhulme Trust for enabling me to conduct this research, I am also highly appreciative of their general attitude towards grant holders which makes them the human face of research funders. In all my dealings with the Trust I have found them consistently supportive, understanding, flexible and truly interested in promoting good research, particularly when it tackles real-life problems. I am also grateful to Brunel University, UK, for granting me a BRIEF award, which funded the pilot studies.

The studies would not have been possible without the amazing participants, who truly and passionately engaged with the project. I am very grateful to them for their generosity and the honesty of their comments. Many thanks go to the final year Psychology students at Brunel University, who used the pilot studies for their dissertations and supported me in the various phases of the research. Particular thanks go to Simon Goodman and Julie Trevor.

My biggest intellectual debt is to the late Stan Cohen for the clarity of his vision, his extraordinary mind and his deep understanding of psychosocial phenomena. I was immensely fortunate to have the opportunity to spend many invaluable afternoons with Stan at Cafe Delancey, our designated 'denial spot', discussing denial, human rights and psychoanalysis. Those long and intense discussions, and the sharpness and compassion of his insights, influenced my thinking enormously, and without them this book would not have existed. I am grateful to Stan for too many things to mention here; his precious friendship and the largess of his heart are simply irreplaceable. I miss him terribly.

Many people contributed in various ways to this book. I am grateful to the many who read and commented on early drafts of my work, either for intellectual content or for proofreading, in particular David Sutherland, Stephen Frosh, Shani Orgad, Sharon Shoesmith and Camilla Sutherland, and the members of my writing group, in particular Ros Gill, Ann Phoenix and Rose Capdevila. Thanks also to Jasper Sutherland for the 'web of passivity' drawing and the many imaginative suggestions for the 'perfect book cover', and to Camilla Sutherland for her patience and perseverance in tracking down those ever elusive references. I am really grateful to the Palgrave editor, Nicola Jones, for her understanding and calm and clear support throughout, and to the series editors, Stephen Frosh, Wendy Hollway and Peter Redman, for going through the manuscript with a fine-tooth comb and for their many helpful comments; the book is greatly improved as a result.

Many other people made this book possible in various and invaluable ways. Thanks go to dearest Ros Gill, muse and auxiliary ego, for being who she is and for her precious friendship. I am grateful to all my friends for their trust and support, in particular Wilma Mangabeira, Margit Veje, Julian Ibanez de Opacua, Colleen Heenan, Lindsay Fraser, Graham Pickup, my Sardinian 'sisters' Mariella Setzu and Carla Fumagalli, and Margo Picken. Special thanks go to Monica Steuerman for the many years of vital Wednesdays, and to Anna Ardovini and Martina Peris for all their invaluable work behind the scenes, and the many heart-warming chats and hysterical giggles over *caffellatte*. Really thanks – I could not have done it without you.

Huge thanks go to my family here – David, Lia Marta, Camilla, Jasper – and in Italy – Luciana, Efisio, Stefano e Ornella – for their love, tolerance, help and support. Special thanks go to my wonderful parents for their belief in education, for enthusiastically supporting my studies, and for always making sure I had books even when money was tight. I will be grateful for that forever.

Finally, my gratitude goes to irreplaceable Lenin and adorable Rigo(berta), for their unconditional love and for keeping me company, with their soft eyes and gentle snoring at my feet, during the many solitary hours of writing.

Foreword

Human rights activism involves many aspects – occasionally high-adrenalin, mostly mundane – but one of the most common features of this line of work is how much talking it involves. Staff meetings, informal meetings, corridor talk, debates and arguments over coffee or beer: human rights activists talk a lot. And one of the frequent causes of debate among activists is that elusive creature, 'the general public', or 'the ordinary person'. As researchers, campaigners and others fight over finalising the message of a draft publication, someone among us would always say 'the public is not ready for this', 'the public needs something else', 'ordinary people will react only if we do it like that' and so on. This may not be surprising, but the extraordinary aspect is that very rarely do human rights activists go beyond truisms, clichés and unsubstantiated arguments in these kinds of debates. In view of the meticulous ways in which human rights activists build their fact-finding and legal arguments, it is at times astonishing how little they invest in trying to find out how the 'ordinary person' actually reacts to their appeals. As someone who took part in many such debates over the years in several human rights organisations, I can attest that all too often we simply don't have a clue.

There may be several reasons for that. The belief in the notion of Speaking Truth to Power perhaps takes attention away from how people would perceive that Truth. The justified emphasis on ensuring the reliability and credibility of published information often does not leave time and resources to assess what happens to the information once it is disseminated. Organisations also often end up confusing ends and means, concentrating on counting the number of relevant appearances in the media (and of 'likes' on Facebook) rather than trying to find out how people understand those media reports and what – if anything – they do in response. Organisational inertia and at times a certain sense of arrogance and self-righteousness also contribute to this lack of attention to public reactions. But whatever the reasons may be, it is pretty clear that most human rights organisations do not try enough to understand how their audiences react to the information and appeals they publish.

In *Passivity Generation*, Bruna Seu has finally done just that: systematically investigate how ordinary people react to human rights information. Filling a major gap in the literature, she has used real-life examples of human rights appeals and meticulously analysed the responses of participants in dozens of focus groups, and the myriad ways in which people remain passive after being exposed to information on human rights abuses. This empirical approach, combined with developing a complex theoretical framework, results in a path-breaking contribution to the study of human rights practice as well as social psychology and psychosocial studies.

Seu's research on this topic started earlier with her collaboration with the late Stan Cohen, one of the most celebrated and influential figures in the sociology of human rights and the pioneer in studying how the public reacts to human rights information. He moved from the UK to Israel in the 1980s, already a legendary criminologist and sociologist, and got drawn into human rights work, co-authoring a very high profile human rights report on the use of torture by Israeli security services. The public reaction to this report, and especially the many ways in which Israelis justified their inaction after being exposed to what appeared to be clear proof of the use of torture, led Stan to begin studying the issue of denial in the context of human rights, a research that led later to his seminal book *States of Denial* (2001). Among Stan's many lasting contributions was establishing the notion that the work of human rights organisations could and should become the object of critical academic reflection, even by those who wholeheartedly sympathise with the goals of these organisations. Seu's work continues this approach, and breaks new ground in the understanding of the public reception of human rights appeals.

Passivity Generation set out to explore ordinary people's everyday reactions to information on human rights violations: how people understand and talk about human rights, how they view their responsibility toward victims and how they often justify their inaction. Her research generated a trove of fascinating data which should become required reading for anyone involved in the production or study of human rights campaigning. One of the important findings, for example, is the animosity people often feel toward the human rights campaigners themselves, especially when campaign materials try to elicit guilt from the public. Her theoretical discussions eschew mono-causal simple explanations of inaction, going beyond the one-liners such as 'compassion fatigue' or 'psychological numbing', and instead offer a complex and dynamic explanatory model. Under the heading of 'passivity' emerges a dynamic and fluid picture of personal, social, cultural and political forces interacting with each other to produce the reaction to human rights appeals.

This multi-layered and multi-faceted framework is not only fascinating academically but also points to the potential of interventions and change: audiences are more sophisticated, for good and for bad, than many NGOs and academics assume, and levels of passivity can shift up and down. Therefore, better-attuned materials from NGOs can play a part in reducing passivity. This insight can counter some prevailing views among activists, who often adopt two types of almost fatalistic approaches to this issue. One is of the 'if only people will know' kind: that NGOs should spread the word about abuses, and public action will automatically follow. The other is of the 'people don't want to know' kind: that it is hopeless trying to get people's attention to distant suffering. Either formulation involves a tacit shirking of responsibility, a reluctance to engage with how human rights appeals can be modified to elicit a better response. Seu's work, demonstrating how people process human rights information in complex and shifting ways, also puts the ball back in the campaigners' court: it shows that they should neither be complacent nor lose hope, but should try to understand how they could work more effectively. *Passivity Generation* should, and will, be carefully studied by both practitioners and scholars of human rights.

Ron Dudai
The Martin Buber Society of Fellows,
Hebrew University of Jerusalem

1
Introduction

Human rights violations, including war crimes and crimes against humanity, continue to be a prominent feature of world affairs. Torture, unfair trials, abuse of civilians in armed conflict and discrimination against vulnerable minorities are only some of the abuses that take place, both in autocratic regimes and in democracies. Crimes against humanity are currently being committed in more than 160 nations.[1] Torture is used in one in three countries, often while the society itself continues to maintain formal contours of democracy (Cohen, 2001, 1996). At the same time human rights abuses continue and go unpunished even in countries that have ratified the Convention against torture.[2]

Legal systems and intergovernmental organisations (IGOs) have often proved ineffectual in their efforts to enforce respect for human rights. Consequently non-governmental organisations (NGOs) have disseminated information in an attempt to mobilise action through responses from the public. NGOs have become crucial actors in human rights campaigning (Hopgood, 2006; Price, 2003; Keck and Sikkink, 1998), and a key aspect of their activity is the 'mobilization of empathy' (Brown and Wilson, 2008).

A major part of human rights work is the production of written reports, which are both a means to an end – whereby 'information is collected, checked, standardized, and disseminated as part of a wider strategy to prevent violations and implement universal standards' – and an end in themselves – based on the belief that even without results there is an absolute duty to convey the truth, to bear witness (Cohen, 1996:517). Human rights reports are now considered to have established themselves as a genre (Dudai, 2006) and, arguably, *the* key genre of human rights publications.

A sub-case of human rights advocacy consists in asking Western audiences to act for the benefit of people in distant countries. This type of communication (in the form of campaigns and appeals) is less legal in style and less laden with information than human rights reports, which are designed to circulate within a closed circuit of other human rights organisations, governments or intergovernmental bodies (Cohen, 1996).

Crucially, and in contrast to human rights reports, human rights campaigns and appeals are widely available to the public and, together with what is generated through the media, the most visible source of information on human rights violations. What is common to both types of human rights communication (reports and campaigns/appeals) is that their effect on the wider public remains unknown and unmonitored (Cohen, 1996).

The success of human rights campaigns is increasingly dependent on the ability to successfully elicit an effective response from the public. These appeals are designed to encourage the public to engage with the protection of human rights in two ways. The first is to put pressure on governments, or non-state actors, in order to stop abuse in ways ranging from letter-writing to consumer boycotts. The rise of the internet and internet-based social networks has increased the options for such public pressure, without which few human rights campaigns would succeed. The second is to promote fundraising activities so that independent NGOs and human rights NGOs can continue to operate.

Human rights campaigns and appeals inform the public about human rights abuses in order to elicit compassion and mobilise people to respond and act for distant others. But the assumption that 'if only people knew, they would act' often proves wrong (Slovic, 2007a,b; Cohen, 2001; Geras, 1999). Not only does the public response barely match the scale of the atrocities, but the information seems to drop into some kind of 'cognitive black hole' (Seu, 2011b; Cohen and Seu, 2002; Cohen, 1996). The key challenge in human rights campaigning, therefore, is to understand what happens to human rights information when it reaches the public, in order to avoid its neutralisation and instead promote proactive responses from audiences.

One of the challenges in communicating with the public involves bridging the gap between the concept of human rights in terms of norms and legal structure, and people's ordinary understanding of human rights (Christenson, 1997; Bowring, 1994). While the former is generated within a universalising legal system, the latter is being constructed within people's specific historical, ideological and emotional frameworks. A recent study conducted by the Equality and Human Rights Commission shows basic ignorance and confusion about human rights among the British public (Ballagan et al., 2009). Thus it seems urgent to gain detailed insight into the ways in which human rights information and appeals are understood by their target audience, in order to promote sustainable and successful campaigning. It is essential for human rights organisations to know how their appeals are received so that they can translate people's knowledge about distant suffering into moral response and action whilst at the same time maintaining impartiality and factual accuracy in their appeals (Dudai, 2006). Yet hardly any research has been carried out in this important field, and human rights organisations lack the means to carry it out themselves.

Passivity Generation reports on a series of studies set up to explore what happens to the knowledge related to human rights violations when it reaches the public. The research was designed as an exploratory and inductive 'bottom-up' investigation with the purpose of generating rather than testing theory on this empirically neglected and under-theorised topic.

What happens in the gap between knowledge and action has been of interest to many different disciplines and schools of thought, each addressing specific aspects of the phenomenon from within their specific epistemological and intellectual traditions. This greatly complicates the task of delineating the intellectual boundaries of this book. Literature on human rights and on public understanding of, and attitudes towards, human rights is clearly relevant to *Passivity Generation* and so is the vast literature on prosocial behaviour, social responsibility and altruism. Issues discussed under the umbrella of 'the politics of pity', distant suffering and problems of representation of distant suffering are also important, as are debates in moral philosophy and research into moral reasoning. The bordering fields of humanitarianism and charitable behaviour also bring important insights.[3]

This is not an issue simply of the integration of bodies of research and current debates, but also and more importantly of how to define, and crucially how to *think*, their topic, as inevitably this is determined and constrained by how the issue is framed in the first place. This book aims to understand the psychosocial conditions and processes that generate passivity in members of the public, in the fabled 'ordinary person'. Only a psychosocial lens allows proper nuanced consideration of socially constructed factors, psychological and emotional states, biographical factors and the subjective capacity for agency to resist, comply, integrate and negotiate all these elements. The psychosocial approach offered in this book does not just explore each of these domains independently, but pays attention to the very important dynamics *between* the domains.

A vignette from my childhood might help to convey my view of the psychosocial field I aim to capture. Once I stood transfixed in front of a most curious shop window. I don't remember what the shop was selling; it was either a stationery shop or a hardware store. The 'thing' I saw in the window did not easily fit into a recognisable category. At first it appeared to be a shallow tray full of live buzzing bees. Intrigued by how anybody would want to keep bees in their shop window, I stood there and studied the tray. On closer examination I realised that these were not real bees, but metal ones each stuck, I presume, on a magnet. As each bee was attracted into the magnetic field of another, it moved in that direction, thus relinquishing the bees it was attracting and breaking the original and temporary balance, and in turn generating a series of other attractions which would then be broken, and so on. Because the distance between bees was so precisely calibrated, individual bees never really got very far, but would get in and out of each other's magnetic field, creating a movement in all directions with no discernible order but engaging the bees in a perpetual, dynamic movement.

This curious object, which I now understand to be a miniature version of what would be defined in physics and chemistry as 'dynamic equilibrium',[4] came back to me when reading the data generated in the focus groups as a fitting representation of participants' psychosocial habitus. People, like the bees in the tray, are affected by many forces, ranging from the global geopolitical to the most intimate emotional reactions and personal experiences, through relatively smaller social and interpersonal contexts. All these influences or 'forces' are not passively submitted to, but negotiated with, resisted, accommodated and influenced in turn. Applying the principle of dynamic equilibrium to public responses and reactions to human rights issues enables us to capture the 'hovering' and unstable nature of action and inaction.

The magnetic bee tray thus could be a useful representation of what the psychosocial field of public action and inaction looks like and how it operates. Whilst it is important to know what prompts members of the public to respond proactively – in whatever way – this book is concerned with public passivity, broadly encompassing any lack of response, be it in terms of emotions, cognition and/or action. By viewing public responses in terms of a dynamic equilibrium, I want to resist a simplistic approach to public passivity. Rather, I want to unpack the notion of passivity through the idea that the manifested stillness, here defined as passivity, is the overt manifestation of a dynamic interplay of forces. Thus framing public passivity as a dynamic equilibrium doesn't dispute the end product of passivity, but engages with the dynamism and complexity underpinning and leading to the passivity.

By identifying and engaging with the different forces at play through this model, I want to draw attention to the paradoxically lively and generative potential of what ostensibly appears as inertia. Because a model of dynamic equilibrium describes a precarious stability which, by definition, is constantly under threat of disruption, it is possible to think of points of tension as potential openings for change and intervention. What appears as inertia or overall passivity can then be viewed as amenable to shifting either way: towards further passivity, but also towards active engagement with human rights issues.

The idea of a dynamic equilibrium graphically represents how members of the public are affected by structural and societal conditions that foster passivity as well as personal biographical and intra-psychic factors inhibiting action. All these factors, even when not dominating the individual, are nevertheless always present and interact in dynamic equilibrium with other forces in a constant process of transition, negotiation and movement. The challenge in conceptualising and writing about such a complex and incessantly moving dynamic is twofold. First is how to stay close enough to the details and the interaction of each component which generates passivity in order to arrive at a nuanced and detailed understanding of it whilst simultaneously holding the meta-level of how it is situated within the wider psychosocial field where it interacts with other forces. Second is how to arrive at conclusions that do justice to each force and the interaction between them, without flattening the dynamism of the interactions. Undoubtedly, it is not possible to achieve this through a linear trajectory as the psychosocial processes this book describes are far from 'neat and tidy'.

Passivity Generation is an attempt to engage with, and make sense of, the complex and fluid nature of public passivity. The overarching motivation behind this book is to offer an integrated multidisciplinary exploration of the multifaceted and multi-factorial phenomenon of public passivity in response to human rights violations. The emphasis is on the ordinary person's everyday understandings and reactions to information on human rights violations.

The book has four main aims. First, it aims to map out scripts, 'ways of talking about' and understanding human rights and their violations. How does the public understand human rights? Through which meanings and schema does the public make sense of human rights violations?

The book is not concerned with abstract formulations; rather, it is interested in everyday understandings and in identifying values and beliefs through which information about human rights violations is processed and understood.

The second aim is to understand how members of the public view their social responsibility towards sufferers of human rights violations and human rights in general, and what kind of actions they take, or do not take, to express their responsibility. In this context, the book aims is to engage with everyday moral reasoning. How do members of the public understand their responsibilities and justify their inaction? How do individuals draw their moral boundaries and determine who and what are, and are not, their responsibility?

Third, *Passivity Generation* aims to understand the psychosocial factors that foster or prevent proactive responsiveness towards human rights. What socio-political, ideological, biographical, inter- and intra-psychic events and factors enable meaningful engagement with human rights issues? Through a psychosocial framing, the book pays close attention to processes of denial, both as psychodynamic operations of defence mechanisms activated by information about human rights violations and as ideologically laden vocabularies of denial.

Fourth, the book intends to offer empirically grounded recommendations to policy makers and to NGOs about better ways of informing the public about human rights and their violation, and how to facilitate a more meaningful, deeper and longer-lasting public engagement with human rights issues that goes beyond donations and short-lived participation.

The book opens with a multidisciplinary review of central themes and concerns of scholarly work on public passivity. Chapter 2 schematically charts how public passivity has been understood, discussed and researched so far. As well as providing a mapping of the disciplinary frames through which passivity has been understood, Chapter 2 introduces the psychosocial framework which will inform the book as a whole. It also gives key information about the studies on which the book is based.

Chapter 3 identifies broad patterns of explanations, justifications and reactions used by participants to 'talk about' human rights violations and their response to them. By looking at the most frequently used themes, the intention is to map out a typology of what issues, justifications, reactions and understandings are available to the public when discussing human rights violations. These themes are considered to be similar to Lakoff's (2010, 2008) scripts and frames, whose function is to provide a ready-made understanding of human rights and their violations. In this chapter, as in the rest of the book, these are considered as moral scripts, not only because they are used by participants to reason and differentiate between right and wrong and justify their responses, but also because they were embedded in wider normative considerations about participants' duties and responsibilities. Thus the second aim of this chapter is to reflect on the complex, contradictory and ambivalent nature of everyday moral reasoning. Finally, the chapter looks at how scripts intertwine and link with each other, producing complex and multi-layered justifications and understandings that, like strands in a web, lend support to each other and make the web 'sticky' and ostensibly stable and resistant to change.

The mapping contained in Chapter 3 begins to capture the intricacies of moral living and the complex dynamics taking place between stated values and their application. This theme is developed further in Chapter 4, which looks at the relationship between the public and NGOs, in particular in relation to what Darnton and Kirk (2011) call the 'transactional frame'. One of the unexpected findings of this study was that NGOs mediate the public's relationship with distant suffering and human rights in specific and powerful ways, beyond the obvious function of literally being mediators of the information. The data draws attention to the many ways in which the public experiences and responds to NGOs. Chapter 7 engages with the affective component of the relationship between public and NGOs, while Chapter 4 looks at how it is managed through operations of denial. A close analysis of the repertoires used by participants shows how everyday and banal justifications are used to neutralise Amnesty International's moral claims, thus illustrating the power of denial in contributing to a widespread climate of passivity.

Chapter 5 focuses on how people connect, or do not, with suffering others in distant places. It starts with a brief review of how ideas about geographical distance, difference and otherness have been understood to connect to moral and social responsibility towards others who are distant or not part of one's close group of identification and belonging. Crucial to these debates is the issue of moral boundaries. The second part of the chapter analyses the mechanisms through which participants draw their moral boundaries, whilst the third and final part of the chapter interrogates processes of 'othering' through which populations involved in human rights violations are constructed.

Chapter 6 demonstrates how moral reasoning is profoundly embedded in biography and identity and explores the complex and variable modalities through which they affect individuals' responsiveness towards human rights violations. First, the chapter discusses examples of the identity work performed by participants' accounts of their responses to human rights issues. Participants' narratives make visible the ways in which moral positions are never neutral or pristine. Rather, they are saturated with passionate investment in the individual's identity and the need to establish a good sense of self. The chapter also looks at the role of biography in setting up paths of engagement with others' suffering and illustrates how, overwhelmingly, active engagement is prompted by direct exposure to others' intense suffering, rather than by abstract or normative principles. Additionally, the chapter engages with the thorny issue of what constitutes an optimal amount of personal suffering necessary to connect individuals with the suffering of others. It identifies two psychodynamic attitudes – reparative and repetitive – resulting from personal experience of suffering which determine a proactive or avoidant response to human rights and the suffering of others.

Chapter 7 focuses on the role of emotions in public passivity. It offers a psychosocial model of emotions that is attentive to both personal emotions and socially constructed justifications based on emotions. Particular attention is paid to the phenomenon of not engaging emotionally, or initially engaging then disengaging emotionally, often defined as compassion fatigue or psychophysical numbing. The model I present takes into account the psychodynamic (particularly in terms of intra-psychic conflicts and defences evoked in the process) and social aspects (in the form of socially acceptable narratives used by participants) of such processes. Three modalities in which emotions are involved in public passivity are identified. The first looks at members of the public as 'defended' (Hollway and Jefferson, 2000) and emotionally conflicted subjects and discusses instances in which participants hint at psychodynamic and intra-psychic conflicts evoked by information of human rights violation. In the second the public is the victim of secondary trauma from information about brutalities. The third looks at the commodification of emotions in responses to human rights information through which the public takes the position of consumers.

The concluding chapter draws together the strands of the book and reflects on the insights generated by the data. It considers how the findings might translate into recommendations for policy makers and NGOs on how to foster better communication with the public which engages them in human rights issues in more meaningful and sustainable ways.

2
Between Knowledge and Action: Multidisciplinary Frames and the Psychosocial

What happens in the gap between knowledge and action has been of interest to many different disciplines and schools of thought, each addressing specific aspects of the phenomenon from within its specific epistemological and intellectual tradition. In offering a specific framing, each discipline also offers explicit or implicit solutions and ways to promote change. These universes of understanding have developed in almost complete isolation from each other and have rarely benefited from cross-fertilisation.

This chapter asks the following questions: How has the problem of public passivity in relation to human rights issues been framed and understood so far? How have advocates and activists framed it to capture public attention and promote change?

The first part of the chapter critically reviews existing research, identifying limitations and contributions from various disciplines. The second part presents the theoretical framework of the book and explains why a psychosocial approach is the most fruitful in capturing the multi-layered complexity of public responses. The third and final section describes the study on which the book is based.

Mapping the framing of passivity

Public responses to human rights information involve a constellation of phenomena which so far have been studied in isolation from each other, making simple framing difficult. This greatly complicates the task of delineating the intellectual boundaries of this book.

The first section of this chapter looks at how public passivity has been approached, understood and conceptualised by different disciplines and how each discipline has made a claim that public passivity should be a matter of public concern. The multi-layered and tightly compressed literature offered below maps out the current state of play and how public passivity has been conceptualised and addressed within disciplinary contexts. The review offered here strategically and purposively captures specific intellectual traditions and identifies gaps and limitations in the conceptualisation of passivity.

As for the ways in which public passivity has been framed, the problem for NGOs is in terms of monetary donations and longer-term engagement with humanitarian issues, while Media and Communications attribute public passivity problems to communication and how the message about distant suffering has been constructed. For scholars interested in the 'politics of pity',[1] moral philosophers and some sociologists (e.g. Boltanski, Arendt, Singer, Geras), the problem is one of social responsibility, while social psychologists have concentrated on the factors that enable individuals to respond prosocially[2] or that interfere with helping behaviour.

Knowledge and insights produced by each of these frames rarely cross disciplinary boundaries and, constrained by their own epistemological foundations and interests, tend to offer isolated and insulated understandings. Crucially, and strikingly, in all this, the public, the ordinary person, so highly theorised, remains somehow unknown, but rather constructed deductively on the basis of these frames and the epistemology, philosophy and ideology underpinning them. The ordinary person juggling complex and competing demands has so far deserved little attention.

Public attitudes to and understanding of human rights

Before getting into a discussion about framings of public passivity in relation to human rights issues, it is important to make a short foray into current knowledge of public attitudes to human rights. Recent research into audience perceptions of human rights violations has been almost exclusively quantitative. Among such studies the aims are diverse, though all broadly governed by a common desire to interrogate and confirm a universalist conception of human rights. A dominant approach across these studies is the assessment of respondents' knowledge and support for the 30 articles of the Universal Declaration of Human Rights (Ballagan et al., 2009; Clemence et al., 2001; Doise et al., 1999, 1994; Macek et al., 1997; Diaz-Veizades et al., 1995) in order to quantify and categorise attitudes towards human rights more widely.

The work of Doise and colleagues dominates within this area. Following the social representations model, several researchers (Clemence et al., 2001; Doise et al., 1999, 1993) aimed to isolate the common frames of reference that govern responses to human rights. Their work reveals four distinct orientations towards human rights issues: *advocates* (favourable response to human rights), *sceptics* (less favourable responses to human rights), *personalists* (high personal identification with human rights but sceptical of governmental efficacy) and *governmentalists* (low personal identification but strong belief in governmental role in protecting human rights) (Doise et al., 1999). Stemming from this body of work, McFarland and Mathews (2005) isolate three human rights orientations: *endorsement* (general support), *restriction* (in favour of restricting human rights in moments of crisis) and *commitment* (blanket support regardless of personal or national cost). In terms of factors that inform responses to human rights, they found that social dominance orientation (SDO), dispositional empathy and ethnocentrism dictate support or opposition to human rights. In a similar study, Cohrs et al. (2007) propose that individuals' attitudes towards human rights – and subsequent human rights behaviour – can be categorised (and predicted) according to right-wing authoritarianism (RWA), social dominance orientation (SDO), personal values and political ideology. Since we see two studies that specifically analyse respondents' perceptions of human rights conditions within their own country (Carlson and Listhaug, 2007; Anderson et al., 2002). Both these studies support the finding that perceptions of human rights conditions are determined by the political reality of the country; the higher the level of political terror, the more negatively citizens will evaluate human rights conditions.

Within the UK, *Public Perceptions of Human Rights*, published by the Equality and Human Rights Commission in 2009 (Ballagan et al., 2009), marks an important move towards integrating both quantitative and qualitative approaches to the study of public perceptions of human rights. The study attempts to illustrate how human rights extend beyond the field of legislation into the realm of the individual and the community. It is unique in its attempts to explore if and how negative attitudes towards human rights can be changed through persuasion, debate and argument. The Commission states its intention to utilise results from its qualitative research to improve its communication with the public. Thus, the work pays close attention to the language used by participants when talking about values (which often coincide with human rights) and suggests that the Commission could employ this vocabulary in order to foster public support for human rights. Due to an absence of human rights terminology in respondents' discussions, the study urged the Commission not to assume that the human rights framework is widely understood by the public. The report concluded that there is confusion among the public about what human rights actually are and the legislation which surrounds them. Forty per cent of the public say they know a great deal or a fair amount about human rights generally, compared with 58 per cent who don't know very much or anything at all. Importantly, the results of this study found that respondents do not consider human rights abuses to occur in the UK; rather, they are something that is predominantly deemed to happen in other countries. Despite evidence that human rights have become an integral component of world culture (Meyer et al., 1997; Finnemore, 1996) superseding modernisation theory as the dominant way of discussing social change in the developing world (Rajagopal, 2003), the lack of detailed understanding among the public revealed by the Equality and Human Rights Commission's study indicates a need for more effective communication of human rights issues.

Media and communications[3]

Although Media and Communications has paid a lot of attention to audience passivity in response to distant suffering, the majority of empirical studies draw almost exclusively on textual and visual analyses. These media and communications studies critique media coverage of suffering as producing 'compassion fatigue' or overload in the media of information on suffering (Tester, 2001; Moeller, 1999), and explain audiences' lack of response and engagement as due to patterns of media coverage, such as repetition, routinisation, naturalisation, fetishisation and commodification of suffering, de-humanisation of sufferers, emphasis on certain emergencies and under-representation of others (Chouliaraki, 2006; Tester, 2001; Boltanski, 1999; Moeller, 1999; Benthall, 1993). Some have argued that the failure to represent victims of humanitarian disasters as human beings in their difference, and to encourage a message of an unconditional obligation to help distant strangers beyond borders, has deep connections with, and is partly responsible for, the broader crisis of pity and erosion of solidarity (Chouliaraki, 2012; Orgad, 2012; Lokman, 2011; Ong, 2011; Cottle, 2009; Nash, 2008; Silverstone, 2007). Silverstone's (2007) holistic view of media, mediation and morality suggests that while distant suffering might be one context where the media's moral work is pronounced, because it spotlights the relationship between the viewer here and the sufferer there, it must be concurrently connected to the broader structures of people's morality. Silverstone (2007) insists on a view of morality as inscribed in people's everyday lives, and stresses the need to connect its exploration to the ways in which the media in their multiple platforms, contexts, forms and genres, continuously shape and enact morality.

Most of the empirical studies on the mediation of humanitarianism focus on the symbolic (textual and visual) construction of violence and suffering by mediated images and narratives. Studies in this strand investigate a variety of types of representations, mediated forms and genres of distant suffering including news coverage of humanitarian disasters (Chouliaraki, 2006; Tierney et al., 2006; Moeller, 2006, 1999; Seaton, 2005; Gaddy and Tanjong, 1986), NGO appeals and campaigns (Chouliaraki, 2012; Nash, 2008; Vestergaard, 2008) and their interaction with media narratives and products (Richey and Ponte, 2011; Nash, 2008), celebrity (Goodman and Barnes, 2011; Richey and Ponte, 2011; Chouliaraki, 2010; Narine, 2010) and films (Chouliaraki, 2012; Narine, 2010).

These analyses reveal the visual and textual patterns, formulas, strategies, modes and conventions employed by the media and NGO depictions of distant suffering. Many focus on how sufferers are depicted in the scenes of suffering, and how specific ways of presenting and framing suffering position the Western viewer in particular asymmetric power relations to, and degrees of distance from, sufferers. On the basis of these analyses, authors argue about representations' capacity to shape spectators' understanding and judgements of distant suffering, and the extent and effect to which images and narratives cultivate and/or inhibit humanitarian commitment in the form of compassion, assistance beyond borders, and a sense of solidarity and obligation to act.

These studies highlight the systematic and consistent exclusions and biases in the mediation of distant suffering and how they are implicated in and entwined with cultural, political, economic and organisational interests. These observations underscore how particular choices of depicting suffering are inscribed in and in turn reproduce the power relations and injustices that they may seek to redress.

The psychology of (un)responsiveness

The prosocial literature is vast and diverse. What follows is not a comprehensive review of the prosocial literature but an outline categorisation of issues touched upon in recent psychological studies on public response to distant suffering and charitable behaviour. The literature can be roughly categorised as falling into two groups: studies that apply particular theoretical models to prosocial behaviour (e.g. theory of planned behaviour or social categorisation), and those focusing on specific factors influencing, positively or negatively, prosocial responses or aspects of them. For a critical review, see Seu (2010) and forthcoming.

In the latter category several studies focused on demographic factors, such as social class and gender (Piff et al., 2010; Nelson et al., 2006; Eagly, 2009), people's identities (Crompton and Kasser, 2010), 'altruistic personality' (Monroe, 2004, 2003, 2001, 1996; Oliner and Oliner, 1988), religious affiliation (James and Sharpe, 2007; Jonas et al., 2002), congruence between the 'target in need' and the recipient of aid (Oceja et al., 2010), depleted energy and low level of glucose (Gailliot, 2009), genetic predisposition (de Waal, 2009) and mood (Eisenberg and Fabes, 1991; Salovey et al., 1991; Williamson and Clark, 1989; Yinon and Landau, 1987; Piliavin et al., 1981).

Barry and Wentzel (2006) identified that the influence of friends increased prosocial behaviour, while others found that it was perceiving expressions of gratitude (Grant and Gino, 2010). The vividness, proximity and vicariousness of suffering positively affected the strength of sympathy, although excess of these factors (Loewenstein and Small, 2007) and information overload (Eckel et al., 2007) had the opposite effect. Among other factors, the following have been identified: 'the Scrooge effect', that is mortality salience (Jonas et al., 2002), the endorsing of self-transcendent values (Joireman and Duell, 2005), the relation between the victim and the public, for example, the 'identifiable victim effect' (Friedrich and McGuire, 2010; Friedrich and Dood, 2009; Kogut and Ritov, 2005; Small and Loewenstein, 2003), emotional regulation and varying sensitivity to human fatalities (Cameron and Payne, 2011; Olivola and Namika, 2009), particularly when the fatalities are expressed through statistical means (Small and Loewenstein, 2007).

Important findings have been generated through the application of self-categorisation theory to prosocial behaviour (Levine, et al. 2005; Levine and Thompson, 2004). Additionally, 'societal tilt', 'just world thinking', moral equilibration and similar psychological processes have been identified as important factors in mediating prosocial behaviour towards sufferers who do not share the same social categorisation (Taylor, 1998; Van Dijk, 1993c, 1992).

In terms of structures of values and morality, both social norms and personal standards have been found to affect prosocial behaviour, as well as social sanctions and rewards (Schwartz and Howard, 1982;

Reddy, 1980), fairness and perceptions of reciprocity (Gouldner, 1960), equity (Walster et al., 1978), social justice (Lerner, 1980) and the social responsibility norm (Berkowitz, 1972). Particularly notable are theories on the structure of human values, for example the circumplex model (Schwartz and Boehnke, 2004; Schwartz, 1992) and cross-cultural goals and gender-related patterns (Grouzet et al., 2005; Brock, 1998; Wiggins, 1998; Gilligan and Attanucci, 1988), with people with self-defining moral identities more likely to respond to requests for help (Aquino et al., 2010), while others (Bandura, 1999b) have identified self-regulatory mechanisms governing moral conduct.

Other researchers have focused on the role of ideology and political orientation (Feather and McKee, 2008; Cohrs et al., 2007), individuals' social capital (Brooks, 2005), and conceptions of responsibility and communal boundaries (Smiley, 1992).

A large amount of prosocial research has studied emotions, whether through cost–reward models or as 'arousal and affect' models (Dovidio and Penner, 2004).

There seems to be a consensus that people are aroused by and emotionally responsive to the distress of others (Fabes et al., 1993), with some giving biological and evolutionary explanations (Hoffman, 1990; Cunningham, 1985/1986; Vaughan and Lanzetta, 1980). In opposition to this view, the empathy-altruism model argues for a more complicated picture. The model defines empathic concern as an 'other-orientated' emotional response, such as sympathy and compassion congruent with the welfare of another person (Batson and Oleson, 1991:63), while others (Cialdini et al., 1997) suggest that empathic concern contributes to a greater sense of 'oneness' between self and other.

Two sets of experimental findings are worth mentioning in this context. Shaw et al. (1994) have empirically documented the negotiated nature of emotions by showing that people can actively avoid or resist empathy when they become aware of the potential cost of their help. Other experiments have shown that arousal, far from being universally consistent in its effects, is influenced by social factors like gender and age (Hoijer, 2004; Eisenberg and Lennon, 1983). These findings suggest that socially constructed meanings are never too far away even in what might appear as universal physiological responses.

In conclusion, there is a growing awareness in the field of social psychology that helping is a complex, multi-determined behaviour and is shaped by a mixture of cognitive and affective processes, involving self and other directed motives, and has consequences that are central to one's self-image and social relationships (Dovidio and Penner, 2004:271).

There are several problems with these bodies of work. Although they fruitfully engage with the question of public passivity, and they appear to address similar issues, in fact, they address very different questions. The mismatch is not due simply to disciplinary differences, but also to disparities in epistemology and methodology. To begin with, studies of representations are based on textual and visual analyses of communication and do not tend to involve audiences. On the other hand, the vast majority of psychological studies on audiences are based on surveys and laboratory experiments that use media representations as neutral stimuli.

In terms of the former, it is a common occurrence that findings from studies on communication are applied to audiences despite their not being involved, leading to dangerous assumptions (Ong, 2009). For example, a study that shows distortions in media coverage is wrongly taken to explain audience reactions. Investigating how representations shape and inform knowledge and action exclusively on the basis of textual and visual analysis is limiting, and therefore also misleading. Further, it introduces a risk of reinforcing a mechanistic and over-simplistic view of the relationship between media texts and reception as being a stimulus–reaction, a view that audience research has shown to be reductive and misleading.[4]

Psychological studies, on the other hand, are often deductive rather than inductive and exploratory, and confined to predetermined questionnaire questions. Although social psychologists have grappled to some extent with the complex relationship between what people say and do (the attitude–behaviour gap), overall psychological studies tend to neglect contradiction, ambivalence and dilemmas in moral decisions. Finally and importantly, mainstream scientifically inspired psychological studies actively avoid engaging with the culturally specific, situated and ideologically charged meaning of participants' stated attitudes. In short, societal forces figure very little in mainstream psychological research on helping and prosocial behaviour.

This has been recognised and challenged by critical psychologists. For example, the social psychologist Frances Cherry (1994) has interrogated the political and epistemological implication of the supposed 'neutrality' of psychology in studying bystander intervention. She argues that by moving in as closely as possible to the behavioural phenomena and casting the event in terms of independent variables (e.g. group size that affects dependent variables such as intervening behaviour), these researchers *chose* to 'veer away' from a socio-cultural analysis of the event. She concludes that the use of a 'scientific' approach, at the core of psychology's claim for neutrality and objectivity, is in fact in antithesis to a socio-cultural analysis (Cherry, 1994:40).

Sociology and media studies have, on the other hand, engaged with the political, ideological and cultural meanings underpinning the processes through which distant suffering is 'mediated'. But, by not engaging with the psychological, they are able to tell us very little about what happens in the 'black hole of the mind' – a blind zone of blocked attention and self-deception (Cohen, 2001:6). This 'black hole' describes the unexplored space between reception and (re)action, the space least theorised and empirically explored by any discipline so far.

Similar to Psychological and Media and Communications', empirical studies carried out by the non-profit and voluntary sector are very specialised and tend to mainly concentrate on factors that might increase donations and charitable behaviour. With the exception of the Finding Frames,[5] these studies offer no critical self-reflection of the transactional frame which is assumed as the norm in the interaction between NGOs and the public. We then have survey studies on human rights attitudes, which only provide broad-brush patterns of public understanding and response and don't engage with complexity and contradictions. At the other end of the spectrum moral philosophy only engages with public response in the abstract and is often too bogged down by a focus on normative views of how the public 'ought' to be to produce helpful insights into how the public actually is.

Compounding the problem, these bodies of knowledge almost never communicate across disciplinary divides thus producing a fragmented picture of what the problem of public passivity is about and its solutions.

The collapse of social responsibility: The bystander–perpetrator continuum

As an exception to what is stated above, a disparate group of philosophers, sociologists and social psychologists have found common ground despite their different disciplinary backgrounds, in a shared interest in public passivity. They regard it as failure of social responsibility, primarily in terms of bystander behaviour in the context of the constellation victim–perpetrator–bystander. The main context and focus for this group of scholars has been genocide and, in particular but not exclusively, the Holocaust. Their key concern has been to identify the social, moral and psychological processes in operation when committing atrocities, in particular suspension of moral reasoning, but also the role of the bystander in being aware but not intervening. It is in this latter context that these theorisations of bystander passivity are relevant to this study. It should be acknowledged that this literature pertains to extreme situations in which atrocities are committed in close physical proximity to bystanders thus placing them in direct danger. However, many of these authors believe that what we know about bystander passivity applies beyond emergency and extreme situations and have argued that we need to understand bystander behaviour in its everyday banal manifestations precisely because of the crucial role it could play in preventing or aiding future atrocities. This is because, according to Staub (2003, 1989a,b), bystanders are affected by the same 'societal tilt' of the perpetrator and thus are in danger of also becoming perpetrators or supporting perpetrators through their inaction, or becoming rescuers, as described by Oliner and Oliner (1988) and Monroe (2004, 2003, 2001, 1996). Additionally, the bystander has great power. Through omission, bystanders have the power to exonerate and implicitly condone and encourage perpetrators; through resistance, demonstrating and pressurising government, they can positively impact on the escalation of brutalities (Staub, 2003, 1989b; Geras, 1999, 1995). What connects these specific bodies of research is not only their interest in genocide, especially the Holocaust and bystander behaviour, but that they all attempt to reach beyond the strictly individualistic framing of prosocial and bystander behaviour, to integrate social/structural-political and macro-phenomena with personal-psychological factors.

Public passivity involves a 'mental turning away' or 'moral indifference' and as such is a failure of moral and social responsibility. Human beings need not remain silent in the presence of atrocity; it is the 'responsibility of our kind to constitute a realm of saving norms and sustain these by their actions' (Geras, 1999:10). Geras addresses the 'moral tension set up between the enormous suffering of some people and the blank inaction of others' in the language of political theory by referring to a *contract of mutual indifference* according to which '[i]f you don't come to the aid of others who are under grave assault, in acute danger or crying need, you cannot reasonably expect others to come to your aid in similar emergency'(Geras, 1999:28). This, he claims, is not a purely hypothetical construct set behind a screen of abstraction which separates us from what we know and what we are, but 'it is rather a model of the world we really inhabit [...] The state of affairs described by this contract of mutual indifference is close enough to the actual state of affairs in our world as to portray accurately the relations generally prevailing between most of the people in it (Geras, 1999:29).

This bleak viewpoint is echoed by Bauman (1991), who attributed an important role to the physical and mental distance created by the Nazi regime between the victims and the rest of the population. He argued that "it is precisely the tendency of present day industrial society to extend inter-human distance to a point where moral responsibility and moral inhibitions become inaudible" (Bauman, 1991:192). Similar ideas are put forward by Baum (1988:84), who also uses the definition of moral indifference to describe 'an ethics of distance and distant consequences'.

Public passivity framed as socio-psychological dynamics

The work of Staub (2003, 1996, 1993, 1989a,b) has focused on the study of the socio-psychological mechanisms underpinning genocide and mass killing. He, like Cohen (2001), views the key actors involved in atrocities as a triangle: victims, perpetrators and bystanders. One of the key contributions made by Staub is his theorising of the figure of the bystander as being on a continuum with the perpetrator, always embroiled and implicated in the atrocities through the bystander's potential of aiding through omission or resistance by various means. Bystanders often encourage perpetrators, and they themselves are changed as they passively face the suffering of victims. However, bystanders also have great potential power to inhibit the evolution of increasing destructiveness. The perpetrator–bystander continuum is based on the sharing of the 'cultural tilt', as well as difficult life conditions and resulting motivations.

One of the psychological processes identified by Staub as shared by perpetrators and bystanders is 'moral equilibration' (Staub, 1990), which includes devaluation of groups, just-world thinking, and self-distancing by euphemisms or by an objectifying perceptual stance that reduces empathy. In an earlier work he argues that, because it is extremely difficult to see others' suffering when one does nothing about it, passive bystanders increasingly distance themselves from victims and it becomes progressively less likely that they help them (Staub, 1989b). Further, he suggests that the attribution of responsibility (just-world thinking in terms of the victim and self-serving attribution of low responsibility and controllability to the self) may be self-serving and immoral and used by bystanders to reduce their empathic response to the suffering.

Similar processes are also identified by Albert Bandura (1999a,b), who frames them as 'moral equilibration'. Bandura is interested in explaining the alleged pervasiveness of moral disengagement in all walks of life by formulating an 'agentic' theory of morality, in opposition to most theories of morality which are confined to cognition about morality. Bandura's 'agentic' social cognitive theory looks at the mechanisms by which people come to live in accordance with moral standards (Bandura, 1999a,b, 1991, 1986). It focuses on the self-regulatory mechanisms, rooted in moral standards and self-sanctions, through which moral reasoning is translated into actions. Bandura conceptualises the moral self as 'embedded in a broader, socio-cognitive self-theory encompassing self-organising, proactive, self-reflective, and self-regulative mechanisms' (Bandura, 1999a:193). Central to this theory is the idea that the self-regulatory mechanisms do not come into play unless they are activated through social and psychological manoeuvres [sic] by which moral self-sanctions can be disengaged from inhumane conduct. Particularly important for our purposes is Bandura's theorisation of moral agency as always situated and negotiated through social realities and people's own life trajectories and biographies.

The most robust and nuanced socio-psychological study of public passivity to date is Cohen's (2001) *States of Denial*, where Cohen conceptualises passivity as generated through processes of denial. He claims that expressions of denial are complex, psycho-social phenomena, neither simply 'natural' nor 'static', and that the personal and political ways in which we avoid uncomfortable realities are deeply layered at the level of both personality and contemporary culture (Elliott and Turner, 2003). Thus Cohen's work (Cohen, 2001, 1995; Cohen and Seu, 2002) offers a conceptualisation of public denial as both intra-psychic and social process.

Cohen (2001) draws attention to the culturally available accounts of justifications and excuses that form the vocabulary of moral passivity within our society. He grapples with the cultural, political and psychological factors involved in the complex variety of modes of avoidance we all use to protect ourselves both from unpalatable realities and from our responsibility towards the suffering of others. Cohen offers a typology of three distinct, although at times overlapping, types of psychosocial denial: literal, interpretive and implicatory. In the first – literal, factual denial – the fact or knowledge of the fact is denied: for example, 'my husband could not have done that to our daughter'; 'there was no massacre'. In interpretive denial, the raw facts are not denied but given a meaning different to that which seems apparent to others: for example,

'I am a social drinker, not an alcoholic'; 'this was population exchange, not ethnic cleansing'; 'this was not torture, but robust and legitimate interrogation'. The observer disputes the cognitive meaning given to an event and re-allocates it to another class of events by changing words, using euphemisms or adopting technical jargon. Finally, implicatory denial refers to those explanations that do not deny the realities of the event, or their conventional interpretation, but deny the 'psychological, political or moral implications that conventionally follow'. For example, 'what can an ordinary person do?'; 'someone else will deal with it'.

In the context of this typology, Cohen refers to 'the multitude of vocabularies – justifications, rationalisations, evasions, – which we use to deal with our awareness of so many images of unmitigated suffering' (Cohen, 2001:8). He argues that these vocabularies are increasing and becoming more convoluted as they are used in an attempt to bridge the moral and psychic gap between 'what you know and what you do'. Notably, Cohen states that the techniques of evasion, avoidance, deflection and rationalisation should draw on good, that is believable, stories. He draws on Wright Mills's work (1940), according to which accounts of denial are not mysterious internal states, but typical vocabularies with clear functions in particular social situations. "Accounts are learnt by ordinary cultural transmission, and are drawn from a well-established, collectively available pool. An account is adopted because of its public acceptability. Socialisation teaches us which motives are acceptable for which action" (Cohen, 2001:59). Hence, a denial account does not simply give a plausible, acceptable story about an action ('this is what I do'), but also provides moral accountability for the speaker ('this is why what I do is alright'). Such moral accounting takes a variety of forms in denial: from the psychological techniques of rationalisation, defence mechanisms and disavowal, to the sociological forms of apologies, normalisation and neutralisation.

While acknowledging the socially constructed nature of these vocabularies of denial, Cohen also recognises the co-existence of intra-psychic dynamics in operation in denial. He talks of 'splitting' as a key mechanism in denial that allows people, in both private and public life, to disconnect from painful or uncomfortable realities, thus retreating into a 'twilight zone' of simultaneously knowing and not knowing. While noting that some 'switching off' is necessary in order to retain our sanity, Cohen argues that our rising inability to 'face' or 'live with' unpleasant truths is producing 'wholesale pathologies in the form of alienated individuals and remote communities' (Elliott and Turner, 2003:132).

Conflict, ambivalence, ambiguity, contradiction and complexity are key components of Cohen's formulation. These are also fundamental to the psychosocial investigation of the 'passivity generation' offered in this book. Connecting these theoretical formulations with empirical findings is no easy task as the domains that a psychosocial analysis aims to bring together have historically been kept strictly separate. Socio-political and deep psychological understanding of subjectivity have been considered as belonging to separate, sometimes opposite, realms. Frosh (2003:1547) eloquently summarises the complexities of the relationship between the 'social' and the 'psychological':

> the strict division between individual and social risks the Scylla of reducing one to the other (so that, for example, the social is seen as no more than the free interactions of individuals, or the individual is seen as fully constituted by her or his social class, or gender or 'race' position), and the Charybdis of essentialising each element so that the social is 'bracketed off' in discussions of the individual, or vice versa.

Frosh, with many others, recognises the sheer difficulty in conceptualising the 'psychosocial' as an intertwined entity: 'to see the social as what constructs the personal, without losing sight of the "realness" of that personal domain, is a vastly difficult task' (Frosh, 2003:1564).

Despite these difficulties, a growing number of social scientists have argued for the need for psychosocial analyses that attend to both the socio-cultural–discursive and the personal–affective–biographical in the study of the social phenomena of, among others, public responses to climate change (Weintrobe, 2013), racism and crime (Gadd, 2009), and moral panics (Ailon, 2013). Similarly, I regard public passivity as something generated by a conglomerate of social *and* psychological influences. Geopolitical, socio-historical and contingently localised factors frame how the public comes to understand human rights and the boundaries of social responsibility and action. These social understandings acquire personal meaning and significance through individual emotional, biographical and intra-psychic trajectories (Seu, 2003). It is essential therefore to be attentive both to the social confines of discourse, and to personal and affective resonances and emotional stumbling blocks to higher responsiveness. Related to and underpinning these are personal sensitivities and specific personal and biographical experiences. Denial, both in the strictest sense of intra-psychic defence mechanism and in Cohen's (2001) more psycho-social rendition, is likely to be at play in public responses.

Thus this book is a prime demonstration of the need for both approaches and an illustration of the power of a psychosocial analysis which uses both psychoanalytic and post-structuralist lenses as the best way to capture and creatively engage with the multi-layered phenomenon of public passivity in response to human rights violations.

Theoretical frames and methodological tools

One of the key terms in psychosocial studies and central to 'passivity generation' is that of 'human subject', which reflects a set of fluid and contradictory ideas.

> What is central here is the ambiguity in the notion of the subject: it is both a centre of agency and action (a language-user, for example) and the subject *of* (or subjected *to*) forces operating elsewhere – whether that be the 'crown', the state, gender, 'race' and class, or the unconscious. The important point is that the subject is not a pre-given entity, or something to be found through searching; it is rather a site, in which there are criss-crossing lines of forces, and out of which that precious feature of human existence, subjectivity, emerges.
>
> (Frosh, 2003:1549)

Thus a psychosocial *subject* is

> a meeting point of inner and outer forces, something construct*ed* yet construct*ing*, a power-using subject which is also subject to power (Frosh, 2003:1564, italics in the original). As Butler (1997) put it, subjects are constructed by and in power: that is, they are constituted by social forces that lie outside them, but nevertheless they have agency which enables them to take hold of power and use it. Language is the arena in which this is manifested as language both constrains what can be said and allows space for subjects to exert control over it.
>
> (Frosh, 2003:1552)

Central to a discourse-analytic type of research is the notion that power finds powerful expression in forms of internal regulation, for example when forces from 'outside' work as self-discipline from 'inside'. Through this form of regulation, discourse produces subject-positions. To follow the production of these discourses and the subject-positions created within them is to understand the way power unfolds and oppression is perpetrated, as studying ideology is to study the ways in which meaning (signification) serves to sustain relations of domination (Potter and Wetherell, 1987). This 'lived' ideology' is made explicit in Chapters 3, 4, and 5, through discursive analyses that apply concepts and tools from Foucauldian discourse analyses, discursive psychology, Positioning Theory and Critical Discourse Analysis. The choice of specific discursive method was utilitarian and strategic, and aimed to match the particular aspect of lived ideology under observation with the most appropriate method, following principles which are discussed in detail in each of the chapters. As a whole, these methods are invaluable instruments to get to the collective cultural habitus and the individual strategic operations that foster and justify passivity towards human rights violations. Informed by these discursive methodologies, the textual analysis in this chapter presents a theorisation of the way in which audiences in the focus groups accounted for, explained and made sense of human rights abuses as a socio-cultural practice. As such it contains an analysis of audiences' ideological beliefs about causes of human rights abuses, a construction of the agents involved (in terms of both negative other-presentation of the people living in the countries where abuses are committed, and positive self-presentation) and the strategies used to frame accounts in a particular way.

However, events in the external world are not just mediated by language or discourse but, importantly, by people's states of mind, 'mental states' or 'internal worlds', 'where desire and anxiety act creatively on experience and transform it, so that its relation to reality can never be simply assumed' (Hollway, 2006:17). Internal worlds provide a template for our interactions with the outside world. According to Hoggett (2000:10), debates about identity which are informed by postmodernism seem unable to connect to raw human experience, particularly to emotional experiences such as anger, love or hatred. Others have expressed concern at the limitations of 'too flat, or "unlayered" or disembodied an account of the ways in which people actually form their political opinions and judgements' (Leys, 2011:436).

A psychosocial approach recognises the power of unconscious dynamics and the significance of psychic conflict (Roseneil, 2006). According to Hollway (2004:10), although power is the medium in which all human interaction occurs and the personal is to some extent political, 'there are aspects of our nature which are not only irreducible to the social but which give form and substance to the social itself'. Hollway and Jefferson's (2000:24) definition of the 'defended subject' is particularly germane:

The concept of an anxious, defended subject is simultaneously psychic and social. It is psychic because it is a product of a unique biography of anxiety-provoking life-events and the manner in which they have been unconsciously defended against. It is social in three ways: first, because such defensive activities affect and are affected by discourses (systems of meanings which are the product of the social world); secondly, because the unconscious defences that we describe are intersubjective processes (that is, they affect and are affected by others); and, thirdly, because of the real events in the external, social world which are discursively and defensively appropriated.

The psychosocial analysis presented here assumes that members of the public have emotional investments and psychodynamic inclinations that intersect with what is culturally available to them (Clarke and Hoggett, 2009; Frosh, 2003). However, the study started with a predominant focus on the social and discursive, and aimed to identify broad socially shared patterns of understanding and justifications. Accordingly the study used focus groups, rather than individual interviews, and asked broad and non-personal questions. Yet, despite this setting, most participants divulged personal information and, for the vast majority of time, framed their responses in personal terms, illustrated through individual experiences and anecdotes. Arguably, this could be explained discursively as a strategic move aimed at warranting one's statement through first-hand experience. Notwithstanding the possible truth of such interpretation, it offers a limited and limiting reading, particularly considering the affective charge and biographical significance of some participants' narratives. The affective contents were unprompted and seem to come from nowhere as they did not appear to relate to what had been previously said in the group or by the study's questions. Rather, they seemed to be propelled by an urgency 'internal' to the speaker. These stories manifested themselves as 'ruptures' and/or sudden and unaccounted changes in the speaker's emotional register. These contextually surprising, relatively irrational and emotionally intense communications that broke through the rational surface of otherwise coherent narratives seemed to hint at something else, otherwise unspoken but terribly important.

These affect-laden snippets could not be captured or made sense of through discursive analyses. As eloquently put by Wetherell (2012:128), 'We need an approach that can work with polyphonic and heteroclite subjectivities taking shape in complex, unfinished and plural social relations.' For this reason, psychoanalysis is used in the second part of this book as an alternative theoretical lens to engage with the emotional, affective and biographical contents of participants' narratives. Psychoanalytic readings use concepts of dynamic unconscious, conflicts and defences. The subject is seen as conflicted and defended. Psychoanalytically informed readings add thickness and complexity to participants' accounts. They also provide insight into important dynamics in public understanding of and responses to human rights issues which haven't been documented so far.

In summary, the psychosocial analyses offered in this book situate psychic and social realities side by side, in a dynamic, mutually determining relationship to each other. They offer a psychosocial tapestry of meanings and connections that 'depend on the resources of shared languages and sign systems, cultural and historical repertoires, but worked through personal histories' (Wetherell, 2012:129).

The studies

The data discussed in this book were generated through a series of exploratory studies motivated by the need to know what happens in the gap between knowing and doing, and to understand what ordinary people feel, think and do when confronted with information about human rights violations. As shown above, overall this is empirically uncharted territory, thus the study did not aim to test, but rather to generate, theory and was therefore conducted in a fairly unstructured way, with participants given the lead in the discussion in order to foster the open and free voicing of their opinions and generate 'naturally occurring' dialogue.

Sixty-three participants took part in 12 focus groups to discuss their reactions to human rights appeals and information about their violations.[6] Participants' ages ranged from 19 to 66, and they represented a wide variety of self-defined ethnic and social class backgrounds.[7] The main study took place in multicultural London, UK, which was advantageous for the richness of the data. As well as British, the groups comprised participants from India, Pakistan, Canada, USA, Italy, Sweden, Finland, Kenya, Greece, the Netherlands, France, Spain, Caribbean, China, Thailand, Philippines and Bangladesh. All the main religions – Christianity, Islamism, Judaism, Hinduism and Buddhism – were represented.

The groups were specifically designed to be heterogeneous in order to sample views across a variety of perspectives. Participants were recruited through advertisements asking for volunteers to take part in an informal discussion about human rights abuses. The participants were paid a nominal fee for their participation. The main study took place at the University of London, UK, and was conducted by the author with the help of a research assistant; the first two pilots at Brunel University, UK; and the third in a pub in Middlesex, UK.

Participants were asked to read the material put before them and pay attention to their thoughts and emotional reactions before sharing these with the group.

Although the book discusses a considerable amount of data and ideas, many things are inevitably left out or rendered invisible. For example, despite the obvious advantages of working towards a typology, the effect is that individual extracts are taken out of context and most of the force of the interaction is lost. The other danger is that concentrating on passivity, even though it is the topic of this book, might end up giving a distorted view of what took place in the focus groups and, by extension, the kind of debates that were around at that time. The next, long extract attempts to ameliorate these problems by illustrating the heated dissent that took place in some of the groups. The extract contains some of the themes to be discussed in detail later in the book and exemplifies the contextualised emergence of the themes as they were introduced, picked up and/or dropped in the course of the discussion. As such, the extract gives a glimpse of the frequent and familiar low-level chaos taking place when excited people talk across each other, interrupt and to some extent ignore what has just been said in order to put their point of view across. It also shows the passion as each participant expresses what they believe is right. The affective charge of individuals' positions and statements will be discussed later in the book. Here, the extract aims to give a flavour of the ebb and flow of passions in group dynamics.

The extract comes from the first pilot. Capital letters indicate when voices were raised and square brackets when people talked at the same time.[8]

[P1] Bruna: [...]. I'm sure you're aware there is a campaign going on at the moment about the electrical batons that Britain is actually producing. So there is a case here [Amnesty appeal] about a Tibetan woman raped with one of those by a Chinese soldier. So, we are actually producing them.

Simon: We won't have them used in this country. Xxx[9] I know a lot of countries

Bruna: [Absolutely. So doesn't that bring it a bit, sort of, nearer home?

George:	Well no, because it is not being used here (Bruna: ah..).
Simon:	Well, if they WERE considered. (.) Sorry?
George:	Because they're not being used in this country. All I see is, well great, yeah, bring the economy back up a little bit selling them to everybody else.
John:	It's funny, because you're talking about that (.)
Simon:	[Well I haven't got a problem with that. [general laughter]
Bruna:	What's your problem with that?
John:	[You're talking about that and, and I saw something on television that showed you this baton and what it does and, and you (.)
Simon:	[Which batons are you talking about? I'm not talking about
John:	[Well the whole lot. They, they've shown you (.)
Richard:	[Look what happened in the Kibbutzes, it xxx a nightmare (.)
Simon:	[NO, no. I agree with you. But it's a step up (.)
Richard:	[OR, WHAT.
Simon:	If, if they, they weren't produced in this country, (.) there's people backing an awful lot of money on it.
Richard:	If we don't produce them, someone else will.
Simon:	RIGHT. All right, so that's, that's that country's problem and you can put pressure on them to, to cease production. (.)
Richard:	[It's. The thing is, I don't think (.)
George:	[THE THING IS. HANG ON (.)
Simon:	[IF, if, if they want to produce the electric batons in their own country and use them in that country (.)
Richard:	[Yeah, but if they can't buy them anywhere at all, alright. (.) That's what you're saying. They'll find something else. They'll go back to sticks, or anything.
George:	The thing is, if we, if we. Do we have to be (.)
Dawn:	[That's not a very good argument.
Richard:	[NO, it's NOT. It's NOT. But, it, it, it comes down to xxx disarmament.
Bruna:	[Why, why did you not agree with that?
Dawn:	I don't agree with you. Because by producing them and selling them, you are supporting the use of them directly.
George:	[No, but you, do we have to be responsible for everybody using the products that we have made?
Dawn:	YES. Yes you do.
Simon:	[Of course you do. (.)
George:	[If they used, if they want to use a product that we make to do something like, in an incorrect way, then so be it.

Simon:	*So we, so you think that we can make anything in this country, (.) so long as we don't use it here? (.)*
George:	*[WELL NO. No. What I'm saying is, it shouldn't happen on your own doorstep. WE DON'T have to be responsible if they want to use the products to do whatever. (.)*
Dawn:	*[But what else do you use that for? It can't be used for anything good. IT'S NOT like (.)*
George:	*[Yeah I know, but I'm saying why should we take on the responsibility of everything else (xxx).*
Richard:	*I think, I think it comes down to economics to a certain point.*
Bruna:	*So economics are more important than human rights?*
Richard:	*[If you decide xxx (.)*
Simon:	*[That's exactly what you are saying to the politicians. You're saying that economics are more important than human rights. (.)*
John:	*[To the politicians. Yeah.*
Richard:	*Well it is. Otherwise we wouldn't have them (Bruna: but we are saying). Isn't that the catch. We could chuck all our defence money at human rights issues. Just abandon all defensive spending whatsoever and chuck it at human rights.*
Simon:	*But we're not talking about defence money. We're talking about (.) producing things for export. Who did we supply? Just about every bloody land that's killed thousands (.)*
Richard:	*[WE DID YEAH. Thousands. And that's supposed to be stopping them.*
George:	*But if we stop everything, (.) it's not going to stop these bad elements (xxx). That's what I'm saying. (.)*
Bruna:	*[So, so. I think we (.)*
Simon:	*[We're doing one thing at a time, surely. You know, you don't have to generalise and say, you know, stop everything. You can deal with one thing at a time. If electrical batons is the place to start, then so. These electric wire shields that can kill people and (.)*
George:	*[Lets, let's take on xxx the electric batons. You're going to say, well we're not going to export that to those countries. So basically everybody's going to lose their jobs of making them. So therefore you're going to have more unemployment in your own countries (.)*
Simon:	*[That's not an argument at all, it's complete bollocks, George.*
George:	*[Well no, no. It's, it's another side of the argument.*

My interest here is not in the content of the discussion, which is the topic of the rest of the book, but in the group dynamics. The extract illustrates the 'natural flow' of the conversation and how members of the group engaged passionately with each other while ignoring me most of the time. The quick retorts and switches in arguments show that the positions and arguments were familiar and well rehearsed, demonstrating that they pre-existed the group and that they were available in the social domain. Each view expressed in the group was taken as a token of that view being present in the population of which the group formed a small segment. This in turn points to the crucial role played by the wider social context in which the group operated.

To further demonstrate the importance of context, some of the comments can only be correctly understood within the localised context. For example, we can understand that Simon's comment in line 16 is ironic only in the context of what he says afterwards and because people laugh in response. The crucial meaning added by the tone is not conveyed by the words alone. Similarly, Richard's final comment in line 72 is quite ambiguous, and only by looking at the context we can see that it is sarcastic. The sarcasm comes at a key moment in the discussion when the group is becoming polarised and emotions are getting high. Just before Richard speaks, Simon swears in delivering his highly charged speech '*Who did we supply? Just about every bloody land that killed thousands.*' When Richard continues equally passionately, he drives the point home by shouting '*WE DID, YEAH*', followed by his corroboration that Britain contributed to the killing of thousands of people. His concluding sarcastic remarks might be an implied criticism of the rhetoric that justifies supplying arms in order to stop atrocities. It's unclear from what George says in response whether he just misses the sarcasm or whether he deliberately ignores it to strategically use Richard's words to argue for the benefits of continuing the production and export of weapons. This is followed by my attempt to summarise what is going on '*So, so, I think we..*', which is totally ignored. Simon then tries reasoning again and puts forward a 'one step at a time' kind of argument. George jumps at the opportunity to return to the previously used 'it's good for the economy' argument. At that point Simon loses his temper and attacks George: '*That's not an argument at all, it's complete bollocks, George.*' George is unperturbed and does not contribute to what seemed likely to escalate into a full-blown confrontation.

Beyond the importance of context, this commentary acknowledges the lamentable but inevitable loss of the richness, dynamism and complexity of group interactions which results from zooming in for a capillary reading of the data. It also illustrates the immense passion and intensity of feelings that human rights and their violations arouse in people. This is really important when thinking about public passivity, which in this study was rarely synonymous with indifference.

The groups were given three visual prompts: an appeal from an Amnesty International UK (AIUK) campaign for Afghanistan (Appendix 2), an article from the liberal British newspaper *The Guardian* (*The Guardian* (2013a) 'West "turns blind eye to Saudi torture"', http://www.guardian.co.uk/world/2000/mar/29/saudiarabia, accessed 21 June 2013), and a second appeal from an Amnesty International campaign against torture (Appendix 3). The first item, captioned 'This is an appalling story, don't read it unless you are prepared to help', started with the description of how a woman who had left her children at home while she went in search of food had been raped by soldiers, held for days and then found her children dead of hypothermia on her return. The item was chosen in collaboration with a fundraising officer at AIUK. I wanted an appeal that would be representative of AIUK's work, but that would also address the gap between knowledge and action. The appeal ended with the following statement: 'We have run out of words to describe pain and grief. The rest of the page is for you. Use it to write down your reasons for reading these stories and still refusing to help. If you can't think of anything to write, please fill in the coupon' (through which readers could join Amnesty International).

The theme of knowing but not acting also determined the selection of the second item. The caption of *The Guardian*'s article read 'West "turns blind eye" to Saudi torture' and depicted a man lying on the ground being flogged. It contained, as well as a standard article on human rights violations in Saudi Arabia, two case studies and a link to Amnesty International's Saudi Arabia campaign. I selected this article for several reasons: the information about human rights violations was coming from the media rather than an Amnesty Campaign, and I wanted to see whether audiences react differently depending on the means of information. The article, like the previous item, also addressed issues of passivity and hinted at political and economic reasons for the West's non-intervention. Furthermore, the reader was not asked to do anything or to give and, in the context of the article, Amnesty appeared as a figure of knowledge rather than a fundraiser.

Finally, the third item (Appendix 3) portrayed a steam iron and was captioned: 'Now imagine this was your face. If you can't imagine what it's like to be tortured let's bring it closer to home.' The image came with a Saturday newspaper and was chosen because it was geopolitically de-contextualised and invited the reader to identify with a victim of torture, rather than to engage with a particular political or humanitarian situation. At the end, the reader was invited to join Amnesty International.

The group leader (the author) followed an interview schedule in which participants were asked if and where they had seen human rights appeals and were invited to describe their emotional and cognitive reactions to the appeals. If they had noticed them they were asked whether they felt responsible and/or able actively to respond. There were also some general questions about what they knew about human rights, which human rights they considered important, whether they thought human rights were violated in the UK, and who they thought should be responsible for protecting and upholding human rights. The three pilots were used to fine-tune the focus group schedule, the final version of which was used unchanged for all the focus groups in the main study. The questions were introduced at different and opportune times in each group to respect the 'natural' flow of the discussion. The discussions were transcribed, made anonymous and re-read many times. A thematic analysis was used in the first instance to identify answers to the research questions as well as broad recurrent patterns not directly related to the original questions.

Reflection on the research process

Carrying out this research was an intensely rewarding experience for me. Most of the participants also seemed to find it, if not rewarding, at least interesting. Many recommended it to friends and some asked me at the end of the focus group to donate the nominal fee for their participation to Amnesty International. I declined, in order to preserve the study's autonomy, but invited them to do it themselves if they so wished. I think this gesture was an important statement that something meaningful had happened for the participants. It is banal to say that many factors contribute to the resulting data in a study, and that many of these factors inevitably remain unknown. It is still important to reflect on what can be gathered, if not fully known.

To begin with, participants seemed to be motivated by several factors. Here I am referring exclusively to observable factors, such as participants' behaviour in the group or information shared during discussion. Some wanted to take part in the study ostensibly because of their pre-existing, ongoing or past involvement in human rights issues. Others had an interest in the topic but no direct experience. These participants seemed to use the group as a way of thinking through their undeveloped positions and attitudes towards the topic of discussion. Others came because of circumstantial and particular reasons. Some came for the experience after feedback from a friend, and others were studying in related subjects. Curiosity drove other participants, while a minority came for the money (two participants who did not say a word). Additionally, because the first two pilots took place in the university where both the author and the research assistant were based, it is likely the participants would have come as favour to the research assistant, who was using the data for her final year project. That certainly was the case for the third pilot study, which was conducted in a pub where another supervisee of the author worked part time.

The initial question ('What are your thoughts and feelings reading this information?') tended to elicit stock or short answers to begin with. Then, after most participants had spoken and a sense of safety had begun to develop, the group relaxed and participants seemed able to share more personal details. Although group members were overall respectful of each other's opinions, discussions were often conducted passionately.

It is important to consider, although difficult to gauge, the effect of group dynamics on participants expressing their opinion in a focus group: for example, participants' desire to conform to the group, stand out from the group, or otherwise react to the situation. Peer pressure also seemed to play a role, with some dominant members of each group being very vocal and assertive and steering the discussion in a particular direction.

Equally, as part of group dynamics it is important to consider the effect of the research set-up. The participants were told very little in the recruitment information apart from being invited to a group discussion on human rights issues. However scant the information, this invitation conveyed the message that the project, and therefore the researcher (the author) considered human rights important. It is impossible to know exactly what impact this had on the participants, but it is likely that the advert attracted people who were either interested in human rights issues or felt they had some knowledge and expertise on the subject.

Regardless of the variety of individual motivations to take part in the study, it would be fair to expect that participants were inadvertently set up in a defensive position and felt that they had to prove their commitment to human rights issues and find explanations and justifications that would make sense to others. The fact that a view was heard in the group was taken as a token of that view being present in the population of which the group formed a small segment. Nevertheless, it is important to be mindful of the potential impact of the micro context of the study when thinking about the defensiveness in the participants' accounts.

Equally, my passionate interest in human rights inevitably influenced my approach to the research and the analysis of the data, which at times might appear to be judgemental towards the participants. This is certainly not my intention. My aim was never to judge individual participants, but rather to target the climate of acceptable passivity and denial towards human rights violations that in my opinion permeates our society. It is important to know and understand how members of the public resist appeals and 'do denial', not to blame individuals but in order to turn denial into acknowledgement. This, in my view is an urgent task and the primary motivator for the study.

I do not consider myself immune from the allure of the vocabularies of justifications used by the participants. Like them, I also struggle to resist the vocabularies' everyday and ostensibly innocuous familiarity and acceptability. At times I see through some of these vocabularies very quickly and I am able to resist them; other times I am hoodwinked more easily or find it harder to resist the allure of denial. It is from this sense of 'being in the same boat' with the participants that my doggedness comes, rather than from a position of judgemental superiority.

Equally passionate is the despair I frequently experience at the state of the world and with how quickly and how often history seems to repeat itself. At times I also feel the helplessness and futility so often expressed by my participants, when thinking of the number and scale of the obstacles preventing the principles contained in the Universal Declaration of Human Rights from becoming a reality for humanity as a whole.

These ongoing passions motivated me to undertake this research as an attempt to understand how a member of the public, an 'ordinary person', makes sense of the Declaration, its application, and what prevents human rights principles from being applied more successfully. It is also an attempt to identify and engage with the ideological habitus generating passivity towards human rights violations. This is what I want to challenge. The intensity in my analysis is not meant as an indictment of individuals, but rather as an attempt to unmask and confront the everyday, banal climate of acceptable passivity. The unmasking is not a 'truth-finding' mission; rather, it stems from the belief that only by identifying mechanisms and vocabularies of passivity is it possible to fight them and counteract them with alternative scripts. The aim of this book is to understand and to challenge this passivity and, in doing so, to contribute to greater social responsibility in regard to human rights violations.

The next five chapters present the data. Chapter 3 uses a thematic analysis to present a typology of vocabularies of justification for passivity, described as a web of passivity. Chapters 4 and 5 use discursive analyses to discuss in detail vocabularies of denial as human rights practices and contributing to public passivity. Chapters 5 and 7 apply psychoanalytic theories to understand participants' emotional responses to human rights violations and the role played by their biography in informing their responses. Because of these theoretically diverse, multi-methods analyses, some quotes will be discussed more than once, which is inevitable when wishing to engage with the complex and multi-layered nature of participants' contributions.

3
The Web of Passivity: Everyday Morality and the Banality of a Clear Conscience

This chapter concentrates on patterns of explanations, justifications and reactions used by participants to discuss human rights violations and their response to them. It has several purposes.

In charting the public's responses the chapter aims to identify, at the simplest level, how 'people talk about' (Augoustinos and Every, 2007) human rights violations by identifying the key broad patterns of explanations and reasoning used by participants. In line with the 'bottom-up' approach of this book, the offered typology is intended to firstly report on, and illustrate, the key themes that participants spontaneously made use of in discussing human rights and their violation.[1] These themes were used in all the groups, although in different measures and proportions by specific groups and individuals. This suggests that the typology represents 'what is around': that is, the range of issues, justifications, reactions and understandings available to the public at the time of the focus groups to discuss human rights violations. As such, these scripts are considered similar to Lakoff's 'explanatory conceptual models' (2010, 2008, 1987): that is, scripts and frames whose function is to provide a ready-made understanding of how some part of the world works (Darnton and Kirk, 2011). What is presented does not claim to be an exhaustive or static map, as new scripts emerge as society evolves.

Second, the vast majority of these scripts were structured as *topoi* (Wodak, 2004; van Dijk, 2002, 1993b): that is, common-sense narratives followed by an implicit or explicit conclusion deriving from them, often in the form of justification. Consequently, this thematic exercise also charts the participants' justifications for their passivity as well as for what they find difficult or problematic in human rights issues (such as '*I don't have the time to deal with this*' or '*it's too complicated*'). The fact that participants framed many of the themes as justifications automatically makes them moral scripts, underpinned by implicit normative beliefs. As commented above, this is not a static map as vocabularies of denial adapt and metamorphose with changes in society. Rather, it is meant to identify and label moral scripts, and draw attention to their importance in expressing and shaping public understandings of human rights issues and how they are incorporated into people's everyday lives. The next two chapters will analyse some specific scripts to highlight their ideological function as human rights practice. This chapter presents the typology but also reflects and comments on the moral domains that underpin and sustain these scripts, thus illustrating the banal quality and ideological connotations of everyday moral reasoning which contribute to their normalisation and invisibility.

Third, the chapter also considers the clustering of individual scripts. In doing so, it is possible to observe how the individual types of justifications are put together in specific intersecting combinations that strengthen each script's contribution towards building a reasonable 'story' that is competent and recognisable, and that works. The point here is not to reify specific groupings, as there are many potential combinations, but to introduce the idea of the scripts joining up to function as a web, combining different logics and moral imperatives.

This highlights the importance not just of the individual strands of moral reasoning but also of how they coexist and intersect (not always harmoniously) with each other. Contradiction, ambivalence and 'messiness' are intrinsic parts of these dynamic interactions. Equally, extracts using a conglomerate of scripts convey a sense of the subject being weighted down by the web of scripts which, like strands in a spider web, might look flimsy when taken individually, but joined together exercise a compelling 'stickiness'.

This knitting together of diverse types of explanations is not necessarily a Machiavellian exercise. Rather, it illustrates the dilemmatic nature of moral reasoning (Billig et al., 1988) and how people arrive at moral judgements (i.e. how they differentiate between right and wrong). It also exemplifies the way people talk and think – they make lists, reflect on them, explain them, and reach some kind of more or less stable conclusion. The clustering indicates a kind of moral 'mix and match' approach to human rights issues, which brings together ready-made and socially available moral scripts. Personal agency operates within a broad network of socio-cultural influences. In these agentic transactions, people are producers as well as products of social systems (Bandura, 1999a; Butler, 1997). While not neglecting individuals as moral agents, the focus of this chapter is on the 'cultural supermarket' of moral scripts through which members of the public put together complex and multi-layered moral accounts. These findings are important for the way we understand moral reasoning, the daily process through which individuals arrive at moral judgements through rationality and logic.

Moral reasoning and the everyday

Jean Piaget (1932) and Lawrence Kohlberg (1985, 1963) contributed greatly to the understanding of processes of moral reasoning and how they develop through the conceptualisation of stages of moral development. Societal norms play a crucial role in these stages of moral development by motivating individuals in different ways through life stages: for example, first to avoid punishment, then to gain peer approval, and finally to benefit society as a whole.

Carol Gilligan's (1982) groundbreaking critique of Kohlberg's theory proposed important differences in the way boys and girls arrive at moral judgements and actions. More recently, Jonathan Haidt has put forward a social intuitionist model for understanding the process of moral judgements, one that challenges the 'causality of reasoning in moral judgments' (Haidt, 2001:815). He aligns his approach with what he describes as the Thomas Jefferson 'head-heart model of morality (HHM)' (Haidt, 2002:54) and David Hume's assertions regarding the nature of reason: 'reason is and ought only to be the slave of the passions, and can pretend to no other office than to serve and obey them' (Hume, 1969:462). In common with these two approaches, and counter to the Kantian alignment of morality with rationality, Haidt's social intuitionist model asserts that 'moral judgements are like aesthetic judgements: they are gut feelings or intuitions that happen to us quickly, automatically, and convincingly' (Haidt, 2002:54). Rather than moral reasoning informing moral judgements, Haidt proposes that the process of reasoning occurs after the intuitive decision has been made. Haidt highlights that his model is a social one that accounts for the influence that peers and broader social/cultural factors have upon both the reasons an individual gives for their moral judgements and upon the instinctual moral decisions themselves (Haidt, 2001:814). Thus, Haidt's formulation highlights the negotiated and complex nature of moral reasoning and the key role played in it by societal forces.

As discussed in the previous chapter, Bandura also looks at the social embeddedness of the mechanisms through which moral reasoning is translated into action. He identifies four key manoeuvres: (a) the reconstrual of the conduct itself so it is not viewed as immoral; (b) the minimising of the agent's role in causing harm; (c) the minimising of the consequences of their action; and (d) the devaluation and blaming of the victim. Although these mechanisms are identified specifically in relation to inhumane actions, as operations of moral disengagements they are nevertheless highly relevant too when the result of moral disengagement is moral inaction.

In terms of the first category, the reframing of one's immoral conduct so it appears moral, Bandura gives examples of what could arguably be defined as rhetorical operations: for example, moral justifications through which people can act on a moral imperative and preserve their view of themselves as moral agents while inflicting harm on others (e.g. brutal dictators might justify the atrocity they commit by reframing them as necessary acts to protect their country's values or from preventing it from falling into chaos). Language is key in these operations. Some examples of Bandura's euphemistic labelling are highly resonant with Cohen's interpretive denial: for example, the killing of civilians defined as 'collateral damage'; bombing missions described as 'servicing the target'; employees being not fired but 'given a career alternative enhancement'. Exonerating comparisons rely heavily on moral justification by utilitarian standards. According to Bandura (1999a:196):

> cognitive restructuring of harmful conduct through moral justifications, sanitising language, and exonerating comparisons, taken together, is the most powerful set of psychological mechanisms for disengaging moral control. Investing harmful conduct with high moral purpose not only eliminates self-censure, but it engages self-approval in the service of destructive exploits.

Displacement and diffusion of responsibility are two other powerful techniques, as well as disregard or distortion of consequences.

Finally, self-censure for cruel conduct can be disengaged by stripping people of human qualities. The process of dehumanisation, as argued by many (Staub, 2003, 1989a,b; Bar Tal, 1989; Levi, 1987), is an essential ingredient in the perpetration of inhumanities. As this and the next chapters will illustrate, many of the mechanisms of disengagement described by Bandura were apparent in the focus group participants, thus demonstrating their social embeddedness and that they play an important function in moral inaction, as well as immoral action. Bandura (1997) states clearly that the self-regulation of morality is not entirely an intrapsychic matter, as rationalists argue. Instead, Bandura (1999a:27) claims that people do not operate as autonomous moral agents impervious to the social realities in which they are immersed. Moral agency is socially situated and exercised in particular ways, depending on the life conditions under which people transact their affairs. Moral actions are the product of the reciprocal interplay of personal and social influences. [...] Human behaviour cannot be fully understood solely in terms of social structural factors or psychological factors. A full understanding requires an integrated perspective in which social influences operate through psychological mechanisms to produce behaviour effects.

Some of the moral disengagement practices, such as diffusion of responsibility, are rooted in the organisational and authority structures of societal systems. The ideological orientations of societies shape the form of moral justifications, sanction detrimental practices, and influence which members of a society tend to be cast into devalued groups. These socio-structural practices create conditions conducive to moral disengagement. However, people are producers as well as products of social systems, as social structures – which are devised to organise, guide and regulate human affairs – are created by human activity. According to Bandura, neither situational imperatives (Milgram, 1974) nor vile dispositions (Gillespie, 1971) provide a wholly adequate explanation of human malevolence. I would add that, similarly, neither personality traits nor situational factors can account wholly for inaction.

Lakoff (1987) has also explored the socially constructed nature of moral reasoning and in particular the role played in it by language. In *The Political Mind* (2008), he puts forward a compelling explanation of how the public ends up taking one political position instead of another. Lakoff (2008:8) starts with critiquing the 18th-century view of reason which makes the Enlightenment problematic: conscious – we are what we think; universal – the same for everyone; disembodied – free of the body and independent of perception and action; logical – consistent with the properties of classical logic; unemotional – free of the passions; value-neutral – the same reason applies regardless of your values; interest-based – serving one's purposes and interests; and liberal – able to fit an objective world precisely with the logic of the mind able to fit the logic of the world. In opposition to the Enlightenment model of how human beings reason, Lakoff argues that individuals are complicated and commonly use more than one mode of thought, and that these can only be understood contextually and in relation to others (e.g. neoliberalism can sometimes look conservative to progressives and socialistic to conservatives).

In this process, language is at once a surface phenomenon and a source of power. It is a means of expressing, communicating, accessing and even shaping thought:

> If we hear the same language over and over, we will think more and more in terms of the frames and metaphors activated by that language. And it doesn't matter if you are negating words or questioning them, the same frames and metaphors will be activated and hence strengthened.
>
> (Lakoff, 2008:15)

According to Lakoff (2008), complex narratives – the kind we find in anyone's life story, as well as in fairy tales, novels and dramas – are made up of smaller narratives with very simple structures, called 'frames' or 'scripts'. The neural circuitry needed to create frame structures is relatively simple, and so frames tend to structure a huge amount of our thought. Each frame has roles, relations between these roles, and scenarios carried out by those playing the roles, and words are defined relative to frames and conceptual metaphors.

On similar lines to Bandura and Lakoff, this book as a whole is interested in scripts throughout – moving from the broad socio-cultural to the specific and personal (biographically informed and emotionally laden). This chapter maps out the scripts, metaphors and frames used by members of the public to think and talk about human rights and their violations. A thematic analysis is used to map out the web of scripts and get a sense of how the identified scripts intersect at micro, macro and meso levels.[2] As such, this chapter is the first building block of a narrative that criss-crosses these domains.

My first inroad into the vastly complex narratives generated in the focus groups was to isolate the recurrent 'smaller stories' or 'scripts' that were used repeatedly by different participants in different groups and times. The first part of this chapter looks at them as distinct entities, for the strategic purpose of illustrating how each is underpinned by particular understandings or constructions of human rights, and is ensconced in specific moral principles, generally in contrast with those of universal human rights. Later, I will give a few examples of how they cluster to form more complex narratives.

The scripts were selected on the basis of appearing in different focus groups, being used by more than one participant in a particular focus group, and when the specific script was not questioned but implicitly recognised by other group members. That these scripts were repeated in some form or another independently in all the groups suggests that they play a role in the current understanding of human rights and delineate the boundaries of how the subject could be talked about at that particular time. For ease of presentation, only one or two quotes will be used to illustrate each script.

As well as being looked at as 'surface phenomena' (Lakoff, 2008), the scripts are considered as socially accepted vocabularies of denial. As a system of public knowledge and socially shared beliefs, the scripts operate as *topoi*: that is, a discursive resource in which one may find arguments for sustaining a conclusion (van Der Valk, 2003:319; Wodak and Meyer, 2001). This is made particularly clear by how the scripts in the web are not *specific* to human rights but, as rhetorical resources, could be used in many other contexts. They are considered vocabularies of denial when they go beyond providing a particular view of the world – 'this is how are things are' – to accounting for the speaker's actions and attitudes in moral terms – 'this is why what I do is right' (Cohen, 2001). Thus, in so far as they are employed to directly or indirectly explain and justify the speaker's reactions and action or inaction, they are human rights practice. In Wetherell's view (2012:125), 'Practice draws attention both to a transpersonal "ready-made" we confront and slip into, as well as to active and creative figuring.'

The multiple nature of moral imperatives underscoring the crisscrossing scripts illustrates the unstable and ambivalent nature of engagement, oscillating between activity and passivity, constantly negotiating between different moral imperatives and needs. One of the points made by this chapter and the book as a whole is that while there is some resemblance of stability or settlement into patterns, these are never properly fixed. This in turn shows how participants' subjectivities are each disputed sites where opposing forces of engagement, disengagement, distancing and rapprochement fight for the upper hand.

Vocabularies of denial

'It's too much to ask': demand fatigue/caring overload[3]

[4] Joel: *I think something like Ethiopia where there's another famine after the one previously where there were thousands of children dying and we had Band Aid and that sort of thing, and that was supposed to help, of course it didn't help at all, if anything it harmed [...] so*

> *when you see that constantly coming on your screens, at that point compassion fatigue occurs, I think.*
>
> [6] Colin: *and also the fact that the increases in information sharing around the world means that you've brought you know us here in a nice Western democracy are brought face to face with this kind of story more often, from all round the world, and there's almost like a caring overload. It's like well I care about this, this, and this, but can I really care about every single country in the world in every, you know, you know, it's a, I I often feel like (.) you know, how, how, how much can I care about, you know, how much can I get involved with, how much can I actually do anything about?*

This script, used by many participants, problematises human rights issues because of their nature and sheer number, presented as one of a vast number of issues, some of which are intractable, demanding care and attention. Human rights are thus positioned as adding to the incessant flow of demanding causes. The comparison between human rights violations and African famine implies that human rights causes are also intractable.

Recent studies carried out by NGOs (Darnton and Kirk, 2011; TW Research, 2009; Creative, 2008) claim that the British public is stuck in its perception of Africa. Darnton and Kirk (2011) have argued that a more accurate way of interpreting the survey data is that the UK public is stuck in the frame it has been given for tackling poverty by Live Aid, creating a one-dimensional picture of Africa that has endured for 25 years. The narratives about Africa thus tend to feature African babies with pot bellies and famine, and construct Africa as a bottomless pit into which the UK public has poured resources with no discernible effect.

Joe's account features many of these tropes and concludes with another well-known element of this type of narrative: compassion fatigue, further discussed in Chapter 7, showing how the term 'compassion fatigue' has become ordinary in its everyday acceptability. The focus of this script, however, is not compassion fatigue or Africa in the specific, but the public's sense that there is a constant flow of demands made upon them. This is expressed by Joe as *'constantly coming on your screens'* and similarly by Colin as being brought more often face to face with this kind of story. Colin calls it *'caring overload'*, which he then differentiates into three separate but related stages: caring, getting involved and doing something about. Colin's use of hyperbole – he perceives the demand on him as asking him to care about every single country in the world – draws attention to his perceived need to draw boundaries but also to his experience of being under siege.

However, this sheer accumulation of atrocity images does not necessarily cause indifference to suffering, at least not with Colin. Neither is this stimulus overload, but rather seems more akin to demand overload (Cohen and Seu, 2002; Cohen, 2001). It fits into a more universal cognitive combination: on the one hand, the oppressive difficulty of knowing that there is too much to do; and on the other, too many demands even to discriminate between them. While caring overload, as defined by Colin, does not involve a lessening of compassion as in Joe's compassion fatigue, they both make reference to a perceived increase in media exposure and demand on the ordinary member of the public.

The 'too much to ask' script illustrates how members of the public's understanding of, and reactions to, human rights violations knit together geopolitical issues with a personal sense of being bombarded by demands, especially the role of the media in the flood of information and the popular discourse of 'compassion fatigue'.

'It's all relative'

In this script, as in the next three, human rights, rather than their violations, are presented as intrinsically problematic. Thus the scripts touch on a range of human rights issues and share the common feature of being presented through reasonable and reasoned arguments, each connecting to existing debates on human rights and their violations. As vocabularies of denial, they also share a quality of rationalisation whose ambiguity as a term is intentional. Rationalisation is defined as both 'the act of making something rational' (Oxford English Dictionary) and 'the attempt to present an explanation that is either logically consistent or ethically acceptable for attitudes, actions, ideas, feelings, whose true motives are not perceived' (Laplanche and Pontalis, 1985:375). The next two extracts hinge on whether human rights should be universal or relative, in one case because of questions of cultural relativism, the other in terms of who decides that something should be considered a right or not.

> *[3] Elsa: Just just picking up from [Terry]'s point I think there's another issue arising from this and that's how different people view human rights. The whole erm culture relativism what the West may consider wrong erm and outright torture, Saudi Arabia with its Islamic laws may consider it just in a way. And I think that it is important to view this, this piece (R/yeah) in a different perspective.*

Elsa makes reference to the long-standing debate on how cultural relativism fits in, or not, with a universal declaration of human rights, implying that there isn't an absolute and universal right. Elsa's narrative thus taps into a well-known argument against intervention which is presented as respectful.

Other comments fit in with continuing debates about the content, nature and justifications of human rights to this day. Indeed, the question of what is meant by a 'right' is itself controversial and the subject of continued philosophical debate. Harriet, for example, makes reference to the multitude of 'rights' (I imagine she is referring to the 30 human rights articles), thus pointing to the difficulties inherent in deciding in the abstract what and how many human rights should be (already she seems to think that 7 would be unmanageable, while the Universal Declaration lists many more than that).

> [7] 172: *Harriet:* *The problem with people, I think the problem when people think that and they sit down and have certain representatives to sit down and er write them down. They start writing a list er where does the list end? You know, what's, how many rights are there exactly? Seven?*

She is also concerned with the complexities of a proclamation of human rights in the absolute and how it could be read differently depending on the parties' interests.

> *Harriet:* *well, well there is there is erm I mean anybody can have, anybody is likely to have er an intuitive reaction of 'that's wrong' if you see someone slaughtering loads of people. So that can be like the basic, er one of the basic er rights that, I think it's right to life. But then if you if you bring that to another, that right to life, you can bring that to another issue say abortion, it gets very very complicated. Er so erm it could be for a, like as a [xxx] negative, erm, that you have rights, or you shouldn't have the right or the arrogance to kill. Like that would be, I think that would be slightly less confusing, [laugh] and slightly more useful, 'cause right to life is such an absolute.*

Without going into a detailed analysis of Harriet's words, it's important to stay with the end of her statement which implicitly constructs human rights as confusing and not very useful.

Finally, Alf takes to the extreme the issue regarding the difficulty of deciding when something is a human rights violation.

> *Alf: my nephew would say that if I take his Pokemon cards away it's torture.*

This script offers a good illustration of the dilemmatic nature of morality in particular when applied to human rights issues. In terms of human rights, the extracts are exemplary of a widespread confusion about the nature and number of rights, by whom and how it is decided what they are. The challenge of their application as universal rights against localised norms and interests features particularly strongly in this script.

'I didn't cause it, why should I have to fix it?'

The next two extracts, from Mary and Betty, use a legalistic type of rationalisation, often used by other participants too, to discuss issues of accountability in human rights violations. As such, this script is a good example of implicatory denial.

[9] 118: Betty: *I don't feel guilty at all. I, it's not the people I know I haven't contributed anything at all towards this kind of system. I have never done anything like that which will bring out er that barbaric behaviour from a person. I don't feel guilty at all.*

[5] 131: Mary: *But, the thing that really gets me is that there are people who are so responsible for it and they're the ones who are just sitting there and (A: doing nothing about it really) sitting around and drinking cocktails. [...] I think it's a conflict for me to try and do something about something when there is somebody else that's causing it to be that way and who've got the power to change it and who is the one who should take action and change it. So I've got a conflict there although I think given the fact that they're not going to do anything about it, I mean it's not going to change it if we leave it in their hands, we should do something about it, but then....*

These two extracts voice a powerful approach to the issue of human rights and whose responsibility it is to uphold them. Both Mary and Betty seem to think that the responsibility should be laid at the feet of the perpetrators or the corrupt governments (or at least this is how I read the reference to those who are in power, are responsible for '*this kind of system*' and spend their time drinking cocktails) who are not intervening. This kind of moral reasoning relies on a legalistic principle of duty to repair the harm done, which automatically exonerates the speakers. As a rendition of culpability and responsibility it is selective, but it was commonly used in the groups. See, for example, the discussion about arms trade on page 48. The subscript is that asking the speakers to feel responsible and take action is simply unfair.

Mary's account is more complex, however, and illustrates the dilemmatic quality of moral reasoning. Mary starts from premises similar to Betty's but spontaneously she subsequently questions her own position and realises that if she were to take her argument to its consequences it would mean that nobody would ever do anything about human rights violations. She goes back and forth between the two arguments, and she concludes with 'but then ...', suggesting that this argument is far from being resolved. The dilemma involves two types of morality: one based on legalistic principles, the other on universalism and social responsibility. The first allows both Mary and Betty to identify a rule that clearly demarcates moral boundaries and allows them to reject responsibility. But this clashes with the principle of 'universal brotherhood' and duty to help.

The next script deals with another familiar way of arguing where individual and state responsibilities and accountabilities should stop.

'We are not accountable for the misuse of what we produce'

The notion that those who trade in human destruction do not do it alone is not a new one and has been central to much research, particularly on bystander phenomena. Among others, Bandura (1999a) claims that perpetrators depend heavily on the moral disengagement of a network of reputable agents who manage respectable enterprises. He reports on the research carried out by Thomas (1982), who interviewed an American weapons dealer. When asked about his feelings about supplying torture equipment to Ugandan president Idi Amin, the dealer justified this as a legitimate business based on 'consumer needs' and, using advantageous comparison, he replied:

> I'm sure that the people from Dow Chemical didn't think of the consequences of selling napalm. If they did, they wouldn't be working at the factory. I doubt very much if they'd feel any more responsible for the ultimate use than I did for my equipment.
>
> (Thomas, 1982, cited in Bandura, 1999a:204)

Similarly, when interviewed about the lethal potential of weapons, an executive of a trade group representing gun manufacturers justifies the business he represents thus:

> We design weapons, not for the bad guys, but for the good guys. If criminals happen to get their hands on a gun, it is not the manufacturer's fault. The problem is, you can't design a product and insure who is going to get it.
>
> (Butterfield, 1999, cited in Bandura, 1999a:205)

Some of these rationalisations were also used in my focus groups. Here is an extract in which Adam is justifying Britain manufacturing and exporting electric batons to be used as torture instruments.

[4] 343: Adam: Yes, but for all the thousands of electric batons that are produced, it is only a very small percentage that are used on people, most of them are used on cattle, in places like Argentina. [...] some of it [is propaganda] because I mean you can't stop all batons just because they are, a lot of them may actually be used on cattle and things like that. And just because a small number are used on people, it you don't use batons, electric batons, they'll use something else. It's not like land mines, well mines, or things like that which are specifically aimed at people, specifically aimed at maiming people as opposed to killing them, because they know it's going to be used to maim somebody. So you use (xxx) thousands of things that, maybe one, two, three four five whatever are going to be used on people. I mean you can't stop the entire thing (xxx) because of that. It's like if I poked you in the eye with a sharp stick, you'd (xxx) say you're not allowed sharp objects. [...] we can't be held accountable for the misuse of one tool. [...] Oh, if we changed from batons to double barrelled shotguns, the majority of double barrelled shotguns are used for shooting crows, rabbits, and vermin, one or two people use them for holding up banks, that doesn't mean to say that we shouldn't have double barrelled shotguns. Does it?

As in the examples before, we have a clash of moralities and Adam is clearly carving out a very thin slice of moral acceptability by avoiding the moral implications of legitimising the UK involvement in the production of torture instruments. Adam's argument cannot be faulted logically, or morally, if, , the 'potential misuse' argument is bolstered by economic discourse constructing the closure of factories impacting on the workers' rights to a job and the negative impact on our economy. Bandura (1999a:205) argues that by fragmenting and dispersing sub-functions of the enterprise, the various contributors see themselves as decent, legitimate practitioners of their trade rather than as parties to deathly operations. Self-exonerations are needed to neutralise self-censure and to preserve self-esteem. In line with Bandura, I would also argue that Adam's use of rationalisation enables him to use this script as implicatory denial to disconnect from the moral implications of producing and exporting electric batons to countries where they will be used as instruments of torture.

'Like Sylvester Stallone'

The next couple of examples use a different kind of rationalisation, mainly based on hyperbole, willful misunderstanding or reduction to absurd.

Colin: *That's right. I'm going to invade xxx Afghanistan single-handedly and [all laugh] I'll be like Sylvester Stallone, you know.*

Alf: *I'm going to give them money so that they can what, topple the Saudi Arabian government? […] I can see my money going towards helping someone who's starving. I can't see my money going towards toppling the Saudi Arabian government which is one of the richest governments in the entire world. You know my ten dollars is just not going to do a thing.*

The reduction to absurd is intriguing as a moral script. However tempting it is to read it in that way, taking account of other comments from Colin and Alf, I don't think it is an attempt to mock human rights; rather, these two accounts are very successful in conveying the frustration and helplessness experienced by the participants in all focus groups. The reference to the 'tough guy' who in action movies accomplishes the impossible captures the fanciful nature of isolated individuals shouldering the responsibility for ending human rights violations. Some of the recurring features, such as helplessness and the contradictions involved in asking for monetary donations to support human rights causes, will be discussed in detail in Chapters 4 and 8. Another recurrent feature of this script is its highlighting of the contrast between the perceived inadequacy of the individual, expressed through ludicrous comparisons, and the scale of geopolitical complexity of human rights violations.

'It must be human nature'

The next two scripts use essentialist ideas of humanity to explain both human rights violations and participants' own passivity. Underpinned by a view of humanity that is inevitable and unchanging, they in turn construct human rights as inevitable because human beings are quintessentially nasty.

> [4] 112: *Emma: Erm more or less, because I mean the story has happened already and after the Second World War they said 'no more' but and again. It must be something in human nature.*

This script presents human rights violations as due to human nature, thus removing human rights violations from their political and historical contexts and attributing them instead to inevitable human characteristics. As Mandy comments, *'it's more of the same really'*, thus stripping each conflict of its political and historical meaning and reducing it to yet another burst of brutality. Geopolitics, history, colonialism, inequality are rendered irrelevant by this essentialist script. Constructing human rights violations as inevitable makes this a self-exonerating script of implicatory denial. Essentialist ideas of human nature are also brought in to justify human rights abuses.

> [9] 305: *Trudy: Yeah but on the other hand, supposing I had a child and someone kidnaps my child, I've got the kidnapper and he's not telling me where my child is. Boy, I'd torture him until he's spoken. I'd appeal to him and if he didn't hear me that's it, I'd do whatever I could to get him to tell me where my child is. Because that's human nature. I wouldn't care how much pain it is.*

Trudy's account, although also hinging on the explanatory power of an alleged human nature, is quite different from the previous ones. Hers is a familiar script, similar to the utilitarian justifications of torture for the good of many, but relying on the primacy of maternal feelings as a moral principle. In terms of moral reasoning, Trudy's account is surprising in a focus group on human rights violations and it did provoke dissent in the group, but clearly Trudy is confident that motherhood trumps human rights in the moral hierarchy. For our purposes, this is revealing of how the universalism of human rights has to contend with local and personal moral imperatives. Human rights as universal and absolute are implicitly downgraded as abstract principles and eclipsed by more immediate personal demands. In terms of scripts, anything presented as human nature clearly carries strong argumentative powers.

'You should care for your own first'

[3] 104: Paula: Yeah I just think that, you know, we've got our lives and country to look after.

[6] 32: Mandy: Maybe it's the same with this, it's kind of like you've got to let go of those because there's enough to do at home

These are familiar scripts: 'look after your own first', 'care about what is on your doorstep' and so on. Singer (2009) addresses parochialism in his denunciation of passivity in regard to world poverty. He would recognise the sentiment expressed by these participants, and in fact would identify with it, in his careful observation of his own reactions. When the tragic earthquake struck China's Sichuan province in 2008 – killing 70,000 people, injuring 350,000 and making nearly five million homeless – he felt sympathy but, as focus group participants described, it did not affect his everyday life or capacity for enjoyment. He reasons that we intellectually register faraway disasters, but we are rarely disturbed emotionally by tragedies that occur to strangers far away with whom we have no special connection (Singer, 2009:50). Singer supports this claim by showing striking differences in US donations to domestic and to foreign disasters and wonders whether this might be hard-wired through kin selection for evolutionary reasons, even though he strongly questions the normalisation and naturalisation of parochialism in traditional moral philosophy. The power of this script is in drawing moral boundaries and resisting moral responsibility beyond the most immediate lines of identification and care. The use of the metonymy 'home' is representative of that immediate core of connections, yet its vagueness is also significant in leaving unclear exactly who is inside and outside the definition of 'home'.

'I don't want to be tied down'

This script uses a very different set of arguments based on liberal principles of individual freedom and free choice. This script was very popular in focus groups, particularly in discussions around individual anonymous donations versus committing to a standing order.

[P2] *Tina: I think depending on what we see as our freedom, or whatever,
it's like having our own car, or whatever, you know, that it's not
helping out. BUT, you know, I want my car, I want my, to be able
to go around when I want, as I want. Um, it's, it's like, like, yeah
I can do something on my own, but if I join a group then I'm
committed to certain times and that's restricting my freedom, so,
you know, that kind of idea. So it's about, um, (.) responsibility
and committing yourself to something that might not suit you one
day. Or rejection about not wanting to get tied into something. Or
knowing that something like Amnesty, you know, once you've got
into it then it's, (.) um, um, things that get sent or letter writing,
it's, it's perpetuated. It takes more to get out, than it does (.)*

A neoliberal discourse underpins this script, which could be summarised
as 'I want to keep my options open'. In the same way that Tina wants
to be able to take her car and go where she wants, she rejects the idea
of commitment, which is viewed pejoratively as being 'tied into something'. In contrast to commitment, Tina expects respect for her right to
change her mind. The power of this script is revealed in the way Tina
expresses it as her unquestionable right, which she doesn't expect to be
disputed (and indeed it wasn't). This demonstrates that individualistic
neoliberal principles are considered legitimately moral and can be used
to counter appeals to support human rights organisations.

'It's not how it looks'

This script is a good example of interpretive denial to then bolster
implicatory denial.

[4]: *Adam: I don't, I don't, no, there will always be homelessness, and I've
been homeless myself, and there's a lot of fraud (xxx) goes on in
the homelessness. You'll probably find a lot of people out there on
the street (Joel: they want to be (xxx)) have a lot more money than
you do.(Joel: yeah and a lot) That's right, and a lot of people who
sell The Big Issue⁴ are actually claiming dole and housing benefit.
(Joel: yeah) And there's a lot of fraud that goes on*

In response to a member of the group defining homelessness as one of
the human rights abuses taking place in the UK, Adam is talking about
homelessness to counteract the claim that human rights are abused
in his country. He uses first the fatalist notion that there will always
be homeless, thus presenting it as a fact of life and implying that we

shouldn't make such a fuss about it. He then warrants his position by saying that he had been homeless himself, thus attributing to himself the status of an expert and also pre-empting potential criticisms. Finally, he uses interpretive denial to imply that the situation is more complicated so not as bad as it looks. In fact, he undermines empathy for homeless people by creating antagonism (*'you'll probably find they have a lot more money than you do'*) and accusing them of benefit fraud. It is clear from Joel's eager support that this is a highly resonant narrative. The urban myth that most homeless people are benefit scroungers continues to get a high profile on the right-wing press.[5] Interestingly, one of the cases discussed by the *Daily Mail* argues that benefit scams have been made possible by current human rights legislation,[6] thus alluding to a link between this kind of script, which basically undermines the victim's credibility, and the dangers of liberal principles underpinning human rights principles. It also further illustrates how these scripts are not the speakers' personal creations, but circulate in society.

'Out of sight, out of mind'

The issue of distance was frequently brought up as a reason why the participants did not actively respond to information about atrocities. There were two specific ways in which distance was discussed. The first was a concrete understanding of distance in terms of physical distance; the second referred to a cognitive and symbolic distance. The latter was referred to either in terms of how the physical distance affected the person's capacity to understand and therefore to care or hold the atrocity in their mind; or in terms of hierarchies of importance, with what happens round the corner as more relevant. The first, concrete modality, exemplified by Karen's quote, will be discussed in depth in Chapter 5.

> [9] 162: *Karen:* It does. It doesn't affect my day-to-day life. It does affect my conscience. But it doesn't disturb my day-to-day life because it's something far away. Out of sight, out of mind.

The morality underpinning this script is complex as it hints at a disconnection between Karen's morality – '*It does affect my conscience*' – and her daily life, which goes on undisturbed. This is really important in terms of the gap between morality and action (how knowing that something is wrong does not translate into action), and points to how unintegrated human rights issues are in ordinary people's lives. It speaks of the power of parochialism, but also of a belief, consistently expressed in all focus groups, that human rights issues are not relevant to the UK, but only pertain to faraway places.

'I don't have the time'

[6] 141: Neil: *We don't have the time, if we had the time we could sit down, think about it and come to a conclusion and think it out but we don't, in the Western world time is becoming more and more a precious resource. And because we don't have time, we can't deal with human rights abuses and they get jumped, they get bumped straight from top to bottom. When is your next appointment, when is your next meeting [...] I say, yes? [all signal their agreement] I feel responsible I want to help but there isn't the time, there isn't money, I haven't got the options.*

This script hinges on lack of time, thus making it immediately recognisable. Neil focuses on having time as a necessary condition to think through human rights issues. Thus, time seems to pertain less to the modern pace of Western life (although Neil puts the two together) and more to human rights issues being experienced as intricate and complex. Neil seems to be saying that because human rights issues require complex solutions and understanding, and because time is a rare commodity in the West, personal and relatively smaller-scale commitments become pressing, immediate demands which take priority over 'bigger than self' problems (Schwartz and Boehnke, 2004).

The power and appeal of this script is not just that it constructs human rights issues as demanding and time-consuming, thus echoing the sense conveyed by earlier scripts (that they problematically make demands on the individual), but that its reference to paucity of time resonates so strongly.

Vocabularies of action

Even though this book's main concern is to understand what fosters passivity, participants did not only provide accounts and justifications for passivity. The extracts discussed in this section are both expressions of individuals' political positions and counter-arguments to some of the scripts discussed in the previous section. It is important to include these alternative vocabularies for several reasons: first, insofar as the purpose of this chapter is to map out ways in which people talk about and understand human rights violations, these accounts present quite different ways of understanding human rights; second, these accounts illustrate the dissent and differences within focus groups; third, it is important to include scripts that resist the overwhelming legitimation of passivity, to remind ourselves that, however powerful and seductive, vocabularies of denial can be counteracted with alternative scripts.

'Leading by example'

This script is exemplified by extracts from Jill from Finland and Dahlia from Sweden, whose comments on intervention and international solidarity and aid paint quite a different picture from what we have heard so far.

[2] Jill: Oh yes, I mean, well, Scandinavia is so ah, we have a very high level of living standards. We don't have people begging on the streets, you just don't see them because the government takes care of them. And then you, you, you do see this kind of articles [referring to the focus groups' props] all the time because we are such a small country we can't afford to ignore everybody else so we do get lots of information about what's going on. And it is terrible. I have to admit I'm very proud of my country because we send people to work with, in these crisis areas and even working lots with Amnesty International.

This account provides important information on what might foster proactive and socially responsible reactions from the public. First, we see the introduction of an ethics of care offered by a government that leads by example and 'takes care' of the vulnerable and needy. Second, in terms of knowledge – similarly to what has been repeated in all focus groups – Jill reports a large amount of information on human rights violations; but unlike the others, she frames this positively, as an essential for a small country to be connected to others. In terms of action, Finland actively intervenes in humanitarian crises, which makes Jill proud of her country. There is no sense of helplessness in Jill's account; rather, her narrative upholds the importance of connectedness, and thus the information about atrocities is integrated through this logic and is not felt as threatening. The active and caring stance taken by the government clearly plays a crucial role in the alternative moral reasoning presented by Jill

*[5] Dahlia: I think also that it depends on where you're coming from as
you said because (Ann: exactly) if you come from a country like
Sweden where we're from erm you can't really say Q< well you
need to look in your own back yard >Q[7] because our problems
[laugh] are ridiculous in comparison to this. Our economy is so
strong, our country has no problems if you look on an international level. (Ann: exactly) it's seriously it's like, you cannot use
that argument uhm coming from that background because I can
see how you can say that in India, of course (Ann: I totally agree
(xxx) with what she's saying) there are so many issues that you
have within your own country. Er, so that looking to Saudi Arabia
may might not make sense. But if you come from most of Europe
(Ann: then xxx, yeah) our relative problems are very minor. And
also I was just thinking when they, when Sweden's economy erm
went down, together with everyone else's I guess, er, Sweden has
always had one per cent given to the third world of the GNI[8] and
they made that half. Half a per cent all of a sudden and there
was, people were so upset and people were so, there was a large
going on and people were like Q< this is just unbelievable >Q
like this is one of the very very few years we've had very left wing
government for very long, not very left wing but social democrats
in power. Erm, and that, those were during the few years that
there was a right wing government I think. Erm, and people were
extremely upset because of this like Q< we may have problems,
our economy may be in a down period right now but if you look
at the third world then we can never ever like defend that kind of
actions >Q*

Jill and Dahlia thus propose an alternative causal explanation for
parochialism to those given by Adam Smith and evolutionary psychologists, based on education and political climate. Dahlia's comments in
particular provide evidence that if a country leads by example, and
leaders foster a climate of social responsibility and universal solidarity,
their citizens will internalise those values. Citizens protesting because
the government has cut their foreign aid sounds like science fiction in
the context of the preceding scripts, but Dahlia's account explains it as
a natural corollary of years of Swedish government taking a responsive
approaching to Third World problems. A morality of connectedness and
contextualisation, rather than individualism and insularity, is key to this
script.

'Deeper changes are needed'

[9]: Karen: Er, it's it's always in my mind what happens is wrong, but er since I can't help as a single person we need a big, much bigger force, much bigger feeling to make things change. One person here feeling sorry for a whole nation is not much of a help.

[6] Lorna: I know but that seems like in such a short term sort of immediate reaction (Colin: yeah, yeah, 'cause when the guilt wears off) I mean you, you know that a lot of these they're real long-term global problems they're not just going to go because I feel guilty today, you know, it needs a lot more sort of, erm, deep-rooted sort of real long-term measures.

Karen's and Lorna's accounts take us full circle to issues of helplessness discussed earlier. I want to suspend for a moment the consideration of this script as an excuse and engage with the emotions conveyed by these two participants. There is something poignant in Karen's sense that her feelings are not big enough and that they do not amount to a force strong enough to change anything. Her formulation is unusual, not so much in terms of the familiar expression of helplessness, but rather her sense that if others' feelings joined with hers it would make a 'bigger feeling', a bigger force that could bring change. She paints a tragic picture: many isolated individuals having feelings for distant others, but without the chance of joining forces with other like-minded individuals these feelings evaporate and turn into helplessness. As Lorna and Colin put it, 'the guilt wears off' at an individual level while what is needed is 'deep-rooted and long-term measures'. The suggestion is that human rights issues are not amenable to individual solutions or benevolence. Deeper political, economic, social changes are needed.

This theme is pursued further by Colin.

Colin: I'm sure that's part of the trick isn't it? a really effective way of not having to do it is to bring it all back to individual responsibility, you know, if you doing this rather than it being absolutely assumed that it's a collective action, a collective society action that can get rid of these problems and the acceptance that as a group we're going to contribute to it. And instead it's, there's all this active rhetoric about, you know, keep taxes low, you know, and don't give money to anybody. And erm and as a result of that the money isn't available to make the changes the changes that are necessary and the collective will isn't there either because we're such individualistic culture. Ah, it's so paralysing.

Colin raises the extremely important issue of the pitfalls of the individualistic way in which human rights appeals are constructed, and how this individualistic framing generates in turn individualised responses and understanding. Colin's account is in stark contrast with Dahlia's, and suggests that a government's focus on the individual is a successful 'trick' not to do anything about human rights violations. Despite the differences in localised contexts, Colin is in agreement with both Jill and Dahlia that human rights issues should be considered a problem of collective, rather than individual responsibility, and addressed through collective action.

'We should be encouraged to be social creatures'

The issue of individualism features also in Anna's contribution, which pines after the 'golden era' of political activism:

Anna: *I wish there was more of erm a collective erm conscience. More now. I think there was more twenty years ago, thirty years ago. I think now it's, it's very much the cult of the individual and I think, er a lot, a lot has gone by the way, you know by the wayside. Uhm,Q< oh well I can't change anything so I won't do anything >Q and that's it, erm. And I, you know, and and it's not people need to be, people don't need to be led but I think, you know, to get people to to to follow you or to to accept you, you have to lead by example. And when you look at what NATO is doing or whatever you just don't feel, you know, you are in the hand of people who are wanting the best (B/uhm) and therefore I think people are fed up, don't believe in anything and I think that's very sad, and unless you can, I think it will produce (xxx) you know, I don't know, maybe I shouldn't xxx. I just feel, I work for a university and I, I see people every day and I just feel there's a lack of social conscience in most of the students I see. Maybe I'm not, you know, maybe they're it's not the right university, but I feel, you know, people are interested in their well-being, how much money they can make, how much will they xxx make in the future and the material side, the materialistic side. There was more of a conscience before. I really feel that very strongly and and I think we're losing all that, you know, we we just, you know, it's more more more more more more.*

Anna's account is very rich in identifying the blocks to proactive responses to human rights issues. She first of all identifies the cult of individualism which militates against a collective conscience. Anna claims this is what underpins apathy. She then, like Jill and Dahlia, also claims that more proactive public responses can only be fostered by a moral leadership which she laments as absent in the UK and NATO operations, thus contextualising geopolitically issues of human rights as well as the spiral of distrust that untrustworthy leadership engenders. She then identifies education as an important moral tool, and yet her current experience working in a university is that students are encouraged to prioritise material values. Her six times repetition of 'more' conveys powerfully her sense that greed is a powerful driving force that militates against social responsibility.

This account is echoed by Neil, who is studying in a UK university

Neil: I think so. I think there's a severely large culture in individualism because I grow up during the nineteen nineties and I go to [prestigious London university] as well which is a very materialistic university. There's no need to nod quite so viciously, erm, there's no need to nod quite so quickly, [all laugh] I'm not that bad, [all laugh] erm but there is, they are a very materialistic university. You can, even now you have careers talks all the time, we're invited to meet the big employers we're we're told that we're going to get good jobs, we're told that we're going to get good money and we are encouraged to do this from birth and so I think when you say there's a there is a there isn't a a social conscience I think that's probably because there can't be anymore. We're just not encouraged to do it we're not encouraged to be a social creature in the Western world. And I think when we're trying to discover the the rhetorical arguments one of them has to be your entire life conditioning in in a Western culture is is individualism so why should you help someone else? You first, them second. I think that's one of the arguments.

Whether they call it 'bigger feeling' or 'bigger force' or 'collective conscience', all these and many other participants are identifying the need for a collective conscience and for collective responsibility for human rights violations, and the difficulties in generating a collective political effort in individualistic societies (Hoggett, 2009).

The geopolitics of intervention: 'Economics always rule'

While the previous script focused on the detrimental effects of individualism and narcissism on the capacity of individuals to feel willing and able to respond proactively to human rights violations, this script contextualises non-intervention in human rights issues in terms of geopolitical and economic interests.

[3] Carol: No I feel empathy. I feel completely sorry for them (B/right) and people if I had anything within my power to help them I'm sure I would do that but I don't have that power as an individual, but Amnesty is an organisation I'm sure does have (.) some say, but not a great deal of say I don't think so. I think all they can do is lobby (.) (B/yeah, put pressure) and put pressure on them, but, by the same token they cannot bear that much pressure on a country which (B/no) basically (.) can do what it likes because of its commercial viability in oil. Therefore all the other nations are going to close down to it anyway and say Q<yes whatever you want we will do for you, you can carry on doing whatever you like in your country because we need your source of oil to feed the rest of the world>Q and therefore in that respect economics always rules rather that humanity, effectively, human concerns always take a second, a second tier (xxx) on that xxx. So much I always think there's never going to be something you can do.

The script used by Carol is one in which humanity takes a second tier after economic interests. She focuses on oil, but her point has a wider reach in highlighting the collusion of entire nations in condoning human rights violations through passivity because of economic interests. According to Carol this is why individuals end up feeling helpless. She also ends with fatalism – *'I always think there is never going to be something you can do'* – but this seems to come not from folk wisdom about the inevitable harshness of life, but from a consideration of the contribution of large international economic and political interests in the perpetuation of human rights violations.

The politics of resistance

Vicky brings her own experience of political resistance to illustrate the power of collective actions in changing the course of history.

[2] Vicky: I remember about in the early 70s late 60s in Greece where I was at the time there was this military quandary (R/yes) Well it is not nearly as horrible as this (R/no) but there were tortures, it was the police mainly (R/yes yes) The, I mean I was a student at the time, we were chased by the police you know, I felt this helplessness that you couldn't say I mean what you wanted to say (R/yes) because you might end up, that was for me the freedom of speech was so horrible because you know, I mean, it's really I felt really I had to

say what I felt and I was right. And I felt that, you know, sense of helplessness, and then there was, I'm not saying that was a student and lots of people in Greece will overthrow the government, I know it was more I mean general political interest, and also pressure from other countries, it wasn't the students who got killed OK, but that helped. The fact that they wouldn't shut up, they wouldn't just, all revolutions in countries, you know it's similar. If you don't shut up and you shout and some get killed, some get tortured, and then they'll leave, that's how you get freedom, otherwise, I mean you don't do anything, you know right from the beginning you're not gonna get anything. At least if you try, you have examples, whole histories full of examples, revolutions and er people getting killed and tortured among their lives. You know well, eventually, I mean there will be sacrifices yes, but you will (xxx) you know free them eventually. I mean we have recorded history so I'm hopeful I mean I'm really optimistic about this.

The web in action

Having ended the previous section with a rare note of optimism on the capacity for citizens to intervene and mobilise themselves against injustice and human rights violations, this section takes a less optimistic view to look at the cumulative effect of scripts functioning as a web and trapping individuals in passivity. As stated many times, the analysis is not meant to blame the individual speakers. Rather, it wants to exemplify the 'mix and match' approach to morality through which members of the public construct complex and multi-layered accounts. This section illustrates how the weaving together of scripts adds to their individual power of persuasion, like strands in a web.

[3] 47: Tracey: *It's a very difficult situation considering if you try, it's people themselves who suffer if you try and you know?*
             (Bruna: are you talking about sanctions?)
Tracey: *yeah. It's very very difficult and I personally prefer to remain ignorant, because I just think there's so much (xxx) well no I do in some ways because I think some of it is so hard to (read) and that there's often a lot going on places at home and I just think you can't take, you can't take all this in. What can one person do? I personally wouldn't join Amnesty*

> *reading this still (xxx) now. No. Erm, it makes me feel sad,*
> *you know and I just think it's it's it's a shame but I also*
> *think unfortunately that's life and, but I for one don't have,*
> *well, the strength, I don't have the, you know, I don't want*
> *to change that, I'd rather change something closer to home,*
> *there's other issues that I'm more involved in, however awful*
> *these are.*

Tracy's account uses a multiplicity of scripts. She starts with a rationalisation, that it is better not to intervene for the sake of the victims of
human rights violations. Then she uses avoidance as defence against
demand overload, followed by a script on the complexities of the violations, followed by parochial scripts. Then she moves to a fatalist
approach and returns in conclusion to parochialism. Tracy's account
is a good example of how diverse scripts, underpinned by different
discourses and moral codes support each other to present an unassailable logic. The extracts also illustrate the dilemmatic nature of these
justifications in how Tracy contradicts herself and seems to go back
and forth in her reasoning. Finally, it also illustrates an important
point to be fully discussed in Chapter 7, that having an emotional
response is not a guarantee for action. It also shows how, as in a web,
each strand contributes to Tracy being bogged down into inaction.
So much so that it is hard to know to what extent she felt helpless to
begin with or whether it is the constraining result of this avalanche of
justifications.

The progression of passivity is also illustrated in Tina's account,
which gives a chronological account of her reactions, thoughts and
feelings.

[7] *Tina:*   *I think it was similar to what [Leila] was saying. I was kind of*
           reading it and reading it and then it came to the rape and because
           it kind of, got worse, it was she was raped then it was, you know,
           twenty-two men and then it was three day there was a point at
           which I not quite switched off but, the horror sort of subsided and,
           I don't know.
Bruna: *How did that happen?*
Tina: *I think it's, in a way it's because it's like a defence mechanism.*
           We hear this so much that, you were saying that, 'is it covered in
           the media?' but I think it is covered a lot in the media the same with
           the stories like this. And the problem is that we do now xxx switch
           off. I think, or some of us do and so I can be horrified, immediately

> *horrified by the stories but then, there's a way of thinking well, telling yourself you can't do anything about it. So then going off and sort of making yourself a cup of coffee or something and switching off and getting on with your life*

Tina starts with being engaged ('*I was kind of reading it and reading it*') then the information becomes too traumatic for her and she switches off. When asked to explain her response, Tina uses a psychological script of defence mechanism seamlessly mixed with habituation due to over-exposure, followed by a script on helplessness. She concludes with a very familiar narrative of cups of coffee or tea, the British comfort drink, and '*getting on with your life*'. Thus Tina's narrative gives an eloquent snapshot of the short-lived disruption to ordinary life caused by human rights information: how the disturbance starts, how it is managed and how it is justified.

Again, short-lived emotional reactions (contradicting that the best responses are caused by emotional messages) in themselves are no guarantee of action. The idea of human rights violations as a contained short-lived disturbance of everyday life is also described in Pip's account, from a different focus group.

[9] 155: Pip: *Isn't it our human nature that if there is something going around like on the other end of the, this country. Like suppose there is some problem in Green Street or somewhere, because it's not near our home we will sort of feel sorry for an hour or two and say Q< oh did you hear, those Bangladeshis are attacked, oh have you seen that they burnt the Mosque>Q and all that. And after a day or two, even if they're killing each other, that thing is gone, lie low because it's not nearer on this street or in the area in my neighbourhood that I'd be up tight. For a day I'll feel sorry and I'll talk to anybody, whoever phones me or whoever talks to me I'll say Q<did you hear what a nightmare, people have been killed and all that>Q and then after a day or so... Don't you think it's a human nature?*

Like previous examples, Pip's narrative contains several scripts; there is human nature, primarily parochialism, and an 'out of sight, out of mind' script. Notably, like Tina's, Pip's feelings evaporate after a couple of days and other, more immediate demands, physically and emotionally closer to her, take precedence.

Summary and reflections

This chapter has offered a bottom-up mapping of the discursive territory of passivity in relation to human rights violations and prosocial responses. I will briefly summarise some key points in relation to human rights issues and morality.

In terms of human rights, if we take Lakoff's (2008) view that social action is filtered through socially constructed scripts which determine in some way or other public responses to social issues, the scripts discussed in this chapter provide important information on how the public thinks and talks about human rights issues. The first finding is that the public appears to be confused on human rights. The accounts display an alarming lack of clarity on how many human rights there are, what they are and who decides what they are. This lack of detailed understanding of human rights and the legislation which surrounds them confirms the findings from Ballagan et al. (2009).

Second, and of equal concern, the public experiences human rights as not pertaining to their daily realities, but as abstract and disconnected rather than integrated in meaningful ways in their moral existence. Third, when informed about human rights violations, members of the public tend to feel disturbed. Although this is inevitable due to the horrific nature of crimes against humanity, it also seems to reinforce negative attributions to human rights issues as complicated, intractable and hopeless. Fourth, there seems to be a lack of clarity regarding individuals' expected roles in the safeguarding of human rights. This is accompanied by an overall sense that people are surrounded primarily by bad examples of corruption and a widespread prioritisation of economic and political interests over human concerns. In general, people convey a sense of being left alone with knowing about human rights violation, without the support of proactive leadership and having to justify their own lack of action, which they do with complex and sophisticated justifications. It is important to listen to these scripts as 'face value' experiences and understandings of human rights and their violations independently of their function as vocabularies of denial, which will be pursued in the next two chapters. It is alarming how isolated and impotent individuals feel in the face of human rights violations.

In terms of moral reasoning, the accounts have illustrated the plasticity of the moral scripts and suggest that the displaying or rehearsing of these ordinary 'making sense' accounts should not be taken for fixed positions, personality traits or enduring attitudes. It is not just that speakers use the same scripts for different purposes, but that using a particular script doesn't necessarily turn it into a predictable or guaranteed action or inaction. Thus, even though it becomes immediately clear that the vast majority of these scripts are implicit justifications for inaction, this should not necessarily be taken as a demonstration that the participant uttering it is 'passive'. As mentioned in the previous chapter, conformity and other group dynamics should also be taken into consideration when a particular participant seems to take a stable position. The mapping presented in this chapter allows for contradictions, ambivalence, uncertainty and, importantly, changes of heart, thus suggesting that the public can go either way, provided that alternative scripts can be generated and internalised.

Nevertheless, the focus groups demonstrated some relative stability. That the scripts were repeated in some form or other in all the groups independently suggests that they play a role in the current understanding of human rights and delineate the boundaries of how the subject can be talked about at this particular time. As such, the mapping offers a snapshot of the discursive environment and ideological habitus generating passivity towards human rights violations. This is what I want to challenge, not in an accusatory way towards individuals, but rather as an attempt to unmask and confront the everyday, banal climate of acceptable passivity.

The graphic representation of the themes as a web (see Figure 3.1) is meant to illustrate visually how the scripts dynamically intersect and interact with each other and, in doing so, trap or sustain members of the public in their individual passivity through culturally shared accounts.

As for everyday morality, moral hierarchies of goals are important in terms of frames and values and quite in contradiction with Schwartz's circumplex model of motivational types of values. Schwartz argues that people find it difficult to hold certain combinations of values at the same time, when there is incompatibility among them. In particular, according to surveys carried out by Schwartz, people who hold self-enhancement values (achievement and power) would not hold in the same measure self-transcendence values (universalism and benevolence). This model conceives of individuals as holding relatively stable values which are, according to Schwartz, mutually exclusive. As values are the rules by which people make decisions about right and wrong, Schwartz's model offers a polarised view of morality with individuals holding fairly stable positions at either pole. This polarised view of morality is not supported by the data from the focus groups, which

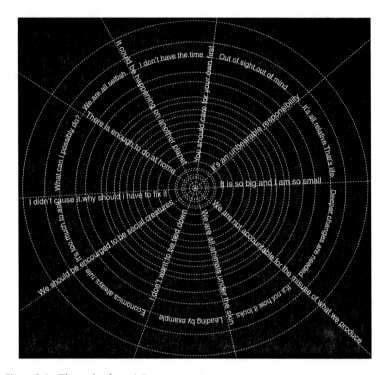

Figure 3.1   The web of passivity

show contradiction and ambivalence and individuals holding opposing views. Morality is far more messy, fragmented and conflictual than
Schwartz's polarised model would suggest. One example is Neil's complex negotiations of values and goals whereby he proclaims universal
values and benevolent intent, but he behaves according to simpler,
ordinary, pedestrian motivations: having to respect appointments, be
present at scheduled meetings and so on. Neil thus graphically illustrates how human rights issues do, from time to time, come at the top of
the commitment hierarchy, but only temporarily, to be quickly pushed
down to the bottom by everyday banal demands.

Another important critique that can be moved to polarised and relatively stable models of morality is that such models assume a straightforward relationship between members of the public and their moral
values, thus neglecting the active interplay people engage in with their
consciences. Stating and believing in one's moral values is one thing;
applying those values is another. As the data will repeatedly illustrate, a
lot happens in the space between values and action. Having provided a

map of the discursive environment and ideological habitus generating passivity towards human rights violations, the next two chapters look at how denial mediates values and action, and operates as human right practice. My target is not individual inaction or self-deception per se, but the lived ideology of passivity as a pervasive and compelling social context. My intention is not to accuse the individual but rather to unmask, confront and challenge the everyday operations of acceptable passivity.

4
The Public and NGOs: Neutralisation and Denial in Response to Human Rights Appeals

As mentioned in Chapter 2, the majority of empirical research into public charitable behaviour focuses on monetary donations. This psychological research has generated a fragmented and disconnected list of factors that positively or negatively influence monetary donations. For example, monetary donations are positively affected when information is provided about other people making gifts and when affordability is reinforced (Bartolini, 2005). A token given in exchange might facilitate donations by signalling a reference price; however, requests for donations accompanied by a specified amount have an even stronger positive impact on donations (Briers et al., 2007). Finally, Sturmer, Snyder (2010) and Omoto (2005) demonstrated the key role played by whether the recipient of assistance is an in-group member. In terms of clusters of motivational factors of charitable giving, Hur (2006) found six: a good deed, altruism, a desire for social responsibility, a desire for the common good, mass psychology and reward expectation. Polonsky et al. (2002) identified charity brand, appeal, facts and images, mode of request, portrayals of individuals in need, demographic characteristics, past experiences with the cause, feelings of pity, social justice, empathy, sympathy, guilt and fear, and the need for self-esteem.

Some personality traits also appear to correlate positively with donations. Agreeableness as a dimension of personality (together with prosocial cognition and motives, as well as helping behaviour across a range of situations and victims) was found to be linked to helping (Graziano et al., 2007). Higher cognitive ability has been correlated to higher probability of charitable giving (James, 2011); mood management (i.e. the projected expectation of how good the donation would make the donor feel and the level of regret if they did not donate) was found to be predictive of donation decisions, while empathic feelings were predictive of donation amount (Dickert et al., 2010). Dispositional values also affect donations (Dovidio and Penner, 2004).

As well as the epistemological and methodological problems identified in Chapter 2, these studies display two problematic tendencies. First, they clearly prioritise monetary donation. Even though a primacy attributed to monetary donations is undoubtedly the symptom of larger economic and structural forces, including struggles within the charitable sector, the repetition of this primacy in psychological studies lends legitimacy to and inadvertently normalises it as the desired response. Second, these studies implicitly promote a mechanistic view of the public that frames people's passivity as a stimulus–reaction problem, which to some extent perpetuates the belief that the more factors can be identified, the easier it will be to manipulate the public into behaving differently. I will address the two problems in turn.

The prioritisation, normalisation and expectation of monetary donations as the canonical public response is highly problematic in many respects. In its deeper and wider significance it is testament to the urgency of a critical consideration of what is meant by passive and active response. For example, an undifferentiated definition of passivity risks morally privileging donations, while making a donation might be an effective shortcut to a good conscience while disengaging from the issue.

Fundraising might be essential to the survival of NGOs, but the side effects of appealing to the public through a 'transactional frame' are explored by Darnton and Kirk in their recent report *Finding Frames* (2011). The report sets out the findings of an extensive study on the values and frames used by the public to engage with global poverty. The study was motivated by wanting to understand the dynamics of public engagement and by attempting to make sense of the discrepancy between a steady growth in NGO fundraising revenues and the public understanding of global poverty that is stuck in the 1980s. The researchers found a paradox at the heart of public engagement with humanitarian issues. They claim that while income through public donation has steadily increased, the level of public concern and engagement with global poverty and its causes has been on a downward trajectory. Speaking of the research evidence on the continually changing nature of public engagement, Darnton and Kirk cite Hilton et al.: 'Attention has been drawn to how face-to-face member participation in voluntary associations has increasingly been displaced by a more distant, "cheque-book" relationship between NGOs and their supporters' (Hilton et al., 2010:4).

In Hilton's model a social movement gains big numbers of supporters by changing the relationship with them to one that is more at arm's length. This change in the nature of voluntary sector organisations has been written about since the mid-1980s, when the phrase 'cheque-book member' was coined by Hayes (cited in Jordan and Maloney, 1997). The phrase sums up the transformation from group member to supporter: that is, someone whose main relationship with the social movement group is a transactional one. This is the principal means by which Hilton explains the inexorable increases in revenue on the CAF chart. Darnton and Kirk (2011:6) argue that 'increasing incomes have been gained by changing the nature of engagement by turning members into support-ers, and setting them at arm's length'. They conclude: 'the sector's engagement models have achieved big numbers and ever-increasing incomes, but with what impact on the quality of public engagement?' (Darnton and Kirk, 2011:6). Darnton and Kirk argue that the 'transac-tional frame' has become a normative script in the NGOs relationship with the public and is employed by both actors. This echoes Zizek's (2001) comment on the narcissistic traits of what he calls the capital-istic subjectivity in which we are superficially touched and give money to charity just in order to keep the distant other at arm's-length (cited by Hoijer, 2004:527–8). It could be argued that this is particularly problem-atic when human rights are concerned for two reasons. First, it is easier in humanitarian emergencies – particularly when not man-made, such as floods, earthquakes – than with human rights violations to make an immediate logical connection between monetary aid and an immedi-ate amelioration of the problem (by providing shelter, food and safety for the victims). Second, even though geopolitical causation is never too far away even in 'natural' disasters, human rights issues are always underpinned by on-going political issues. In this situation the role of monetary donations becomes increasingly complicated.

Judging from the consistent focus in the prosocial literature on mon-etary donations, this tendency does not just pertain to NGOs and the public but is widespread. There is thus a problem of circularity where a pattern of behaviour has sedimented into a 'lived' ideology, practised and perpetuated by NGOs, the public and the 'expert' studying their interaction. The short-term advantages of this 'arm's-length' approach for all concerned are clear: NGOs get revenue through 'cheap participa-tion', and the public get a clear conscience by it allowing them to briefly engage and disengage.

The question for us is what kind of relationship does this transac-tional frame engender between NGOs and the public, and between the public and the problem of distant suffering? These two levels are often collapsed and differences ignored. Yet, while related, the public engagement with distant suffering on the one hand, and the public engagement with NGOs on the other, are very different and both deserve proper scrutiny. This chapter concentrates on the latter.

The role of NGOs in public engagement with human rights and humanitarian issues has been largely ignored by psychologists interested in public passivity. When attention has been paid to it, it has treated NGOs as simple intermediaries, playing either a neutral or an irrelevant part. This attitude also informed this study's original approach and consequently the interview schedule did not contain any questions related to Amnesty International or NGOs in general. What emerged in the focus groups, however, speaks of a fundamental role played by NGOs and is testimony to an intensely passionate relationship between the public and NGOs. The data also illustrate how this passionate relationship is key to the public's attitudes towards human rights and distant suffering. The fact that the data emerged spontaneously, vigorously and consistently indicates the widespread and socio-cultural nature of what participants said, rather than the expression of individual attitudes.

In my data analysis it became clear very quickly that NGOs mediate the public's relationship with distant suffering and human rights in specific and powerful ways, beyond the obvious function of literally being mediators of the information. Patterns emerged, which consistently appeared across focus groups and were saturated with emotions. These patterns will be taken both at face value, as testimony of the public's perception of NGOs and their role in human rights issues, and as vocabularies of denial.

To provide a nuanced analysis of accounts of denial, it is important to pay attention to both content and strategies of denial: for example, what these accounts say and through which means they operate effectively. In terms of content, as 'interpretative repertoires' (Potter and Wetherell, 1995; Wetherell and Potter, 1988) they represent the building blocks speakers use for constructing factual versions of reality, making evaluations and performing particular actions. They are also social resources available to all who share a language and culture and are used by the speaker to justify particular versions of events, to excuse or validate their own behaviour, to fend off criticism or otherwise allow them to maintain a credible stance in an interaction (Wetherell and Potter, 1992).

Interpretive repertoires can be drawn upon by virtually anyone in order to bring about a particular, desired representation of an event

(Edley, 2001). Because interpretative repertoires are part and parcel of any community's common sense, providing a sense of shared understanding, they convey a sense of familiarity and everyday recognition. In the sense that they are banal, they are extremely powerful as 'ideology in action' because they appear so obvious: not the personal opinion of a particular individual but what 'everybody knows' (Edley, 2001:202). Each repertoire contains 'argumentative topoi' of denial. A *topos* is a system of public knowledge, a discursive resource in which one may find arguments for sustaining a conclusion (Van Der Valk, 2003:319). Wodak and Meyer (2001) add that they refer to socially shared beliefs and, crucially, they function as content-related warrants which connect the argument with the claim. As such, they justify the transition from the argument to the conclusion.

The analysis presented in this chapter identifies three interpretive repertoires, defined on the basis of their focus. The first, 'the medium is the message', focuses on the attributed manipulative function of the appeal. The second, 'shoot the messenger', attacks the sender of the appeal, primarily Amnesty International (AI) but also humanitarian organisations and charities in general. The third, 'babies and bathwater', questions in various ways the validity of the action recommended in the appeal. The repertoires are discussed in terms of how participants use them to weaken the standing of the appeal-makers and to ascribe a moral position to themselves while remaining passive to the appeal. As previously stated, the intention here is not to judge individuals, but to make visible how the everyday use of banal justifications contributes to a morality of unresponsiveness. Thus the operations of denial discussed here acquire meaning and significance through their imbeddedness in the micro (the study) and macro (socio-cultural) contexts in which they are used.

If we accept that denials are part of a strategy of defence, presupposing implicit or explicit accusations, or that they may be pre-emptive (van Dijk, 1992:91), the *topoi* are the explanatory links to the unspoken question: 'Why don't you actively respond to these appeals?' Hence, each one can be paraphrased, in turn, as 'because there is a problem with the message'; 'because there is a problem with the messenger'; 'because there is a problem with the recommended action'. In terms of strategies of denial, by looking at repertoires in terms of addressivity – which focuses on the speaker as agent using particular discursive strategies – the analysis makes visible the (more or less intentional) practices adopted to achieve a particular social aim. In line with van Dijk (1993a,b,c), Wodak and Meyer (2001) and Wodak (2004), it focuses primarily on the persuasive dimension of text, that is, argumentation strategies, style and rhetoric. Specifically, the discursive analysis identifies and discusses strategies of:

- perspectivation, nomination and predication (e.g. the use of particular characterisations of the other – in this case AI and other charities) to achieve a particular rhetorical effect;
- argumentation which identifies the arguments, either explicit or implied, the goals of the speaker in using them, and the strategies used to provide backing to the arguments.

These strategies are, to different extents, all aimed at positive self-presentation and negative other-presentation and are intended to warrant the participants' moral stance and undermine Amnesty's appeals. Additionally, the analysis further explores the performative function of accounts of denial through the concept of 'speech act' (Austin, 1962; Searle, 1969), which views what people say as having a function within an interaction and achieving an effect for them. In short, accounts of denial as speech acts 'do' things: warrant the speaker's position, undermine the other's action, convince, justify and so on.

The discursive analysis proposed here explores what subject positions are made possible for both the speaker and the other through the use of particular accounts or storylines and the consequences of such positioning for self-image. Thus the ways in which participants position themselves in relation to appeals and campaigners are looked at as performing particular rhetorical functions to achieve specific ideological and (local) moral effects: namely, to discredit campaigners, thus morally justifying speakers' passivity. Indirect or presumptive positioning has been defined as 'the use of attributions of mental (stupid), characteriological (unreliable) or moral (puritanical) traits to position someone, favourably or unfavourably, with respect to oneself and one's interests' (Harré and Moghaddam, 2003:6). To position someone negatively denies them specific rights and grants the speaker the moral high ground. This 'malignant positioning' (Sabat, 2003, 2001; Kitwood, 1990; Gilbert and Mulkay, 1982) is often part of a dynamic process of repositioning where the speaker is resisting or challenging an original positioning of themselves. 'To engage in repositioning oneself or others is to claim a right or a duty to adjust what an actor has taken to be the first order positioning that is dominating the unfolding of events' (Harré and Moghaddam, 2003:7).

The analysis contained in this chapter focuses on such repositioning. It assumes the unspoken first order positioning whereby Amnesty occupies the moral high ground and positions the speakers under the moral responsibility of acting prosocially in response to the appeal. The analysis illustrates how by 'malignantly positioning' Amnesty, the speaker manages to undermine Amnesty's moral authority and remove its right to demand proactive response by claiming that Amnesty might not be trustworthy, might not be telling the full truth, questioning how the donations would be spent and, ultimately, positioning Amnesty as manipulative and self-serving. This operation allows the participants implicitly to regain a moral positioning for themselves while resisting the appeal.

'The medium is the message'

I start from the assumption that Amnesty International's mandate is twofold: as a campaigner for human rights (striving to inform the public and to raise awareness of human rights abuses) and as a maker of appeals (aiming to raise funds by focusing attention on the specific current issues they are working on). In both instances, they address audiences as moral agents. The first repertoire began to evidence a striking mismatch between campaigners' intentions and audiences' reception of appeals, in that participants positioned themselves as critical and discerning consumers rather than as moral agents. The 'medium is the message' repertoire appeared in all interviews and was the most agreed upon, suggesting that it is a much used 'ready-made' story, already current in the wider social context (Fairclough, 1995), particularly when participants position themselves as 'savvy' consumers. Participants used this repertoire to disregard the function of the message as a plea for emphatic, moral responsiveness to the information and focused instead on the message itself which is scrutinised closely for its style and function.

> *[9] Trudy:*   *It's a very clever campaign; I mean it does actually do what it's supposed to do [...] And when you read that, the first thing you want to do is put your hand in your pocket and send them a cheque. That's what it's supposed to do and it will. It does do that because you get so moved by it, you think, well I'll do anything to help and then it's got this thing about donations at the bottom of it and after reading that you would ...*

Trudy introduces a theme, echoed by other participants in various ways, that the message is 'doing some kind of work', well beyond informing the reader about suffering in a distant place, which hardly gets mentioned. Thus, according to Trudy, this is a 'clever' and successful piece of text; it operates by giving a moving story which gets the reader to feel s/he 'would do anything to help', then the reader finds a strategically located box asking for a donation. The emotionally aroused reader is offered a release through the action of giving a donation. The extract contains several important semantic moves. There is, first of all, the use of referential ambiguity (*'when you read that, the first thing you want to do is put your hand in your pocket'*). By giving agency to a generalised 'you', the speaker invites consent and warrants status of general knowledge to her statement. The use of the figure of speech *'put your hand in your pocket'*, with its implication of immediate unthinking response, intensifies the power of the statement by conveying the strong impression of a mechanistic, automatic exchange (stimulus–response). This is immediately followed by an apparent agreement, *'that's what it's supposed to do'*, followed by a deprecatory qualifier *'then it's got this thing about donations'*, which reveals the discursive intentions of the speaker. The semantic move of showing understanding functions as a disclaimer as it positions the speaker as even-handed and sympathetic. In the final sentence, through a referential move, Trudy constructs a generalised 'us' as emotionally responsive (*'you get so moved by it'*) and profoundly altruistic (*'we'll do anything to help'*) in opposition to, although this is only alluded to, manipulative campaigners who take advantage of 'our' noble response.

I decided to start with this quote, even though it comes from the last focus group, because it contains several elements which appeared throughout the groups and gives a flavour of the types of argumentation used by the participants. For example, it contains the oppositional stance of 'us and them', public and campaigners, which runs throughout the data, even in statements ostensibly sympathetic. Also, and equally omnipresent, there is the persistent and intractable connection between Amnesty's campaigns and money. As a strategy of argumentation, this connection firmly places the debate within a materialistic and consumeristic discourse as opposed to a moral one. From within this discourse, the participants position themselves as reflexive, neutral assessors and critical consumers, who use sophisticated analytical skills to evaluate and judge the effectiveness of the campaign as demonstrated by the following:

[6] Neil: Again even even with this article, even with this article from Amnesty International. It is a rhetoric in a way, because when Amnesty give

> *us this they give it to us in this formula. We always read that we're*
> *about to give you a horror story, we give you the horror story, now give*
> *us your money. It's always every single time you read anything from*
> *a charity it comes with that formula. And that in a way is rhetoric.*
> *I think in a way you feel responsible but then you start question-*
> *ing then you don't have time and then you stop. Your responsibility*
> *fades.*

Neil describes a chain of events similar to that in Trudy's account, but the reaction here is less appreciative and the appeal is presented as openly cynical, mechanistic and manipulative: '*we give you the horror story; now give us your money*'. The fact that there is a horror story in the first place is obscured by the function it serves. The quote is bursting with discursive moves and peppered with intensifications through repetition ('*even*' is repeated three times in the first line) and extreme case formulations ('*We always read that …*'; '*It's always, every single time*'). Neil also uses 'pars pro toto' to back his central argument that what Amnesty communicates is nothing but rhetoric, and to bundle Amnesty together with all other charities. This discursive move obfuscates their specific mandate and dismisses Amnesty's communications by intimating that they are formulaic. This suggests that NGOs' attempts to focus on branding seem doomed to fail. Crucially, as a speech act, these discursive moves invite the listener to (a) focus on Amnesty's technique, rather than its mandate; and (b) accept the argumentative thrust that it is because of this that 'your responsibility fades'. There is a sense of antagonism with Amnesty International, as if Neil felt that he had cleverly avoided a trap. The strategic use of referential ambiguity through the impersonal 'you' generalises the effect of the phenomenon beyond himself, thus normalising it.

[6] Lorna: Once they sort of start talking about, you know, you are their
> *only last hope. I think that's when you see a clear sort of twist*
> *in the tone of the reading and, yeah, it's very irritating and, I think*
> *there's definitely a sort of overkill there you know. It's, they're sort*
> *of forcing you to give money that you're not entirely comfortable*
> *with …*

Lorna's statement describes a very different kind of emotional response from the expected sympathy, empathy and pity. Lorna feels 'irritated' and that she is being 'forced' to do something against her will. The lexical style is revealing here; through exaggeration and the use of strong words like '*twist*', '*overkill*' and '*forcing you*', Lorna intensifies her statement and warrants her '*irritation*'. It is striking that the emotional response to the communication is directed at how the message is put together or at Amnesty, rather than at the horrendous details of the appeal.

In summary, in the 'medium is the message' repertoire, audiences construct the appeal as a cleverly devised marketing campaign which is, nevertheless, manipulative and formulaic. Participants position themselves as being resentful of manipulation and cleverly seeing through such attempts. There is a further twist in this tale, in that participants simultaneously position themselves as discerning consumers and yet express resentment at being addressed as consumers. The attribution of negative actions (such as '*twist*', ' *force*', '*extract money*') convey considerable anger and justify the self-righteous response of self-defensive shutdown. Non-responsiveness is justified by presenting it as resistance to manipulation.

'Shoot the messenger'

In the 'shoot the messenger' repertoire, audiences position themselves in relation to the 'messenger' – Amnesty International in this instance. It marks a shift in the moral gaze from the audience to the agency as participants question the integrity and trustworthiness of the campaigners and charities in general. This repertoire conveys a lot of emotional force and two distinct *topoi* – 'Is this a true story?' and 'Should we trust them?' Each provides a specific warrant to the unresponsiveness. They can be paraphrased as making the claim: 'we don't actively respond to this message because there is a problem with the messenger'. The most deleterious ideological impact of this repertoire is that, by undermining the messenger, it potentially weakens the impact of the appeal.

'Is this a true story?'

In this *topos*, participants are at their most explicit in using a mixture of literal and interpretive denial. The speakers fluctuate between openly doubting the truthfulness of the events reported in the Amnesty appeals (literal denial), and a more subtle intimation of distortion of the truth on the part of Amnesty (interpretative denial). Both have the effect of undermining the force of the appeal.

[6] *Mandy:As I was going through some of it I was thinking oh, I know somebody who actually works in Afghanistan and I'll check with him.*

You know what it's like. I know somebody who lives in the Middle East and was married to a Middle Eastern man, I'll check with them. And then I began to think, I wonder how many of these are actually true. I know it probably sounds terrible to say it because Amnesty wouldn't pick a story up, wouldn't create a story, but there is such a thing as marketing, and you sort of wonder ...

Mandy gives a remarkably elaborate denial account of her action and the moral justification for it. Mandy starts by expressing doubts about the truthfulness of Amnesty's story to the extent that, while reading it, she goes through a list of the possible people she knows with whom she can check the details. She uses several semantic moves to warrant her credentials and insinuate doubt about Amnesty. For example, by referring to her source as someone who '*actually*' works in Afghanistan, she implicitly introduces a difference between those who '*actually*' know (her source) and those who only claim to know (Amnesty). As a speech act, this invites the listener to question the truthfulness of Amnesty's statements. She continues with this discursive strategy through a statement that implies common knowledge and invites recognition and complicity from the listener: '*you know what it's like*'. This informal type of argumentation is designed to get the adherence of the audience to a thesis (Carranza, 1999). The narrative style illustrates how one thought led to another in her head and her suspicion of all the stories reported by Amnesty grew ('*I wonder how many of these are actually true*'). This display of reasonableness rhetorically demonstrates that Mandy is a reasonable person and warrants her good faith by showing how the suspicion comes from the text and not from her. However, having openly introduced distrust, she shows reflexive awareness that what she says about Amnesty might sound bad and contextually unacceptable ('*I know it probably sounds terrible to say it*'). In a spectacular attempt to hold on to two mutually exclusive claims – that Amnesty is simultaneously making up and not making up the story – she offers hope of moral expiation for all through the semantic move of showing apparent support ('*Amnesty would not pick a story up, wouldn't create a story*'), followed by a 'but', which reveals that these statements are simply disclaimers. The parallelism, in the form of repeated negation, backs her statement and intensifies its effect. Amnesty campaigners are lying, not because they are dishonest, but because they are forced to by marketing – '*there is such a thing as marketing*'. She thus positions herself as someone who appreciates the complexities and moral dilemmas of the world we live in and is not a bad person for thinking in this way.

The theme that Amnesty is somehow tweaking the truth proved extremely popular and appeared consistently, even though only a few examples can be discussed here. For example:

[7] *Tina: I was partly thinking are they putting several stories together but then I thought well it doesn't really matter, you use any kind of trick you can [...] There might be some manipulation, there might be. There's certainly some leaving out of details. It's, as someone was saying, we don't know exactly we don't know who the men were, we don't know ...*

[8] *Alf: They are presenting the truth and they are dressing it up.*

The statements varied in details, but they all openly made use of discursive moves such as disclaimers (e.g. '*I think they are true but ...*') or lexical choices ('*they know how to play with the information*'), just to mention a couple. These statements are important, not only in terms of their content – the fact that the same *topoi* appear in most of the groups shows that this is a ready-made story, recognised and consensual – but also in terms of the 'interpersonal' work of the text. That the speakers use argumentation strategies suggests that they are not just expressing their opinion: they want to convince their audience. This in turn implies awareness of a normative moral imperative, meaning that they were aware that they ought to be responding to Amnesty's messages differently, thereby confirming that denial statements are part of a defence strategy, presupposing implicit or explicit accusations (van Dijk, 1992).

While a few statements verged on literal denial (Abi: '*did it actually happen?*'), most were striking examples of interpretive denial; what Amnesty is reporting happened but it is not quite as they describe it. Crucially, this is attributed to Amnesty intentionally making things look worse 'for a specific effect'. This effective technique of neutralisation has the essential function of undermining Amnesty's credibility.

'Should we trust them?'

The second *topos* questions whether Amnesty's information should be fully believed, thus implicitly casting doubts on the organisation's trustworthiness and undermining Amnesty's moral authority. In the first two extracts the participants, who speak closely after each other, are in agreement that Amnesty tweaks the truth.

[8:31] John: The second one though, I was a little bit almost sceptical. Because I mean, don't get me wrong, awful, but there's a lot of hyperbole in here that I'm a bit questioning of. [...] if this were written by someone who didn't work for Amnesty International and had an objective view on it, it would be just as bad, it would be just as condemning but it would be also somewhat more realistic.

The ample use made by John of self-warranting disclaimers (*'don't get me wrong'*) and his apologetic tentativeness (*'I was a little bit almost sceptical'*, *'because I mean...'* and *'I am a bit questioning of'*) indicates caution and suggests that John might be worried about how his statements are received and that they might be deemed 'improper' by the group, especially since he speaks early in the discussion when still ignorant of how the rest of the group and, indeed, the interviewer might react to his opinion. John's tentativeness is not surprising, considering that he is making indirect accusations that Amnesty's statements are untrue and lack objectivity. 'Realistic', in this context, clearly means more reality-based, more truthful. Alf comes to his aid:

[8:37] Alf: That's, I mean I, I, I was part of the Amnesty International disarming club[1] in high school grade nine and ten. I'm a big fan of Amnesty International. But no absolutely, I don't expect them to be objective. Erm that's not what they're, that's not their job. And they're not going to work as well if they're objective. And I don't, I don't fault them for that.

Alf's statement is an endorsement of John's. By simultaneously ratifying the claims that Amnesty is not objective while justifying the organisation on the basis of its mandate, Alf seems to mean here that Amnesty cannot be neutral because of its mission; yet he invites a questioning of Amnesty's words and undermines its moral standing. Importantly, while Alf refers to Amnesty as committed and partisan, John's positioning of Amnesty as manipulative and exaggerating the facts is left unexplained, and therefore unjustified.

Variations on this theme appeared repeatedly within and between groups. For example:

[3] Tracy: I think they were true but I think they have to be edited in a way to make them, you know, more shocking ...

[4] Emma: I think that they know how to play with the information.

[8] Elsa: *I'm a bit weary of Amnesty International reports because a lot of it is exaggeration [...] I'm not sceptical of the facts but just how it's reported and how it's been presented. It just makes me step back from it.*

[1] Lisa: *I believe that most of it is probably true. I do think it's somewhat manipulative [...] So I think that's not something that's not true, it's not like they were lying, they were leaving it out for a specific effect [...] it seems like it's, erm, not as honest, hyperbolic [...] like things that catch your eye just like advertising*

[2] Abi: *Well how can one actually say whether they're telling the truth? How can one actually say if they are telling the truth?*

Here we have a variety of denial operations. While Abi's statement verges on literal denial (did it actually happen?), the others are all striking examples of interpretive denial, for example, 'what Amnesty is reporting happened but is not as bad as they describe'. Cohen (2001:8) describes this form of denial thus: 'the observer disputes the cognitive meaning given to an event and re-allocates it to another class of events by changing words, using euphemisms or adopting technical jargon'. Taken at face value, most of these statements don't criticise Amnesty's truthfulness directly, but rather the way in which the information is conveyed. It is important to note this and to acknowledge the ability and willingness of the public not to 'throw the baby (the truth of the information) out with the bathwater' (the way Amnesty uses this information). Yet there was consensus among the participants in criticising Amnesty for *intentionally* making things look worse *'for a specific effect'*, which implies that participants are being manipulated by Amnesty.

Of all the storylines used by the participants, that involving money and manipulation was the most frequent and most passionately discussed. This last storyline could be summarised as lamenting: 'all they want is my money'.

[4] Joel: *It's meant to tear your heart strings and then twice at the beginning and at the end, there's a little form for you to fill in and start giving money.*

[3] Paula: *Their intention was from the outset trying to shock you enough to make you pay.*

Both Joel and Paula, like many others, felt that their emotions were intentionally manipulated for self-serving motives. These participants don't convey any empathetic distress or emotional upset that the horrible things described in the appeals happen in the world, nor do they value the Amnesty campaigning role in connecting them to others' distant suffering. In contrast, through this storyline, Amnesty International is positioned as ruthlessly manipulating audiences to give money.

[9] Trudy: I don't see on anywhere here does it say 'if anyone wants to go out there and help the needy people; if you want to send donations of old clothes' or anything like that. No, it's hard cash. That's what they want.

Trudy does not explain how exactly she could help protect human rights by going in person or sending old clothes to the country where human rights are abused. These actions are not offered as realistic, possible or even desirable alternatives, but used rhetorically to demonstrate Amnesty's bad faith: *'No, it's hard cash. That's what they want.'*

The psychological component of this statement, the difference between helping motivated by 'empathy-altruism' and 'heroic-altruism' is important. The empathy-altruism theory of helping behaviour, proposed by Batson (1991), suggests that when we feel empathy for another person we will attempt to help the person for purely altruistic reasons, regardless of any potential for personal gain. This seems to be the framework used by Amnesty and humanitarian agencies in general. According to the theory of 'heroic-altruism', an individual risks their own well-being in order to help others, even strangers, by engaging in visible, active intervention (Schroeder et al., 1995; Eagly and Crowley, 1986). This form of helping, referred to by Trudy, has become the best known, I expect because of its visibility. It is highly regarded in popular culture.[2] Unlike 'purely' altruistic versions, heroic-altruism offers the secondary narcissistic gain of visibility and social recognition. Without entering the ongoing psychological debate as to whether this is less altruistic than more selfless motivations, it seems to describe the kind of pay-back that participants feel deprived of when asked for anonymous donations. Thinking in these terms could give a different sense to the following refrain.

[4] Emma: This advert makes me feel like they want to just get money.

The more generous interpretation of this quote could be that the participant dislikes the soulless quality of the monetary side of the transaction which turns Amnesty's appeal, in Emma's definition, into an advertisement. It could also be that participants feel 'short-changed' when the donation makes the personal component of their action invisible. When inclusivity, a sense of self as part of a common humanity (Cohen, 2001), is lacking, it might be harder to respond on purely altruistic grounds. However, calling Amnesty's appeal an '*advert*' is an exceptionally powerful speech act that disowns AI as 'moral entrepreneurs', and firmly positions them as skilled brokers. A similar construction of AI as trying to sell a product comes up in group 6 from Neil.

[6] *Neil: Sometimes in fact I actually keep these (appeals), I actually put them in files somewhere [...] I get ten or twelve of these every day from a variety of organisations or people asking for credit cards or pizzas or whatever [others laugh] it goes in the same thing though, it's junk mail you didn't ask for.*[3]

Roy does not waste time expanding on the theme and goes straight to the point:

[7] *Roy: In money terms I don't trust them.*

It seems that as soon as donations or joining Amnesty are brought into the picture, suspicion is aroused, thus adding complexity to the problematic use of the 'transactional frame' identified by Darnton and Kirk (2011). Considering the implicit acknowledgment contained in *Finding Frames* – that NGOs too often address the public with the short term aim of getting donations – what participants are saying seems a pretty accurate perception of NGOs' attitude towards the public. However, the use of this storyline allows an advantageous self-positioning for the participants who, by implicitly positioning themselves as potential victims of a manipulative, self-serving Amnesty, have the right to reject the appeal as a whole. This very effective technique of neutralisation also functions as a speech act undermining Amnesty's credibility and, with the unfortunate effect on potential longer-term public engagement, it feeds into an orientation of disengagement and scepticism.

Unsurprisingly, the storyline of truthfulness often developed into one of distrust, not only of Amnesty International but of NGOs and charities in general. All the distrust statements were negative but varied in terms of accusation. Kate and Stacey, for example, portray Amnesty as a pest.

[3] Kate: *Once you've filled in one of these little boxes then they, they write to you every couple of months and (Stacey: yeah) ask for more.*

Agencies are positioned by Kate as greedy, relentless and demanding. This justifies implicitly participants' non-responsiveness as a reasonable defence against harassment. Carol is more colourful in her description.

[2] Carol: *[…] non-governmental organisations I usually associate with a lot of money and a sort of high-flying red car because in Kenya the non-governmental organisations officials always drive in big four-wheel-drive vehicles. Very comfortable, and they live in very big houses so I mean that I find them removed from the reality yeah so I have erm, I have never seen how Amnesty International can maybe help with HR abuses in Kenya. Yeah, they seem far removed from regular day-to-day lives people lead in Kenya. It had taken a few high-profile cases and made a noise about it maybe to the government. But how accessible it is to maybe that ordinary Kenyan whose human rights have been violated?*

Here employees of non-governmental organisations (NGOs) are constructed as privileged and affluent bureaucrats, totally out of touch with the real suffering of the local population. There is an insinuation that money from donations goes to support their comfortable lifestyles, sports cars and four-wheel-drive vehicles. Additionally, Carol openly questions whether Amnesty is doing what it claims to be doing: '*I have never seen how Amnesty International can maybe help with human rights abuses in Kenya.*' Finally, she belittles Amnesty's operations as '*making a noise*'

Carol's is perhaps the most complex and multifaceted expression of the distrust storyline. She undermines Amnesty's credibility on many fronts by positioning them as potentially corrupt, out of touch with ordinary people and their needs and, fundamentally, incapable of helping the cause they foster. As in all the other statements, while the repositioning of Amnesty and NGOs is open and clearly articulated, the self-repositioning is often implicit. The unspoken implication in Carol's claims is 'this is why I don't trust them and don't donate to their appeals'.

The recent scandal involving an Amnesty International pay-off of more than £500,000 to its former chief, Irene Khan, has been widely discussed in the media where attention has been repeatedly and pointedly drawn to the link between AI receiving donations from the public and the strikingly high pay-off to Ms Khan.[4] It is precisely this kind of scandal that, despite Amnesty's attempt to account for it and to contain the resulting damage to its public image,[5] powerfully resonates with Carol's account and is likely to feed into storylines of distrust and misuse of resources, which position participants as justified in not giving because of doubts as to how their money will be used. For example:

[2] *Jill:* *You don't really know where the money is going. I find I want to know about these organisations, what are they doing. How much of the money, say 90 per cent of what they get goes towards this. I mean yeah I understand that there are always going to be admin costs and there's always people who has to be hired, and I'm willing to donate towards that as long as it's not more than the money that goes to the people that need it.*

What Jill says in the second part of the quote sounds perfectly reasonable, but her opening statement '*you don't really know where the money is going*' is damning and invites mistrust. The fact that it is uttered in the impersonal conveys the sense that this is common knowledge and should be treated as a fact. The second sentence in her statement marks a turning point in the indirect positioning. Her tone is very authoritative when she states: '*I find I want to know about these organisations, what are they doing.*' But by giving herself the right to audit '*these organisations*', Jill turns the tables and implicitly claims the high moral ground. She is not the one who should be questioned on moral grounds; Amnesty is. She is not the one in need to justify herself; rather, Amnesty should account for how they spend her money.

[3] *Stacey:* *If you could guarantee that the money was going to those people, you could see every single penny is going to those people then it would make you do something about it, but knowing, you know, just gut feeling, knowing that it doesn't go to those people not even half of it, most probably doesn't even go to those people it just makes you think, well, sorry, but no.*

[7] *Leila:* *But having worked for a few charities it kind of put me off donating to other charities. [...] one of the charities I worked, I worked in, there was corruption going on with the chief executive, well alleged corruption. I just thought, it just put me off, and having worked at another charity where you just see how much money's wasted while you're working there. And you speak to people in finance*

> who say 'god I'd never donate to this charity if you saw how much
> money was wasted' and stuff like that it put me off.

Here, participants seem preoccupied with charities' alleged waste or mismanagement of resources. Again, participants don't seem to differentiate between individual agencies.

Stacey wonders where the money goes. She demands guarantees that '*every single penny*' is going to the victims in order to motivate her to give. The use of hyperbole shows that this statement is for rhetorical purposes, rather than being a realistic expectation. The referential ambiguity '*if you could guarantee*' instead of 'if Amnesty could guarantee' implicitly insinuates that Amnesty could not provide that guarantee, but without having to openly state that. Her warranting shows uncertainty as she lacks conviction in her own claims – '*just gut feeling […] most probably*' – yet she still claims that '*not even half of* ' the money goes to the victim. Even while uttering such a precise figure, she still uses referential ambiguity – '*but knowing, you know … knowing that*' – suggesting that this is common knowledge, rather than her own suspicion. Her alleged knowledge that her money would not go to the victims is nevertheless used to justify her decision not to donate to charities.

Leila uses a different tactic to undermine charities' trustworthiness. She starts by warranting her credibility as a witness through personal experience. She uses 'perspectivation' by reporting an alleged negative event related to charities. Even though her self-assurance waivers at one point – '*there was corruption going on with the chief executive, well alleged corruption*' – she proceeds unperturbed to provide variations on the theme of charities' corruption and mismanagement of funds. The use of *pars pro toto* is a powerful device inviting the listener to categorise all charities as corrupt.

The implicit message conveyed in this *topos* is that, as with the previous one, giving money is not a good idea. This is not because of doubts about the political and practical effectiveness of such action, but because, it is suggested, donors' money is not spent on humanitarian causes at all.

Scepticism and cynicism appear to be the overarching moral imperatives which are normalised by the overwhelmingly consumerist, rather than moral, discourse taken up by the participants and, arguably, often set up by NGOs themselves. As consumers, participants justify being sceptical, questioning and discerning to avoid being taken advantage of.

*[4] Joel: A lot of these charities the money, just, just goes in people's pockets
           unfortunately, so many cases with, people start up a charity, 'cause
           you can do that easily. You don't have to have a permit by law and
           the money can go straight into some guy's pocket. And I, I'd dread
           to say that happens with Amnesty. I would think probably they're,
           like, bona fide, I don't know. Makes you cynical that you see all these
           different cases and things.*

Joel constructs charities as legalised fraud. He backs this negative 'perspectivation' by claiming that, due to lack of regulation, anybody can
start a charity easily and pocket supporters' money. The expression of
regret (*'unfortunately'*) warrants the speaker's moral position, and by stating that there are *'so many cases'* he backs his (vague) claim that this is
not his bias but a well-known, widespread phenomenon. Lexical indi-
rectness – *'these charities'*, *'people start up a charity'*, *'you don't have to
have a permit'* – is used to amplify his claim. This is followed by the
powerful semantic move of showing apparent support of Amnesty by
singling them out: *'I would think probably they're, like, bona fide'*. But
the tentativeness in *'probably they're like, bona fide, I don't know'* reveals
that, in fact, he is insinuating exactly the opposite, without having to
appear attacking of Amnesty. The return to vagueness – *'you see all these
different cases and things'* – in the warranting of his cynical approach
gives a sense that these events are pervasive and well known to everybody and positions him as a streetwise individual who knows 'the ways
of the world'. Agencies are positioned as liars, manipulative and self-
serving through the use of this repertoire. Conversely, audiences are
the victims and in need of protection. Once more, the storyline is not
one of social responsibility and empathy, but one of assessment of the
trustworthiness of campaigners. The moral imperative resulting from
this repertoire is the legitimacy and normalisation of suspicion and
scepticism.

'Babies and bathwater'

The final target and the focus of the third repertoire is the action
recommended by the appeal. Its *topoi* justify the transition from the
argument to the conclusion by implicitly claiming that audiences don't
actively respond to these appeals because there is a problem with the
recommended action. Money still figures in this repertoire, but the focus
is no longer on the function of the message or the trustworthiness of
the agency. Instead, audiences position themselves as 'savvy' assessors

of the success or failure of the appeal's strategy. This allows participants to avoid moral criticism for not engaging with the recommended action because the action itself is deemed to be failing: 'It addresses the symptom not the cause'; 'Money won't help'; 'Will go in the wrong pockets'. By defining the action in this way, the 'baby' of socially responsible action is thrown out with the 'bathwater' of the partial truth contained in all of these statements. As speech acts, these *topoi* exonerate and warrant the moral stance of the speaker.

'It addresses the symptom not the cause'

Human rights appeals have many purposes: for example, to recruit new members and supporters, to inform the public and to raise funds. As Cohen puts it: ' success means "getting the message across", "waking people up" or "getting through to them"; but also "getting them to do something – donate money, become active and be educated" ' (Cohen, 2001:196). Yet, disingenuously or not, participants selectively register only one part of what Amnesty is asking them to do: give money. Donations, taken in isolation, are then compared to other possible courses of action. For example:

[2] *John:*   *What about the issues that have brought the conflict,*[6] *you know [. . .] but what, what is being done you know to correct the political situation?*

[7] *Harriet*   *They totally appeal to your emotions but what you don't get is the real reasons behind it. And the facts are just numbing 'cause really that doesn't give you any option or other than you write a small cheque.*

[5] *Mary:*   *We have to like address the people who are really responsible and like do something more direct, rather than just say 'let's give money here, money there' [. . .] giving money, to me, it feels like trying to attack, trying to take care of the symptom instead of attacking the real root of the problem. It's like putting a little bandage on some wound and it's like OK, it'll be OK, and then, that has an effect. If we all give a bit of money the situation's going to get better, but we haven't really tackled the root of the problem and that's, I think that's the only way to change things, is go to the root.*

[9] *Karen:*   *The work has to get to the root of the problem.*

In these quotes, Amnesty's operations are positioned as superficial solutions that do not address the problem and discursively construct Amnesty's mandate to be the 'chicken soup' of human rights. While Amnesty is portrayed as inadequate and ineffectual by '*putting a little bandage on some wound'*, the participants indirectly position themselves as better engaged with the problem because they believe in *'getting to the root of the problem'* (Mary and Karen), and *'getting to the real reason behind it'* (Mary). Through a 'realist' discourse, participants contrast real, deep-reaching action with ineffectual, idealistic, vague solutions. This powerful rhetoric allows participants who do not respond to Amnesty's campaigns not only to avoid blame, but also to claim the moral high ground. At the same time, small details in the participants' talk convey an attitude of dismissivness. For example, the way in which Mary says *'let's give money here, money there'* communicates carelessness and a lack of proper reflection and reinforces the sense that asking for and giving money is the wrong thing to do, thus further undermining Amnesty's authority.

As the purpose of this chapter is not a defence of Amnesty, I will not engage with the misrepresentations and distortions of Amnesty's mandate and actions. However, we can see the social force of these quotes in how they position Amnesty's operations as superficial solutions that do not address the problem and discursively construct Amnesty's mandate as an ineffectual, superficial palliative. Conversely, the participants indirectly position themselves as better engaged with the problem because they believe in *'correcting the political situation'* (John), in *'getting to the root of the problem'* (Mary and Karen), and *'getting to the real reason behind it'* (Mary). Thus, this storyline contrasts real, deep-reaching action offered by the participants with Amnesty's ineffectual, idealistic, vague solutions. This powerful rhetoric allows participants who do not respond to Amnesty's campaigns not only to avoid blame, but also to claim a higher moral ground.

'Money won't help'

Here money is questioned in terms of the usefulness of donations in human rights issues. For example:

[9] *Karen: No amount of money is going to help them.*
[4] *Adam: What's the point in giving them money if it's not going to, it's not actually going to help?*

The need for proof of efficacy of one's pro-social action has been repeatedly demonstrated in research (e.g. Warren and Walker, 1991). Certainly, it is hard to fault Karen and Adam's reasoning in terms of needing to see a direct link between money and respect of human rights, in the same way in which, for example, a donor can see the immediate benefits of their £10 if it buys a goat for a family in Sudan. Thus, taking these statements at face value has implications for appeal makers which will be examined later. Nevertheless, these statements also implicitly function as justification for neither donating nor responding proactively to the appeal. The selective representation and carefully constructed positioning of Amnesty casts doubts and undermines it.

[8] Alf: I am opposed to just say give us money and we'll stop torture. How do you plan on doing that exactly? […] I can see my money going towards helping someone who is starving. I can't see my money going towards toppling the Saudi Arabian government which is one of the richest governments in the entire world. You know my ten dollars is just not going to do a thing. […] so let's say someone who doesn't know anything about Saudi Arabia picks this up and goes 'wow Saudi Arabia's a really awful government. I'll donate my pay cheque this week to' (.) what exactly?, bombing them out of existence? How, what, what, what can you do with this?

Alf, who makes ample use of hyperbole and *reductio ad absurdum*, is an active Amnesty supporter, with a long history of humanitarian action, and his claim is therefore likely to derive from a commitment to more successful campaigning. This is hinted at in the use of '*just*' in his opening sentence – '*I am opposed to just say give us money*' – thus indicating his knowledge that Amnesty does not stop at asking for money, but does much more. Nevertheless, Alf's comments are disingenuous despite his likely good intentions. As someone well informed about Amnesty's mandate, he seems to wilfully misrepresent the organisation, as is revealed by a closer discursive analysis of his words. His repeated use of hyperbole, extreme case formulations and false comparisons – his pay cheque with the riches of Saudi Arabia, ten dollars to Amnesty with bombing Saudi Arabia '*out of existence*' – has the effect of ridiculing Amnesty's appeal. The well-known and powerful rhetorical device of repeating things three times – 'what, what, what' – forcefully draws attention to and questions the action proposed by Amnesty and amplifies further the power of the statement. He also uses parallelism: he initially seems to be in apparent agreement with giving money – '*I can see my money going towards helping someone who is starving*' – but this is followed by a qualifier – '*I can't see my money going towards toppling the Saudi Arabian government*'. This semantic move has several effects. By working as a disclaimer, it warrants the speaker's altruism and generosity, but also sets the scene for the ridiculing that follows.

'Money will go in the wrong pockets'

The claim that money will go in the wrong pockets is developed further by other participants and taken to its most extreme with pernicious implications.

[7] Roy: *I mean funds basically go to the so-called government and the government basically will waste it. [...] the government seems to live like kings, no matter what, the little ministers they seem to live like kings while the people live like paupers*

[3] Stacey: *If I could afford to do something about it then I would but it just makes me wonder, you know, how much of this money does go to the right people. You know, it just makes me wonder, you know, that they keep lining these government people that are doing all the abuses anyway.*

While the previous participants using the storyline of mismanagement of funds only insinuated that charities would be wasteful, both Roy and Stacey speak with certainty about worse outcomes to donations. Roy is not preoccupied with wastefulness and mismanagement, but with the final destination of his potential donation. He seems pretty sure that donations will never reach those in need but will end up in the pockets of corrupt government officials. He is therefore suggesting that charities are inept in ensuring that funds will be used for their proper purposes, or even that they collude in this state of affairs. Stacey agrees entirely with Roy's position, but takes it further by claiming not only that the receiving governments are corrupt, but also that the perpetrators *'keep lining these government people that are doing all the abuses anyway'*.

These last two statements not only manage to undermine the moral authority and competence of Amnesty and charities in general but succeed in repositioning the speakers as savvy assessors of charities' operations, thus further justifying their non-responsiveness as reasonable and morally acceptable. In fact, according to Roy and Stacey, non-responsiveness and not giving is morally preferable as it would constitute boycotting corrupt governments and perpetrators. One of the striking features of this storyline is that it highlights a worrying lack of differentiation between Amnesty, charities and development programmes. This could be read in many ways. It could be taken to signify that audiences simply don't understand what Amnesty does – no money from Amnesty ever goes to any government and rarely to victims. But it could also be read as a rhetorical move to tar Amnesty with the same brush as any organisation asking for money, regardless of their mandate.

The claim that money will go in the wrong pockets was taken to its most extreme with pernicious implications by some participants. Here is the 'killer line':

[4] Joel: No, it (the donation) goes to the leaders more often than not, people like Mobutu who was the third richest man in the world at some point with the money that was being given to them by ordinary people in the street mostly. And just to make this ghastly er he got richer and richer stuffing his way in, in vaults in Switzerland, it's ludicrous; if anything we should decide not to give. 'Cause if you know what's going to happen it's not, it's not going to go to the person that deserves it.

Joel is effectively arguing that the Zairean dictator Mobutu, infamously known as one of the worst perpetrators of human rights violations, became the third richest man in the world by using ordinary people's donations. On the back of the rhetorical power of the colourful image of donors' money stuffing the dictator's vaults in Switzerland, Joel can then claim the righteous high ground for not giving.

This kind of argument echoes strongly with Darnton and Kirk's (2011:21) reporting that while the PPP[7] qualitative research consistently found that even the more engaged respondents were unable to sustain a conversation about trade (and somewhat less so debt and aid); corruption was found to be 'the only issue which people will happily talk about in relation to global poverty' (PPP, 2005, in Darnton, 2007). This trait persists in subsequent studies. Work carried out by Creative (2008) for the Department for International Development (DFID) found that 'everyone perceives that money is siphoned off by corrupt leaderships/further down the line or diverted to buying arms'. In a recent study for Save the Children on its child survival initiative, the first 'barrier' reported by respondents to donating to the campaign was '*money not getting through to the end cause*' (Mango, 2009).

Quantitative data back this finding up, and even suggest that corruption is becoming more salient among the UK public. For instance, 57 per cent of respondents to the most recent wave of DFID surveying agreed with the statement 'the corruption in poor country governments makes it pointless donating' (Darnton & Kirk, 2011). This figure rose by 13 per cent in less than 18 months, from 44 per cent in September 2008 (TNS, 2010). It was wisely observed in the PPP research that people often feel uncomfortable talking about global poverty and their role in it. It may be that some anticipate being asked a question at any moment about whether they would be prepared to make a donation, or take action in some other way. The researchers commented that *'the public is looking for an excuse to disengage from stories about poverty'* (PPP, 2007a,b), and added that corruption often provides that excuse. Among more engaged segments of the public, people are more likely to go on giving despite the widespread perception of corruption. Only 12 per cent of those in the top segment of DFID's segmentation model – the Active Enthusiasts – agree with the statement about corruption making donating pointless (TNS, 2010). Yet it is remarkable in the survey data that those in the most engaged subgroups report a stronger-than-average belief that aid is being wasted due to corruption (see Darnton, 2007).

These findings support the view that the identified repertoires are socially constructed, and are used by the public as resources to make sense of human rights abuses as well as their own moral responsibility towards them.

The *topoi* contained in this repertoire, of course, did not emerge in the linear formation in which they are presented here; participants jumped around, doing and undoing their own claims. However, the artificially linear way portrayed in this analysis highlights the cumulative effect of the statements. It illustrates how variations in the weight of the message, from slightly doubtful to openly accusatory, from questions about political efficacy of donations and administrative blunders to insinuations that donors might be inadvertently supporting perpetrators of human rights abuses, contribute to a very negative picture of Amnesty and donating.

Summary and reflections

Cohen defines human rights appeals as appeals for acknowledgement: 'Look at this! Listen to what we are telling you. If you didn't already know about it, now you have no excuse for not knowing. If you don't care about it, you should. Something can be done. *You* can and should do something' (Cohen, 2001:196). Through a storyline of humanitarianism and social responsibility, Amnesty claims the moral high ground and positions members of the public as under obligation. We have seen how the various statements contained in the storylines did not always emerge in the stylistic and linear formation in which they are presented here. However, the artificially linear presentation highlights the cumulative effect of the statements and illustrates how variations in the weight of the message, from slightly doubtful to openly accusatory, from questions about political efficacy of donations and administrative blunders to insinuations that donors might inadvertently be supporting perpetrators of human rights abuses, all contribute to a very damning picture of Amnesty and of donating. Amnesty campaigners, at best, are constructed as clueless dreamers and bad administrators and, at worst, as indirect/unknowing supporters of perpetrators and tyrants. Not giving is therefore justified as reasonable and moral, and in an extreme case even potentially commendable.

This chapter has illustrated how audiences 'do denial', both in terms of the content of the denial accounts, and in terms of the discursive strategies that make them effective. The analysis of audiences' responses to information about human rights violations has exemplified the culturally acceptable justifications and excuses that form the vocabulary of denial and how the moral claims made through Amnesty International's appeals are successfully neutralised, through discursive and rhetorical moves.

The chapter has discussed the implications of such positioning for the local moral order, its wider cultural significance, and its implications for campaigning. It claims that the relationship between appeal-makers and potential moral actors is an important factor in fostering or hindering social responsibility and collective action. As such, it argues for increased attention to be paid to it by researchers.

Speakers' positions appeared self-evident, reasonable and moral. Participants effectively justified their refusal to donate and their general passivity in response to the appeal, while retaining a position as human rights supporter and warding off potential doubting of their moral stance. This could be seen as a demonstration of the dilemmatic nature of 'lived ideology' (Billig et al., 1988), but it also illustrates the complexities of 'doing denial'. The normative implication of audiences' justifications for their passivity is precisely in their banal, everyday contribution to a morality of unresponsiveness.

Audiences' denial, then, is an operation of power and production of knowledge; it enables the replacement of the moral, compassionate subject by the 'consumer-savvy bystander', equipped with sophisticated analytical tools to assess and critique the style, function and effects of the appeal, and the trustworthiness of the appeal-maker, like a consumer debating whether to 'buy' the product. This is a power operation in so far as it plays a role in sustaining and colluding with more systemic and official operations of passivity and denial, such as those described by Cohen (2001) and Van Dijk (1992).

This is not denial in the common sense of the term, however: it is sophisticated and reflexive. This is in clear agreement with the self-reflexivity of campaigns in the context of post-humanitarianism and the 'crisis of pity' (Chouliaraki, 2008; Vestergaard, 2008; Cottle and Nolan, 2007; Boltanski, 1999) and with concerns expressed in recent work on the dangers of increased commercialisation of non-profit organisations' practices (Vestergaard, 2008) and their 'rebranding' in order to counteract the current 'crisis of pity' (Chouliaraki, 2008). While my study corroborates these arguments, it crucially fills in the gap in the empirical by bringing into the debate audiences' accounts and responses. However, it is not enough to know that audiences resist and 'do denial' – it is crucial to know *how* they do it in order to turn denial into acknowledgement. I will come back to these important issues in the concluding chapter, where I will also discuss the implications of the micro-analysis of denial offered in this chapter for wider debates about humanitarianism, helping behaviour, representation studies and everyday morality.

At this point I will only list the insights offered from this chapter.

The first striking finding is the absence of the distant sufferer in audiences' accounts. Indeed, one is left wondering who the sufferer/victim is, as in all the repertoires, but particularly noticeably in 'shoot the messenger', participants repeatedly position themselves as the sufferer and as potential victims of manipulation and exploitation. This finding has important implications for current debates on humanitarianism, and media and communications' preoccupation with how distant suffering is mediated for the general public and how the sufferer is constructed and represented: for example, whether agency is attributed to the sufferer, how proximal or distant the sufferer is from audiences, how similar or different the sufferer is from us as Westerners (Gaddy and Tanjong, 1986). This reversal in storylines and positions shifts the ground from one of social responsibility and empathy to an assessment of the trustworthiness of campaigners. The moral imperative resulting from this shift in storylines is the legitimacy and normalisation of suspicion and scepticism.

It is crucial for campaigners both to know about the *content* of these denial accounts, to be informed of the range of culturally available responses to their appeals and to be aware of the complexity of self-positioning of members of the public. They need to be familiar with the *cognition* involved in this particular type of social action, and the explicit and implicit patterns of reasoning that are realised in the ways that people act towards others – in this case, both others who had their human rights abused and those who appeal on their behalf. To know more about these two socio-psychological components could produce more effective campaigning and a better engagement with the public. Again, I will return to this at length in the concluding chapter

The data also suggest that, even though audiences refer primarily to agencies, they are actually operating within a broader media context, permeated by wider discourses of media as intrinsic manipulators of truth, both in terms of content (an ideological bias) and techniques (such as in the use of Photoshop). This suggests a problematic assimilation between NGOs and medial logics.

In terms of audiences' reception and action, the findings from this chapter are of relevance to psychological debates on altruism and prosocial behaviour and, in particular, to understandings of everyday morality and moral reasoning. When social psychologists have focused on the distance or closeness of the victim, or on whether audiences engage with the appeals primarily on an emotional or rational level as factors which foster or prevent pro-social behaviour, the appeal itself is considered as a neutral stimulus. However, judging from the data discussed in this chapter, the appeal itself is very significant in terms of how it is put together, who the appeal-makers are and what action is being requested. These findings are important not just in themselves (for the light they throw on the strategic and rhetorical use of these factors) but, importantly, because they re-contextualise audiences' responses and re-position participants in the cultural and ideological contexts to which they belong.

I would like to end with a commentary on the perturbing implications of these findings for humanitarianism. The silence around the distant sufferer is deafening in these extracts. The horror stories are obfuscated, thus effectively silenced, by a close analysis of the function they serve. There is no evidence in these data that audiences respond to the assumptions made both by humanitarianism and social psychology in terms of altruistic emotional responses such as empathy, compassion and pity. Most of the emotional force seems directed at campaigners and warranted as self-protection. This, I find, is the most important and troubling finding; we have evidence of a primacy of self-orientation, rather than other-oriented emotional responses which are, in turn, through ideologically laden discursive manoeuvres, justified and successfully made acceptable and reasonable. How and why this might happen is the focus of next chapter.

5
Us and Them

Colin: *and I think there's a lot of mechanisms for putting other people beyond the pale of those people. There's a sort of outsider ring of people who can be cared about. You can do it through religious means, you can do it through, you know, through sexual or racial boundaries whether, you know. And it's not just that people feel, they feel it compassionately, but not for those people who are outside the boundary, you know whatever it may be.*

Neil: *When push comes to shove you're not going to speak up for people because they're outside of the fence.*

This chapter is about how people connect, or not, with suffering Others in distant places. It starts with a brief review of how ideas about geographical distance, difference and Otherness have been understood to connect to moral and social responsibility towards others who are distant or not part of one's close group of identification and belonging.

Crucial to these debates is the issue of moral boundaries. The second part of the chapter analyses the mechanisms through which participants drew their moral boundaries, while the third and final part of the chapter interrogates processes of 'Othering' through which populations involved in human rights violations are constructed.

Distance and moral obligation

The literature on the ways in which distance from suffering Others bears on our moral obligation to care for them is vast, and has been a central focus of much moral philosophy in the last 40 years. What follows is a very brief, general and schematic overview of key themes and bodies of scholarship. It is not intended by any means to be exhaustive, but rather to give a sense of what kinds of arguments have been put forward when debating how 'far' our responsibility should go. It is worth observing from the outset that very little of this literature is based on empirical evidence and it is overwhelmingly pitched at the abstract normative level of 'what should be' rather than exploring 'what is' in terms of people's existing moral narratives.

In pre-modern philosophies proximity and place were strong, indeed essential, elements of relationships of care in the small-scale societies which have existed for most of human history. According to MacIntyre, 'in many pre-modern, traditional societies it is through his or her membership in a variety of social groups that the individual identifies himself or herself and is identified by others. I am brother, cousin and grandson, member of this household, that village, this tribe. [...] Individuals inherit a particular space within an interlocking set of social relationships; lacking that space, they are nobody, or at best a stranger or an outcast' (MacIntyre, 1981:33–4). There was also a well-defined status to which anyone from outside could be assigned; civilised societies were characterised by how they treated strangers (MacIntyre, 1981:124).

The idea of the priority of physical proximity translating into priority of care and, highly relevant for us, of moral responsibility was common to many religious beliefs too. For Confucius, it was a matter of 'concentric circles' or a 'radiating benevolence', in which self-love is strongest, followed by love for family and friends, neighbours and so on, out to a weak concern for the remotest imaginable person (Becker, 1992:716; Tuan, 1989:44–5). Similarly, for Christianity, ethical treatment should be given to the stranger in our midst – the poor, the leper, the sojourner – who is present before us and whom we are enjoined to treat as a guest and as part of our community, instead of as a stranger, an 'other'. However, it did not import a generalised obligation to all suffering others beyond the city wall (Laqueur, 2009).

With the Enlightenment we have the beginning of ideas of Universalism and impartiality. According to Benhabib (1992:32), what distinguished 'modern' from 'pre-modern' ethical theories is the assumption of the former that the moral community is coextensive with all beings capable of speech and action, and potentially with all of humanity. Nevertheless, in practice, many Universalists narrowed the scope of their principles to exclude certain others – barbarians, women, slaves, the heathen, foreigners (O'Neill, 1996).

Moral boundaries were often discussed through metaphorical arguments. For example, the Scottish Enlightenment writer Francis Hutcheson said: 'this Universal Benevolence toward all Men, we may compare to that Principle of Gravitation, which perhaps extends to all Bodies in the Universe, but, the Love of Benevolence, increases as the Distance is diminished, and is strongest when Bodies come to touch each other' (quoted in Tronto, 1993:41). Similarly, David Hume, in his *A Treatise of Human Nature*, argued that: 'the breaking of a mirror gives us more concern when at home, than the burning of a house, when abroad, and some hundred leagues distant' (quoted in Ginzburg, 1994:116–17).

Some contemporary philosophers hotly dispute this principle. According to Peter Singer, for example, geographic and cultural distance is irrelevant as a moral category; no account should be had of proximity or distance:

> [T]he fact that a person is physically near to us, so that we have personal contact with him, may make it more likely that we shall assist him, but this does not show that we ought to help him rather than another who happens to be further away. If we accept any principle of impartiality, universalizability, equality, or whatever, we cannot discriminate against someone merely because he is far away from us.
>
> (Singer, 1972:24)

Singer concludes that we ought to give as much as possible to distant suffering others, perhaps to the point of marginal utility at which by giving more we would cause ourselves more suffering than we would prevent. Singer makes an analogy with the rescue of a drowning child: if he were passing by a pond and saw a child drowning, he morally ought to rescue the child, even if it meant getting his clothes muddy – because this is an insignificant cost compared to the death of a child.

Not everybody agrees with this view. David Miller claims that there are reasons to privilege the needs of people in the same political community/nation as ourselves; compatriots have obligations of justice to each other arising out of their involvement in a distinct culture, and participation in decision-making that affects people's life chances, both economic and non-economic. These obligations of justice do not extend beyond the borders of nation states. However, Miller (2004:126–7) argues that justice also requires that 'a minimum bundle of freedoms, opportunities and resources that are considered universally necessary for a decent life' be secured for everyone, regardless of nationality.

Richard Rorty (1993) gives an account of human solidarity which is created and contingent rather than based on recognition of common humanity. He refers to the 'sentimentalist thesis', which regards grounding human rights in reason as hopeless. The answer to 'why should we care for a stranger?' is the sort of long, sad, sentimental story which begins 'because this is what it is like to be in this situation... because her mother would grieve for her' (Rorty 1993:133). 'But we are more likely to have sympathy for and alleviate the suffering of (geographically and culturally) distant people than men and women three centuries ago' (Laqueur, 2009:31).

O'Neill (1996:191) constructs a general principle of justice based on the prevention of injury through the construction of institutions which 'help to secure and maintain basic capabilities for action for all'. However, she acknowledges that care and concern are bound to be selective and that there are compelling reasons for directing much care and concern to those who have become near and dear, for they have come to expect it. There can be no universal obligation to which rights to care can be linked, only choice and opportunity.

Feminist writers subscribe to these principles of priority of care for those nearer to us, but from a theorisation of the ethics of care founded on a relational, rather than autonomous, conception of the self, which is formed locally in relationship with close others. Many feminists also emphasise the importance of knowing the concrete Other for whom we care, in the active sense of caring *for* rather than *about* (see Jagger, 1995; Noddings, 1984). Caring for distant people is care in name only; we cannot care for people we do not know. Others have argued that spatial extension of caring relationships can and should extend to distant others, but do so in a particular way: for example, Clement (1996:85) argues that 'we learn to care for distant others by first developing close relationships to nearby others, and then recognizing the similarities between close and distant others'.

Although there seems to be general consensus that care 'starts at home', the processes through which this then extends to strangers and distant Others is left vague. As pointed out earlier, these are overall theoretical debates focused on the 'ought' rather than on the 'is' and are unsupported by empirical evidence. We have seen in Chapter 3 that these data also support the view that people indeed care more about those nearer to them and feel this is their most immediate moral imperative. Nevertheless, if and how people move beyond the immediate circle of care remains unexplained. Implicit in this is how people relate to the suffering Other in distant countries. Some of the arguments above identify mechanisms of assimilation (e.g. Clement, 1996) while some social psychologists have argued that social category relations rather than geographic proximity increase donors' helping behaviour, particularly when benefactors share identity with the social category of beneficiaries (Levine and Thompson, 2004). This suggests that what matters is distance or closeness not so much in terms of physical proximity but based on psychological and emotionally meaningful factors such as identity and belonging. Leaving aside philosophical questions of where we *ought* to draw our moral boundaries of care, it is worth remembering that where the public draws its moral boundaries is highly relevant to the everyday application of Universal human rights principles. Indeed, one of the key tensions identified by sociologists of human right is between the association of human rights with universal claims about humanity and 'the specificity of individual experiences formed by the variation of societies historically and cross-culturally, and the differing biographies of individuals shaped within societies' (Levine and Thompson, 2004:812).

This chapter leaves behind the rarefied and abstract debates around what people ought to be doing and engages with the 'messiness' and complexity of the everyday negotiations around moral boundaries. Indeed, sociologists have been urged to engage 'more deeply with the messy realities of interpretation and implementation (Hynes et al., 2011:813), especially those connecting global declarations with local realities' (Hynes et al., 2011; Hynes et al., 2010; Short, 2009). 'Us and Them' definitions are key to these processes, which are explored in the next section of this chapter.

Denial and symbolic boundaries

Lamont and Fournier (1992) define 'symbolic boundaries' as the lines that demarcate particular individuals, groups and objects while excluding others – this process greatly contributes to the creation of inequality and the exercise of power. Interest in symbolic boundaries has a long tradition in philosophy and sociology, rooted in Durkheim (1912) and his belief that society as a whole is governed by symbolic boundaries, or moral order; it is the common understanding of what is morally acceptable and what is not (what is sacred and what profane) that solidifies the bonds of a community. Literature on symbolic boundaries has gained in importance since the sixties, stemming from the work of Douglas (1966), Elias (1982), Goffman, Foucault and, more recently, Bourdieu (1984). The study of boundaries in recent scholarship has been used in discussions of nationalism, immigration and the rules of membership to particular communities (Lamont and *Thévenot*, 2000; Zolberg and Woon, 1990), race and ethnicity (Bobo and Hutchings, 1996), and social psychological studies of processes of differentiating 'us' and 'them' (Tajfel and Turner, 1985). Recently, symbolic boundaries have been discussed in terms of their function in moral exclusion and in determining the so called *moral community* (Opotow, 2008). According to Opotow and Weiss (2000, 1990), the *scope of justice* is our psychological boundary for fairness. Norms, moral rules, and concerns about rights and fairness govern our conduct towards those inside our scope of justice and determine who and what counts. Moral concerns are only relevant for those inside the scope of justice. *Moral exclusion*, in contrast, rationalises and justifies harm to those outside, viewing them as expendable, undeserving, exploitable or irrelevant (Butler, 2004; Opotow and Weiss, 2000:478).

A crucial role in these dynamics of rationalisation and moral exclusion is played by those ideological processes that construct excluded groups as beyond the moral order (Tileagă, 2006; Creswell, 1996). These forms of stereotyping naturalise and essentialise characteristics of the excluded group. In relation to the topic of this chapter, such processes are of particular relevance in dynamics of denial used to justify moral passivity. The discursive use of the trope *'in countries like that'* constitutes an act of implicatory denial because it symbolically and ideologically demarcates the boundaries of moral responsibility towards suffering others. The invisible, movable but crucial line that differentiates 'us' from 'them' when responding to information about HR violations is an important mechanism through which the public ends up deciding, arguing and feeling that the Other's suffering is not 'their business'. In analysing this type of account, attention is paid to *how* moral boundaries are drawn: that is, according to which principles and through which arguments participants position the Other in a moral domain different from their own – and *for what effect* – primarily to demarcate the field of resulting responsibility that pertains to them and excludes the other.

Quotes were selected on the basis of containing a more or less overt reference to *'countries like that'* and show the variety of ways in which they are brought into the discussion.

The analysis is highly influenced by concepts and methodological tools from Critical Discourse Analysis (CDA), which views language as a 'social act' (Fairclough, 1995) and uses the idea of discourse as referring to particular constructions or versions of reality which constitute and sustain a prevailing social order. The analysis presented is particularly attentive to the role played by discursive strategies in discursive practices, particularly those strategies involved in the self – and Other – presentation; for example, perspectivation (reporting, description or quotation of events) and predication (stereotypical, evaluative attribution of negative traits). As for linguistic terms, *allusions* are particularly useful here, as they suggest negative associations without the speaker having to be held responsible for them. The systematic attention paid by CDA to discursive strategies involved in the constructions of *us* and *them* (Wodak, 2004) is germane to our purposes, as it enables us to identify the social and ideological effects of how participants construct *them*, in *'countries like that'*. Of particular importance are the discursive strategies of referential/nomination, through which participants differentiate between the in-group and the out-group (naturalising, metaphors and metonymies, and synecdoches). For example, the trope *'countries like that'* contains metonymy (countries) and metaphor (that). The metonymy conflates the geographic and social world: that is, the word 'country' does not strictly represent the geographical location, but stands for the population that lives in it. Yet, as the quotes will illustrate, this relation is often ambiguous in that using a metonymy of place to refer to a group of people rhetorically allows the speaker to convey a sense of geographical separateness and distance. This physical distance is reinforced by the ample use of determiner pronouns such as 'these', 'that', 'those'. Rhetorically, these words function as ideological markers endowing the speaker with the power to define and label a group of people in a particular way. This process has been described as 'lumping' (Cameron, 2011) and functions in opposition to particularisation (Billig, 1985). As space metaphors, these markers also convey differing levels of distance or closeness between the speaker and the group they are referring to and reinforce a differentiation between 'us' and 'them'.

Discursively, as speech acts, the use of such physical markers is revealing of the speaker's investment in conveying 'a concreteness' to their opinion; it presents debatable personal opinion as concrete factual knowledge, as well as bolstering the speaker's positive identity and moral stance through nationalistic identification.

The offered analysis questions the concrete side of the self–other location, concentrating instead on the symbolic nature of the claimed existence of such factual differences and mythical countries. Specifically, I want to argue that this symbolic drawing of boundaries operates as a form of implicatory denial, refuting the speaker's moral responsibility towards countries placed beyond this moral boundary.

Drawing moral boundaries

What follows are examples of how the trope '*in countries like that*' was used by participants in different groups when discussing human rights abuses:

[1][9:290] Sophie: *I see these countries as lawless and the fact that...*
Bruna: *Say that again, you see these countries as lawless?*
Sophie: *Because human rights (inaudible) in comparison to this country....*

This extract exemplifies the recurring key features in this type of account. First of all, there is the essential vagueness and referential ambiguity of the definition of places where abuses are committed as '*these countries*'. Second, there is a defining of these countries through an essentialist attribution of being beyond the realm of the law. Finally, there is a differentiation of those countries from this country (Britain). Thus the moral boundaries are drawn both concretely – the differentiation is presented as physical – and symbolically on the basis of who has a legal system and who doesn't, who respects human rights and who doesn't.

[3:4] Stacey: *Sick [some laugh] Sick. Ah. It's just horrible, it's really sick and sad for people in these countries really. I just feel lucky that I live here [laugh].*

Stacey also draws her moral boundaries by mixing geographical and symbolic boundaries. She uses a medical/psychological discourse to differentiate between the sickness of '*these countries*' and Britain's implied healthier status. The boundary is made concrete by her firm self-positioning as on the right side of the boundary: she is lucky to live here rather than in the sickness over there.

[7] Tina:[2] *In so many countries there doesn't seem to be a good side and a bad side. [someone makes sounds of agreement] It's kind of, it's like everyone's in there committing these atrocities.*

By using '*in there*' in connection with '*these atrocities*', Tina lexically links the atrocities described in the appeals and newspaper article with countries '*over there*'. This move simultaneously locates atrocities in particular countries (and by implication not in others), and distances our country here from countries '*over there*'.

Tina further strengthens the differentiation between us and them by drawing a moral boundary on the basis of who is good and who is bad. Using generalisation and referential ambiguity she states that in *'many countries'*, in essence, everybody is bad. One of the consequences of stating that *'everyone's in there committing these atrocities'* is that there isn't a 'clean' or, as Reiff (2002) calls it, a 'deserving' victim. What Tina implies is that the victim might also be a perpetrator or somehow implicated in a cycle of violence. Thus while reinforcing the moral boundaries that keep her separated from what happens in *'these countries'*, by negating a differentiation between victim and perpetrator, Tina lumps them together. If the victims are allegedly implicated in the abuses, moral boundaries drawn on grounds of moral purity justify Tina in distancing herself from the atrocities.

[P1] Dawn: I think if it was Switzerland or Holland
John: You'd probably be surprised it was happening in those
*   countries*
Dawn: You would
John: Because you wouldn't expect that sort of thing to start with.

This time *'those countries'* is used to refer to two European countries, Switzerland and Holland, and defines them as countries where atrocities would be surprising. Therefore, the 'other' countries, by contrast, are implied to be places where atrocities are normal and to be expected. The lack of detail suggests that the speakers expect everybody to know what they are talking about and agree with them, as Dawn openly does. In other words, it is so self-evident that 'that sort of thing' does not happen in countries like Switzerland and Holland (i.e. Western nations) that there is no need for further explanation. This quote is particularly interesting in showing how the use of the metaphor *'they'*, *'these'*, and of the metonymy *'countries'* is not a literal description but an ideological tool to differentiate 'us' from 'them'.

The comparison between Western and non-Western countries for rhetorical and ideological purposes is also used by Richard in a different focus group:

[P2] Richard: But, but there's no one thing in that country that you can say,
*   right, you know, Germany was, they're Nazis Q< That's wrong.*
*   We can't accept this behaviour >Q. Whereas in countries like*
*   that, there is not actually one thing that you can identify for*
*   the reason why it's happened.*

Richard also pursues the line of argument of human rights abuses being determined by characteristics of the country where they happen. Richard uses the rhetorical move of false concession (Wodak and Meyer, 2001), through which he admits that atrocities have indeed been committed in Europe too. However, this is presented as an exception due to an identifiable cause, Nazism. Germany is then compared to *'countries like that'*, where it is impossible to identify reasons. This construction serves several purposes. First, it warrants the speaker's credibility by positioning him as capable of fair and rational analysis. Second, presenting Nazism as an isolated incident, by contrast, suggests that in *'countries like that'* human rights abuses are the norm. Finally, to claim that it is not possible to identify one specific reason for the abuses suggests that in *'countries like that'* abuses are committed not because of particular historical or political circumstances, but because this is how they are intrinsically. The reported speech *'We can't accept this behaviour'* is interesting as it implies a judgement and suggests that if something specific can be identified, it can be recognised as wrong and stopped. But, as in the case of *'countries like that'* where no single rotten apple can be identified, the whole barrel *'is beyond the pale'*. It is equally interesting that it is indeed a 'we' that cannot accept this behaviour, rather than a 'they', which not only leaves ambiguous who is making the judgement (Germans, British, Europeans),but also positions Richard as one of them, and within the moral boundary. Richard's account illustrates the sophisticated nature of the processes determining who is 'in' and 'out', but also the complexity of what happens to 'knowing' and what actions, or indeed inactions, knowledge can foster.

Denial in action

The next two, and longer, sets of extracts illustrate how moral exclusion links with and is crucial to implicatory denial, by underpinning justifications and rationalisations for not getting involved. What the participants are describing is not a 'turning of a blind eye' or claiming not to know. On the contrary, participants own their knowledge, and it is on the basis of such alleged knowledge that they justify not taking responsibility and thereby remaining passive.

[7] 150 Leila:[3] *I think when I was reading about Saudi Arabia I think it was those stories there[4] I was thinking that Q< oh that kind of thing happens >Q is the story with the woman who was*

> accused of being a prostitute. I think it was only because of
> one book that I read when it talked a lot about things like
> that and I just thought Q< oh well that's the kind of thing
> that happens there >Q

[7] 151 Harriet: I think it doesn't make it any worse, you know, if it happens
a lot. But just the fact that it happens a lot and is far away
contributed towards the helplessness. And if it's right there
around the corner you can say, you know that it can, that
it's easier to do something about it. And if it's in a country
that where it's less rare then it's more likely to cause like
erm (Bruna: outrage?) Outrage yeah.

[7] 153 Tina: Uhm. I'm not sure. I kind of [laugh] kind of questioned what
I said now. But erm I'm still not sure but I think it's very true
that we do have maybe a belief that, that certain things
happen only in certain countries but on the other hand
I still think that distance doesn't really have that much
effect.

I will leave the issue of distance aside as it deserves fuller attention, and concentrate instead on the self-reflexive dialogue as the three participants grapple with the realisation that they do hold the belief that human rights abuses happen only – or more frequently somewhere else. Responding to the article on Saudi Arabia, Leila implicitly refers to mechanisms of social stereotyping when she tells of the recognition conveyed by *'oh that kind of thing happens'*. This memory is credited to a book that *'talked about things like that'* – like what exactly is unclear: prostitution in general, prostitution being a crime, human rights abuses, Sharia law? This important vagueness is carried out into the final sentence, where *'that kind of thing happens'* turns into *'oh well that's the kind of thing that happens there'*, where the *'kind of thing'* stops being a legal category and becomes representative of a particular country. Truthfulness is not the issue here, but the process of labelling and social stereotyping that is taking place. Vagueness is central to these processes as, by de-contextualising the problem and removing it from its historical and political roots, it feeds into essentialist beliefs about a country and a population. This is how they are, have been and always will be. Particularly revealing in that respect is Leila's resignation, conveyed by her *'oh well'*, and normalisation – *'that's the kind of thing that happens there'* – that contributes to the belief that human rights abuses only take place in countries *'like that'*, and because this is intrinsic to those countries there is nothing we can do about it.

It is Harriet who makes explicit the connection with action by suggesting and linking issues of helplessness and normalisation. Harriet claims that frequency and geographical distance are the blocks to intervention, implying that if it were happening round the corner we would do something about it. There is no space here to discuss adequately how closeness does not, in fact, necessarily make people suddenly proactive. In terms of frequency, however, she makes the important point that it is countries with higher frequencies of abuse that causes more outrage, which challenges justifications based on habituation, desensitisation and normalisation. I imagine she is reconnecting to her previous point that the recent death of asylum seekers in Britain was a human rights abuse but not much was made of it, while if it had happened in Nicaragua it would have created an uproar but would also have been normalised as typical of that country. Thus, she might be reflexively pointing to a possible social and ideological investment in being morally outraged with something happening '*out there*' but it not resulting in action. This suggests that the moral outrage plays a fundamental function in reaffirming moral boundaries and strengthening moral exclusion. Such psychosocial processes of self-referential moral outrage are terribly important in order to understand passivity and how moral boundaries are complicated things indeed; they are not drawn once and for all, have to be constantly renegotiated and propped up, and are disputed and tendentious.

[2:205] *Carol:*[5] *I was thinking that erm could this be erm the issue of difference, uhm, between human beings because erm, I usually feel that erm we have not really yet accepted each other, I mean sort of that there is always the other for us. So that maybe, like I'm African, the Other for me is maybe a white person. I'm African and Christian, the Other for me could be a white person or a Muslim or maybe a Jew, so that erm, or maybe another tribe because in Africa we have our di [different tribes] erm so that if it is happening erm to a white person, a Muslim, another tribe, erm, it's no big deal, it's no big deal really for me because it's them, you know that, it's not me, and it's not the people who, it's not what I belong to. So erm, it's easy to disassociate myself and not really feel or really, or maybe not look at the issues as objectively as possible. And maybe feel erm that in my country I come from one tribe and we have a dominant tribe. But*

> *the general feeling is usually uhm if it's happening to them then they deserve it because of A, B, C they have done or this sort of thing so I have no business you know, caring for such a purpose. [...] But er when I sit, when I sit in my living room in Nairobi it's easy to say when I see Kosovo and everything that's happening, it's easy for me to say Q<ah, look at those Europeans, ah look at what they are doing and they thought it was Africans who who [all laugh] Everyday they thought it would happen in Rwanda yeah? Well let them deal with this >Q And it's no big deal for me over there.*

I have kept Carol's intervention in its entirety because it beautifully summarises all the key stages of drawing moral boundaries through 'us and them' differentiations and prejudicial categorisation, psychosocial processes of moral exclusion and 'just world thinking', and their use to justify inaction and disconnection. The essence of what Carol says is that while we cannot get away from difference and therefore 'the Other', as soon as the Other is defined, something happens to our emotional and moral responses towards the Other's troubles. The resulting attitude could be summarised as 'it has nothing to do with me'. Carol is hinting at the existence of an invisible line of demarcation between what is our business and what isn't. What makes 'the Other' is not fixed – it could be determined by skin colour, nationality, religious orientation or, resonant with Freud's 'narcissism of small differences', might be determined by a difference ostensibly so small and yet so important such as belonging to a neighbouring but different tribe. However, as soon as the victim is *'the Other'*, as Carol puts it, *'if it's happening to a white person, a Muslim, another tribe, it's no big deal really for me because it's them, it's not me, it's not the people I belong to'*. It is acceptable then to turn away and reject any responsibility.

The next section deals with the ways in which 'the Other' was talked about and socially constructed by the focus groups' participants. In doing this, I am particularly interested in how participants' narratives make use of what has been called 'modern' (McConahay, 1986) or 'new' (Barker, 1981) racism, as a discursive strategy that presents negative views of a particular social group, while safeguarding the speaker from accusations of racism or prejudice (Augoustinos and Every, 2007). It also illustrates how the 'ways of talking' about the 'Other' (Augoustinos and Every, 2007:124) contribute to an 'Us–Them' worldview which interferes with and is used to resist a Universal sense of responsibility for human rights.

The ideological function of these accounts is in the way they are mobilised by audiences to resist Amnesty International's appeals and justify their own passivity in response to these appeals. Their rhetorical function is to warrant the speakers' passivity and allow them to preserve a moral and benign position for themselves while doing so.

'The other'

When discussing prosocial behaviour in the context of human rights abuses, the figure of the Other is particularly critical. Considerations of whether to intervene or not are inevitably embedded in wider formulations of causes, effects and modalities of the abuses. Ideological, personal and nationalistic interests impact heavily on the cultural interpretations of how the speaker fits into these worldviews. Thus the relationship 'Us–Them' is not tangential, but rather is at the core of how audiences make sense of human rights abuses and their own responsibility in protecting them.

Social identity theorists have argued that belonging to a *psychological* group defined as a set of people who share a common sense of 'we-ness' and the dynamics of differentiating 'Us' from 'Them' is an essential part in the process of identity formation (Turner, et al.,1987; Turner, 1982; Tajfel et al., 1971). Reicher and Haslam (2010:290) argues that psychological group membership transforms the relationship between people such that what matters is no longer who people are as individuals but rather which category they belong to – notably *'us'* or *'them'* (2010:290). The resulting intergroup bias – a positive perception of *'ingroup'* members and a negative attribution to members of the *'outgroup'* – have been considered by some as an instance of a more general law of human motivation, in some cases preliminary to any social context (Israel and Tajfel, 1972).

Overall, there seems to be multidisciplinary consensus on 'Othering' as a general, universal social process playing a crucial part in individual and group identity. However, it is important to differentiate between such a Universal process and the historically contingent forms it takes. If we accept that Othering is a way of defining and securing one's own positive identity through the stigmatisation of an 'other', we are also saying that this process carries the intrinsic danger of a self-affirmation dependent upon the denigration of the other group. Declaring someone

'Other' involves stressing what makes them dissimilar from or the opposite of another, generally the Self, and this carries over into the way others are represented, especially through stereotypical images. In that difference lies the potential for hierarchical representation: it is not simply that the Other is different; it is also inferior, abnormal, problematic.

According to Staszak (2008), the ethnocentric bias that creates otherness is doubtlessly an anthropological constant. All groups tend to value themselves and distinguish themselves from others whom they devalue. However, Western societies stand out in this process because colonisation allowed the West to export its values and have them acknowledged almost everywhere through more or less efficient processes of cultural integration. Post-colonial scholars have compellingly argued that, while it is widely recognised that having a concept of the 'Other' is an integral and necessary element in the constitution of the Self and does not have to be pejorative per se, it often involves dehumanisation of the other and can be used to justify discrimination and exploitation.

Processes that transform a difference into Otherness so as to create an 'in-group' and an 'out-group' are better illuminated when attention is paid to both the practices and modalities of Othering and the function of particular constructions of the Other. From this point of view, Otherness is due less to the difference of the Other than to the point of view and the discourse of the person who perceives the Other as such. Opposing 'Us' and 'Them' is to choose a criterion that allows humanity to be divided into groups: one that embodies the norm and the identity of which is valued, and another that is defined by its faults, and is devalued and susceptible to discrimination. Otherness, then, is the result of discursive processes by which a dominant in-group ('Us', the self) constructs one or many dominated out-groups ('Them', Other) by stigmatising a difference – real or imagined – presented as a negation of identity and thus a motive for potential discrimination. To state it naively, difference belongs to the realm of fact, and otherness belongs to the realm of discourse (Staszak, 2008).

In psychosocial terms, some have argued that 'the Other' is a primary source of subjectivity and that various kinds of cultural myths arise in the course of history to define certain kinds of Others in order to carry the projections of the majority culture (Frosh, 2005), suggesting emotional as well as political investments in processes of Othering. This particular function of Othering is central in understanding current, typically indirect and subtle forms of racism (Pettigrew and Meertens, 1995).

In more reflexive forms of racism, minorities are not biologically inferior, but different. Because of their often subtle and symbolic nature, many forms of the new racism are discursive: they are expressed, enacted and confirmed by text and talk (van Dijk, 2000). They appear to be mere talk, and far removed from the open violence and forceful segregation of the old racism. Yet, as van Dijk (2000) points out, they may be just as effective in marginalising and excluding others, especially when they seem to be so normal, so natural and so commonsensical to those who engage in such discourse and interaction.

Three recurrent patterns, or storylines, were used across the groups to discuss populations (undifferentiated in terms of whether they were victims or perpetrators) involved in human rights abuses, as follows:

1. The first storyline is one of barbarism. It positions the other as intrinsically belligerent, uncivilised and politically primitive, and implicitly positions the speaker as representative of civilisation.
2. The second storyline is one of arrested development. It constructs the Other as uneducated and in need of the civilised West in order to progress.
3. The third is an esoteric storyline. It constructs the other as a religious fanatic, brainwashed, intractable and quintessentially 'Other'.

The analysis of the three storylines will pay attention to 'Self–Other' positioning, to the ideological function of the positioning and to the discursive strategies (e.g. lexical choices, referential ambiguity, synecdoche, perspectivation) used to perform such ideological operations.

'They are barbaric, constantly at war with each other and uncivilised'

The first storyline is exemplified several times.

[3] Tina: the Western world thinks of other countries like Saudi Arabia and Afghanistan as being really really er third world like, real barbaric. That's how I would say certain (people) define them (.) that is how really, what makes me think.

From the first line Tina's account splits the world in two: the Western world and *other countries*, which are subsequently defined as 'third world' and 'real barbaric'. Tina's narrative from the onset uses geopolitically hierarchical processes of Othering that position 'them', the countries where atrocities are committed, as inferior to 'us'. Several discursive operations are used to do this. First of all there is the 'lumping together' (Cameron, 2011) of *other countries* of which Saudi Arabia and Afghanistan are supposed to be an example. Lumping them together denies individual countries, and consequently their citizens, their cultural and historical specificity and identities. This way of 'talking about the other' (Augoustinos and Every, 2007) is de-humanising and invites stereotypical views of the other.

At a first reading, it is not surprising that Tina talks about Saudi Arabia and Afghanistan together, despite important differences in terms of wealth and technological advancement. Both countries were the subject of two of the prompts: they share particularly repressive ways of treating women and are both Muslim fundamentalist countries. However, she does not talk about them in their specificity but as representatives of a particular group of countries, vaguely described as '*other countries*' which are lumped together in terms of both being barbaric. The important point here is that Tina is introducing a link between barbarism and human rights abuses. The fact that both are Muslim countries helps the manoeuvre, because of current demonising views of Islam (Dunn et al., 2007; Frosh, 2005; Hopkins and Smith, 2008). We will come back to Islamophobia later in the chapter; here, it is important to focus on the ideological operation of the worldview that is being put forward of human rights abuses deriving from barbarism.

The potential criticism of these views being stereotypical and racist is circumvented by Tina's use of the discursive move of *transfer* to attribute these negative beliefs to the generalised 'Western world' – which I imagine she considers herself part of. It nevertheless allows her to not to take responsibility for her views.

This kind of generalised and vague way of referring to populations living in places where human rights are violated as '*they*' was a recurrent feature in all focus groups. See, for example, Trudy [9:32]: '*You almost think they're barbaric that way*'. Here Trudy uses referential ambiguity both when expressing her own opinion, and when talking about the other as faceless, de-contextualised, intrinsically barbaric '*they*'. This rhetorical move generalises her statement and allows her to present it as a well-known and universally shared opinion that she cannot be blamed for.

The next extract exemplifies the processes of positive self-positioning and negative other-positioning, distancing and othering the 'Other', that frequently appeared in the focus groups. At this point the focus group is discussing what, if anything, they could do to stop human rights abuses.

[9:399] Karen: Maybe out of embarrassment if our government will embarrass them into it like they did with the Chinese baby and our government made a comment to the government of China. Did you read that? And the government of China is very embarrassed about,[6] oh no, you know the authorities weren't given the go ahead to drown the baby so we'll look into it they got embarrassed because our government made a comment and said, Q< you know, that's barbaric>Q. (someone makes sounds of agreement) That's the only way that maybe the government and those countries will be embarrassed into making some kind of changes.

Western and, by extension, the speaker's superiority is established in this fictional dialogue between Britain and China. Britain holds the higher moral ground and shames the government of 'those countries' into making some kind of changes. Karen's simplistic rendition – the Chinese drown babies, the British are shocked and condemnatory – is so polarised that it verges on caricature. This self–other positioning is made particularly vivid by the use of reported speech between the morally superior British government, portrayed as saying: '*you know, that's barbaric*' and the scolded, embarrassed China that, like a child caught red-handed, tries to deny its culpability: '*Oh no, the authorities weren't given the go ahead to drown the baby so we'll look into it.*' Regardless of its truthfulness, this statement is a good example of the ongoing attempt by the speakers to position themselves and their country in a positive light. The investment in nationalist loyalties and identities plays a big part in this accounting, and so does the investment in particular self–other positioning – we are definitively the good cowboys, civilised and benign; they are the barbaric, uncivilised Indians. In terms of socio-cultural practices, as in the previous examples, the view is reiterated that human rights abuses happen because 'these countries' are barbaric. The infantilising tone of the account might make it appear benign, but it is also patronising and carries strong echoes of colonialism.

The important role played by lexical choices in processes of Othering is again evident in Neil's account, which also makes ample use of referential ambiguity.

[6] Neil: There has to be, there has to be some basic level of human rights though. I mean, rape is in some African, central African countries accepted as a perfectly normal thing. If if er one tribe, one tribe takes

> *over, one tribe's chief takes over the other tribe by killing their chief,*
> *then the women are raped by the tribesmen. Erm, the rape is per-*
> *fectly accepted and culturally accepted and the women accept it as*
> *happening. So do we have any rights to install such basis, what we*
> *would all consider a basic human right of not being raped, onto other*
> *cultures? It's a very very complicated question.*

This extracts contains two important discursive moves. There is a lexical move that brings together 'some African countries' and 'tribes', thus
implicitly positioning Africans as tribal and pre-modern. There is no
specification of which countries Neil is talking about, thus contributing to a generalisation and de-contexualisation of countries which are
presented as removed from their specific political and cultural histories.
This characterisation is redolent of more traditionally racist constructions of Africa as the 'dark continent', or the 'heart of darkness', where
terrible, unspeakable things happen. This particular rendition is used
to define the conditions deemed necessary to even begin to talk about
respect of human rights: '*there has to be some basic level of human rights*
though'. By stating this *sine qua non*, Africa is intrinsically excluded from
the human rights discourse.

It is interesting how Africa is brought into the debate. None of the
appeals made reference to Africa, suggesting that Africa might be mentioned not because of its relevance, but because it represents what is
quintessentially and hopelessly 'Other'.

The *Viewing the World* study for DFID (2000) found that the general public understood the developing world to mean Africa, which
in turn was associated with poverty, famine and drought. Around the
same time, Greg Philo of the Glasgow Media Group reported that the
public saw African countries' problems, including war and poor governance, as '*self-generated*' (Philo, 2002, cited by Darnton, 2007). These
findings were echoed in the qualitative research on PPP, which found
that the causes of poverty were seen as either '*natural*' or '*man-made*',
but that either way, they were deemed '*internal*' to poor countries (PPP,
2005, cited by Darnton, 2007). One respondent in that wave of the PPP
research was typical in calling Africa a '*bottomless pit*' (Darnton and Kirk,
2011:23).

The second discursive move, made possible by these constructions, uses the liberal discourse of cultural relativism to justify non-
interventionism and passivity as 'respect' of other cultures, thus positioning Neil as thoughtful and reasonable. Augoustinos and Every
(2007:138) also illustrated how ' liberal principles of equality, justice,

and fairness, become ideological resources that can be used in the service of justifying inequities and, indeed, of giving expression to views and practices that can be seen discriminatory.' The positive self-positioning continues through the final statement '*it's a very, very complicated question*', through which Neil positions himself as capable of handling complex social issues.

This is not a criticism of Neil, who is clearly struggling, like many others, with the thorny issue of universalism versus cultural relativism. In that contested territory, particular constructions of the Other matter enormously.

As was the case with other participants, Neil's speech hinges on a negative other-presentation and positive self-presentation. The specificity of the topic – rape – however, is crucial at many levels (I will return to the personal significance of rape for Neil in the next chapter) and has wider implications than those attributed to these undefined African countries. Let's not forget that one of the Amnesty's appeals, used as prompt, also talked of rape. Even though the appeal talked of a gang rape carried out by Afghani soldiers, the idea is introduced that in '*some countries*' rape is not only '*perfectly accepted and culturally accepted*', but also that '*the women accept it as happening*'. It is unclear whether this last statement signifies that rape is totally normalised, thus accepted by women, or rather that women have come to *expect* it. Neil's important appreciation of the complexity of cultural relativism at the same time enables that discourse to justify tolerance as a respectful non-interventionism. Processes of generalisation and 'lumping together' through which historically, politically and culturally different societies are constructed as intrinsically violent and culturally primitive were widely used. For example:

[7] *Tina: In so many countries there doesn't seem to be a good side and a bad side (someone makes sounds of agreement), it's kind of, it's like everyone's in there committing these atrocities.*

Like Neil, Tina uses generalisation and referential ambiguity when referring to '*many countries*' where, in essence, everybody is bad, thus implying that the victim is also a perpetrator or somehow implicated in a cycle of violence. This *pars pro toto* is really damning for victims of abuses as well as for the countries where they take place, where a section of the population is taken to represent the whole. As a discursive move, it has the opposite function of the familiar trope 'a rotten apple in a barrel', generally used to single out bad elements in a group or a community,

thus functioning as mitigation. Here, on the contrary, we have inten-
sification through which entire countries are positioned as totally and
intrinsically bad. As a negative other-positioning it essentialises and nat-
uralises brutalities. It also implies moral exoneration for the speaker: if
they are all committing atrocities, what can we possibly do?

Below is another example of an essentialising negative other-
positioning. Richard is paraphrasing another member of the group's
argument in defence of the UK producing and exporting electric
batons:

[P2] Richard: *Yeah, but if they can't buy them anywhere at all, alright, that's
what you're saying, they'll find something else. They'll go back
to sticks, or anything.*

The rhetorical function of this argument is evident in the repeated use of
referential ambiguity '*they*' to denote all the countries to whom Britain
sells electric batons – a long and varied list – thus lumping '*them*'
together as intrinsically violent. The negative Other representation is
essential in exonerating Britain for selling instruments of torture by suggesting that Britain is only supplying these belligerent countries with
more sophisticated means of fighting each other. The statement '*they'll
find something else*' suggests an intrinsic quality in the other as actively
spoiling for a fight. The spatial metaphor '*they'll go back to sticks*' means
they'll revert to what they were using before Britain supplied them with
better means, but also implies an original sense of backwardness. The
powerful image of someone fighting with sticks in the digital era thus
adds to the construction of the other as primitive.

In terms of positioning, speakers using similar discursive moves are
implicitly positioning themselves as the positive opposite: civilised,
modern and progressive. In terms of the moral implications of this
self–other positioning, it exonerates the speakers from having to take
responsibility

'They need us to progress'

The second storyline is one of arrested development which constructs the Other as uneducated and in need of the civilised West
in order to progress. The binary categorisation of civilised/modern–
barbaric/primitive continues in the second storyline, which also hinges
on an 'us-them' differentiation used to bolster the speaker's positive
self-evaluation and justify their moral stance. However, the relationship
with 'the Other' is different in this second storyline, where 'the Other'

is constructed as suffering from psychosocial arrested development and the self is construed as 'helpful' and benign.

[7] Peter: *That's the thing the government, I think these countries' govern-*
ments haven't haven't been well formed. They haven't got a good
structure, general foundations are not there. They just have to
improve their foundations then human rights will come about after
that.

Peter provides a developmental account for abuses of human rights. Implied here is that human rights are only abused in *'these countries'*, not in 'ours', because they are behind us in developmental terms; in so far as the Universal Declaration of Human Rights (UDHR) is the child of modernity and civil society, these countries are pre-modern. The familiar construction of the other as having bad or weak government is essential to the moral positioning of the speaker and his country: we don't have to do anything; they'll grow out of it.

[9:58] Karen: *I think we, we in this country are very privileged because ah,*
the system of government is such that we can air our views,
we can report crime to the police and if not a hundred, at least
ninety per cent of all crime is attempted and taken to court, and
there is some law in the country. We are privileged to be in this
country, where there is law which is followed, there is police
there's infrastructure, and things are going smoothly. There is
value of human life in this country, whereas in some countries
of this world, I think this day and age, things are as if there is
no civilisation at all.

As we can see from the points made above, the Other, inferior, underdeveloped, backward, is constantly compared to Us, civilised and superior. These particular constructions illustrate the ubiquity of colonialist discourse and its infiltration into everyday talk. They have important ideological effects when used as human rights practice; geopolitically they bolster and legitimise Western supremacy, attribute atrocities to qualities internal to the country where they happen, and are essential in constructing a particular type of Western responsibility – to educate and enlighten.

Miles and Brown (2004) trace the Western 'civilizing mission' back to the environmental arguments around race which became particularly significant in the 19th century. If, as the environmentalists claimed, the savagery attributed to Africans was a human condition, then the savages could be subjected to modification and improvement. This argument was used in America to justify slavery on the basis that it permitted Africans to "'step along the road of 'progress' towards 'civilization'"' (Miles and Brown, 2004:39).

This 'civilizing mission' established a particular relation between the West and the 'Other' that positions the West as civilised and benign, and the other as in need of education and enlightenment to develop from barbarism. Such a rhetorically crafted construction of the West as protective, originally used to bolster colonialist missions, appears to have endured over time and has infiltrated public and ideological discourses about 'the Other' in a much wider and pernicious way. Even humanitarianism, according to Calhoun (2010), has been tainted by it, particularly in its early stages. Calhoun describes it thus:

> humanitarian ideas appeared also as part of the rationale for colonialism. Humanitarianism was often part of the "civilization" colonial powers sought to bring to the peoples they conquered. [...] The *mission civilisatrice* sought to convert "wild" natives into better people, the prisoners of unfortunate traditions and superstitions into modern, rational human beings. [...] Evidence of the barbarity and backwardness of others was put forward in support of the argument that they would benefit from European rule' (2010:10).

Colonialist discourse superficially appears benign and caring, thus bolstering the speaker's (and that of the nation she or he identifies with) morally acceptable self-positioning, despite the underlying condescending, patronising and racist connotations of what they are saying. In this sense, this second storyline provides a slightly different opportunity for positive positioning and justification for passivity. While in the first the essentialist construction of the other as intrinsically barbaric and belligerent justifies passivity, this 'colonialist' storyline allows the speakers to position themselves as active and already helpful in the role of educators and of example setters, as we can see openly in the extracts from Pip and Karen. In their accounts, we can also see how these operations of 'Othering' connect and bolster a position of not responding to Amnesty's appeal.

[9:81] Pip: And the main issue is not the money. It's the mentality, their way of thinking, their education, their system. One needs to put a system

a very very strong system to change their behaviour (B/uhm) and
to change behaviour you don't need money, you need education.

Karen picks up Pip's point and develops it further:

[9:89] Karen: Money is not going to help. We need people, professional people
from overseas, like trained teachers, trained doctors, you know
people going there, basically educating those people. Getting it
out of them from the dark ages. And then educate them, educat-
ing them about the daily, day-to-day life. You know those little
things which can sort of bring them out. (B/uhm) Because they
have been suppressed and going back to history what's happen-
ing there has been suppressed for years and years and years if
you go back into history they have always been suppressed by
big powers. They have never had their own freedom.

Pip is relatively more straightforward than Karen in her 'Othering'. The main storyline – money versus education – appears at the opening and the closing of the speech. The main body of the account is taken up with the work of positioning, implicit for the speaker and overt for the 'other'. The two *topoi* – *'money won't help'* and *'you need education to change their behaviour'* – run in parallel and support each other. Discursively, they serve the purpose of constructing the other as having bad mentality, bad behaviour, bad ways of thinking, bad education and, summing it up, a bad system. '*Their*' system is in fact so bad that it would take a '*very very strong system*' to counteract it. Implicit in this is that *our* system is, of course, what they need to change their behaviour. Lexically and discursively, it is important to notice the lumping and distancing in this speech – the other is referred to as a generic '*they*' – which, paired with the referential ambiguity – '*one needs*', '*you don't need money, you need education*' – operates as a speech act by giving a personal opinion the semblance of objectivity. Thus the speaker is simply voicing '*what everybody knows*'. While Pip's self-positioning is only implied in Pip's speech, Karen elaborates on it and fully brings out the underlying colonialism.

It is tempting to go along with Karen's account. It makes sense, is familiar and appears to be brimming with sympathy, particularly in the second part when she talks about '*those people*' being '*suppressed for years and years and years*'. And indeed, Karen's approach seems altogether benign and helpful. Karen and Pip agree that '*money is not going to help*'. This is, of course, crucial in terms of the appeal which both Pip and Karen position as a simple plea for money. At a first look it seems that one of the main functions of their narratives is to resist Amnesty's appeal and justify it through the familiar trope 'money won't help', as has been discussed in the previous chapter. But the narrative goes further than that and presents us with a powerful self–other representation. The implied 'we' is what 'those people' need. Thus, 'those people' are constructed as living in the *'dark ages'*, while we are the *'professional people from overseas'*. The phrase *'people from overseas'* is particularly poignant as it evokes the iconic image of Colombo's ships arriving on the shores of the new world. *'Getting it out of them from the dark ages'* is equally powerful and leaves no doubt as to how countries where abuses of human rights are committed are constructed. The other's position as backward is further elaborated and refined through the infantilising claim that 'they' need to be taught by us about *'the daily, day-to-day life'*. Another powerful phrase follows on – *'you know those little things which can sort of bring them out'* – which could easily be taken from a dialogue among teachers or mothers of developmentally delayed children. Discursively, however, the referential ambiguity again protects the speaker who evokes consent by assuming agreement from the listeners via the use of *'you know'*.

These narratives confirm Darnton and Kirk's (2011:6–8) belief that the public views the causes of poverty as internal to poor countries: famine, war, natural disasters, bad governance, overpopulation and so on. They argue that public perceptions have been stuck in this frame for 25 years because of the Live Aid Legacy which has generated a dominant paradigm characterised by the relationship of 'Powerful Giver' and 'Grateful Receiver' (Darnton and Kirk, 2011:6). They identify a 'moral order' deep frame in which 'undeveloped' nations are like backward children who can only grow up (develop) by following the lessons given by 'adult' nations higher up the moral order (Darnton and Kirk, 2011:8).

There is clearly a lot of identity and Othering work in these brief sentences, and the lexical choice is particularly stark and evocative – the other is from the dark ages, we are the professionals from overseas. It determines not just who is doing the 'doing' and who is that being done to, but also establishes the moral underpinnings of what 'we' do to 'them'. As Calhoun (2010) points out, colonial projects shaped a 'first world' consciousness. They divided the world into actors and those acted upon. This division is significant in many respects, particularly for the geopolitical causal explanation of why 'these people' are still in the dark ages. Karen is particularly keen to establish two ideas: one is that *'they have been suppressed'* – which appears three times; the other is that this suppression has continued over time – established through the repeated use of *'back in history'*, and strengthened by the well-known rhetorical move of three times repetition in *'suppressed for years and years and years'*, by *'big powers'*. Who the *'big powers'* are is left unspecified but, surely, it cannot be us because we don't oppress, we send doctors and teachers to help. I am thus suggesting that Karen's statement operates at many different levels by offering and legitimating colonialist explanations to geopolitical problems, while simultaneously warranting her identity, moral position and resistance to Amnesty's appeal through these specific other-representations.

'They are esoteric, brainwashed and intractable'

The third storyline is enacted through specific constructions of the Other as indoctrinated, fanatical and brainwashed (overall by religion, but sometimes by political leaders too). It is also enacted through the recurrent use of vagueness and referential ambiguity in talking about places where abuses of human rights occur in *'countries like that'*, discussed earlier. As in the first storyline, the self-positioning is overall implied in this storyline and is constructed in opposition to the negative other-positioning. Like examples discussed previously, these constructions are employed ostensibly to give a psychosocial accounting of why human rights abuses occur, but also to justify the speaker's unresponsiveness by essentialising the abuse.

> [8:5] Alf: *Because I think religion is probably the source of the greatest good and the worst evil of mankind at the same time, and I think it's something that controls people's hearts and minds far more than any piece of paper will, or government or anything else. And I think if you get someone who's truly truly devoted, and there's a lot out there, then whether you call it a fatwa or a jihad or a breaking or violation of religious law, then people are going to get hurt and killed. And you can't get rid of religion.*

To begin with, Alf's negative other-positioning relates to religion in general as *'something that controls people's hearts and minds'*, but from later references to fatwa, jihad and religious intolerance he is clearly referring to Islam, or rather a selectively negative, but currently familiar, representation of Muslims as intolerant and as religious fanatics. This theme resonated across the focus groups; sometimes only implied, at others openly stated. Rhetorically, Alf's account is nicely crafted to appear fair by opening with a balanced view of religion as potentially both good and bad and by referring to mankind in general, rather than to a particular religion. He starts by talking in general terms of mankind, religion and governments and he is not afraid of owning his position: in the first three lines he claims three times that what is saying is his opinion. It is only subsequently, when his statement moves away from platitudes and makes uncomfortable claims, that he steps out of the picture through referential ambiguity: *'if you get'*, *'whether you call it'*, *'you can't get rid of religion'*. His statement uses metaphors very effectively to support a mono-causal explanation of human rights abuses. For example, he likens religion to a force capable of controlling people's emotions and reason – *'hearts and minds'* – and compares it with the ineffectual flimsiness of laws and treaties – *'any piece of paper'* – and governments. I imagine the *'piece of paper'* he is obliquely referring to here is the Universal Declaration of Human Rights: a powerful rhetorical move. To complete the crowning of religion as the most powerful influence of all, he concludes that it is stronger than *'anything else'*. This absolutist claim is crucial to his implied conclusion that, as *'you can't get rid of religion'*, human rights abuses are inevitable and attempts to protect human rights futile.

This attributed inevitability of human rights abuses is the first warranting step for Alf's self-exoneration for his passivity. The second is the modality of Alf's self–other positioning. The rhetorical power of his statement hinges on the 'cause and effect' accounting that he gives in the middle section of his statement: *'if you get someone who is truly truly devoted... then people are going to get hurt and killed'*. This unassailable logic constructs human rights abuses as something intractable and successfully leaves Alf out of it, both in terms of cause – he is not a religious fanatic – and solution – or rather the inevitable lack of one. That Alf is attempting to distance himself from all this is captured by the geographical metaphor of the perpetrators as *'there is a lot out there'*. Thus, by constructing the other as religious fanatics and separate from himself, he is implicitly constructing himself as different, capable of analysing and understanding the problem but unable to help.

This kind of construction appeared in various forms in most of the focus groups. For example:

[3] *Tracey: I think there was quite I believe there was quite a strong religious aspect from the second story.*

[P1] John: But, but, I also think that you've got the doctrine there you've got
a religion, that's very powerful. That's an emotional thing that's
moving people to behave in a certain way, by the, barbarically, or
just seeing what they can get away with. [...] I think, I think the
religion, the religion, um, governs the people and their behaviour,
because they believe strongly in that religion. And they're just very,
they just don't see anything else [...] And they just won't budge.
They won't actually sit down around a table and sort of discuss
things, because it's so indoctrinated in the way they think.

[7] Roy: Overall what I think of these people is, I mean, most of these here
are Saudi Arabia, Syria, or Afghanistan. Most of the countries that
are here follow the Islamic regime [...] These people take certain
aspects over the limit fanatically which erm and some of them is,
how should I say, total rubbish, some of the things they follow, for
example.

I'll come back to Alf and Roy's personal investments in their positions
in the next chapter. Here it's important to recognise how participants
use familiar constructions of Islam as a resource. Dunn (2001) identified clear patterns of Islamophobia in Australia that depended heavily
on stereotypes of Islam as fanatical, intolerant, militant, fundamentalist, misogynist and alien, with Muslim men specifically constructed
through themes of animality – of lesser civility and humanity. A range
of commentators, from different disciplinary angles, have implied a new
and globally dominant racialisation axis – Islam and the West. Frosh
(2005), for example, has identified Islam as the latest manifestation of
the racialised figure of the Other, while others have pointed out that the
global War on Terror has the potential to construct a racialised binary
of the (non-Muslim) West and the Muslim world that will have local
effects (Hopkins and Smith, 2008). On similar lines, van Dijk (2000:36)
has argued that most mentions of terrorists (especially in the US press)
will stereotypically refer to Arabs.

It is easy to get sidetracked into seeing just Islamophobia in these
accounts, rather than seeing religious fanaticism as only one aspect
of a more complex construction of the Other as esoteric and, importantly, resistant to change or influence from the West. This is revealed
in basic and straightforward statements like the one from John: '*they
are just very, they just don't see anything else, they just won't budge*'. The
three-time reiteration stylistically strengthens what is expressed in the
content: '*these people are stubborn, it's impossible to get through to them,
they won't listen to "reason"* '.

It is not just the constructions *per se* that are important, but *how* these are used to build an essentialist representation of the Other as not just a religious fanatic but also esoteric, intractable and resistant to change. Religion is only the first step in this process. The statements regarding the Other's religiosity are consistently intensified, so the Other is not simply a person of faith, but a religious fanatic and indoctrinated. The element of extremism in the Other's behaviour is pursued further through attributions of over-emotionality, lack of reason and unreasonable behaviour. Alf claims that *'religion controls hearts and minds'*, Roy that *'these people take certain aspects [of the religion] over the limit fanatically'*, Tracey identifies *' a strong religious aspect'* in one of the human rights abuses, and John claims that religion is *'an emotional thing that is moving people to behave in a certain way, barbarically'*. Thus a particular link emerges, at times more explicit than at others, between religious fanaticism and human rights abuses.

It is in this context that other, ostensibly milder versions of the same theme of the quintessentially 'Other' begin to make sense in terms of how they function both to create, by contrast, a positive subjectivity for the speaker, and also to justify passivity.

These are rich statements that cannot be fully unpacked here, but they all share essentialist constructions of the other as intrinsically different from us. This difference is explained in various ways and attributed sometimes to culture, legal systems or species. Sometimes it is attributed to something more impalpable, which implies not only an intrinsic difference from us, but that this difference is such that 'we' cannot begin to understand 'them'. They are unfathomable, so profoundly different and impossible to get through to that, as Fred candidly puts it, *'the easy thing is to say "this is nothing to do with me" '*.

Summary and reflections

When discussing prosocial behaviour in the context of human rights violations, the figure of the Other is particularly crucial. Considerations of whether or not to intervene are inevitably embedded in wider formulations of causes, effects and modalities of the violations. Ideological, personal and nationalistic interests impact heavily on the cultural interpretations of how the speaker fits into these worldviews. Thus the relation 'Us–Them' is not tangential, but rather is at the core of how audiences make sense of the violation of human rights and their own responsibility in protecting them.

The extracts contained in this chapter have illustrated how spe-cific representations of the 'Other' infiltrate into participants' accounts even when a participant's stated intention is benign. The use of these culturally shared constructions has important implications for the understanding of human rights violations and where they are being committed. Three distinct but overlapping constructions have been identified through which the Other is presented as barbaric, underdeveloped and esoteric. These constructions de-contextualise the violations and essentialise characteristics of these populations, thus construing the causes of their suffering as internal. These rhetori-cal manoeuvres feed into the symbolic and ideological boundary-making that excludes entire populations from deserving care and protection. While bolstering the speaker's subjectivity and moral stance by differentiating the Self from the Other, these narratives also justify speakers' passivity by constructing human rights abuses as a non-Western problem. As such, this form of accounting is a human rights practice, promoting particular worldviews and under-standings of causes of human rights abuses with important ideological implications.

Leaving aside the moot point of whether 'Othering' processes are intrinsic and/or a natural part of identity formation, the data suggest that in the context of human rights and social responsibility they per-form specific purposes. Their performative function illustrated in this chapter demonstrates the socio-political nature of the way in which the public thinks of human rights and highlights the importance of contex-tualising public understanding through what is socially and culturally available.

The narratives discussed in this chapter by all means do not repre-sent the entirety of the participants nor audiences in general. But they certainly represent the majority or consensus view of participants on what is acceptable to say about the Other. These contextually accepted constructions of the Other are not accidental: first, because they pre-exist the focus groups as currently available narratives about the Other; second, they are also not accidental because they play the important function of protecting the speaker from moral criticism, by expressing their views and justifications in a way that is acceptable to the social group.

This chapter has focused on only one type of account which, in any event, wasn't used by every participant, and represents only one ele-ment in a complex range of responses. However, this account remained consistently unchallenged across the groups, which suggests consensus on what it is acceptable to say about countries where human rights are abused. The discursive strategy of allusion, which depends on shared knowledge, captures this phenomenon. The person who alludes to something counts on preparedness for resonance: that is, counts on the preparedness of the recipients consciously to call to mind the facts that are alluded to. As negative characteristics attributed to others are not openly stated, but only alluded to, the speaker does not have to take responsibility for them because they involve familiarity and rely on the assumption that '*we all know what is meant*'. In other words, the world of allusions exists 'in a kind of repertoire of collective knowledge' (Wodak, 2004:195). This type of account clearly pre-existed the discussion and expressed something acceptable to the social group. Its acceptability was essential to protect the speaker from moral criticism.

The consistent juxtaposition of negative Other and positive self-presentation, tells us that this type of account also performs important identity work: it bolsters the speaker's self-perception by warranting their moral stance, avoids guilt for their passivity, and overall confirms their positive identity. Yet, by determining who is within and who is without a 'moral order', using this trope when thinking about human rights issues has serious implications in terms of how large sections of humanity are understood, related to and treated both on the geopolitical scale – for example, in terms of foreign aid and openness or closeness to asylum seekers and on the micro scale of neighbourly relations. It certainly militates against campaigners' attempts to bridge the 'us–them' divide through principles of shared humanity, universal compassion and international solidarity.

I will return to this important issue in the conclusions, and consider for the time being possible investments in using these narratives. If the speaker's moral positioning is so dependent on constructions of the Other, then perhaps these *have* to be negative and damning. Frosh (2005:205) makes an important philosophical point: 'the outside Other is primary, built into the structures of a society premised on difference and division and it is in relation to this primary Otherness that each individual subject emerges. ' Frosh refers to an ontological function of Othering, while in this chapter we have seen how 'Othering' is also used to bolster speakers' subjectivity in general and to warrant their moral stance. 'Othering', then, is in this sense highly functional. Speakers *need* the other to be barbaric, underdeveloped, belligerent, brainwashed and religious fanatics, to distance themselves, to avoid being implicated globally, historically and individually. The next chapter explores further the complexities of negative other and positive self-presentation, by moving beyond the socially constructed scripts, to explore personal investments and emotionally charged positions taken up by individual participants.

6
Identities, Biographies and Invested Narratives

This chapter continues to investigate the role played by identity in participants' accounts. In the previous chapter the focus was on the discursive and rhetorical function of 'self–other' constructions in bolstering the speaker's positive self-image. Here, the focus is on the emotional component of identity-based accounts.

The role of identity and biography in participants' responses and attitudes towards human rights, atrocities and suffering of distant others has only been implicitly referred to so far. They are this chapter's focus, marked by a move away from discursive to psychoanalytically informed readings of participants' accounts. Psychoanalysis is used to shed light on the important juncture at which information about human rights violations emotionally intersects private lives and acquires personal meaning.

Thus this chapter engages with the ways in which the information, filtered through personal experience and biography, emotionally affects the subject's overall response to and understanding of human rights issues. Psychoanalysis is used as a theoretical 'lens' to attend to the psychodynamics of participants' affective responses to human rights information

Attention to biographical and identity elements was not originally driven by a pre-existing theoretical orientation, nor did the interview schedule contain any questions directly eliciting biographical details. All the instances reported here emerged spontaneously; participants used biographical details of their own accord to explain their positions and beliefs. As a spontaneous occurrence, biographical information did not present as standalone and coherent narratives. Rather, snippets of life emerged erratically here and there. Yet their consistent appearance signalled not only that people think through personal narratives – something narrative theorists have been arguing for a long time – but that moral reasoning is profoundly embedded in biography and identity and as such is emotionally charged. Human rights scripts and prosocial attitudes are no exception. How they are embedded, though, is complex and variable.

Three modalities emerged as to how identity and biography were woven into the participants' discussion of their relationship with human rights, and these will structure this chapter.

1. The first modality, identity dilemmas, refers to the identity work performed by participants' accounts. While the book so far has looked at the rhetorical and ideological work performed by participants' narratives, here I'll make visible the ways in which, however hard the speakers worked at trying to construct their opinions as objective and rational, they unwittingly illustrated how moral positions are never neutral or pristine. Rather, they are saturated with passionate investment in one's identity and the need to establish a good sense of self. Some of the accounts in this section have already been discussed in previous chapters to identify the ideological and social dynamics underpinning them. Revisiting them in terms of emotionally invested biographies and identities not only adds complexity to the participants' moral positioning, but opens up a completely different way of understanding the impact of human rights information on the public.

2. The second modality, paths to engagement, looks at how events in participants' lives led to initial and/or continuous engagement with Others' suffering through accounts of participants' prosocial and charitable behaviour. Overwhelmingly, active engagements seemed to have been prompted by direct exposure to Others' intense suffering, rather than by abstract or normative principles. This section will discuss biography as 'path to engagement',[1] vicariously experienced through friends or family members. The focus is on the emotional charge of particular events in spurring people into responding proactively, as well as a consideration of the 'optimal intensity' of emotions to effect that. While in this category participants seemed to be driven by a desire to repair suffering by preventing others from having to go through it, such 'reparative' trajectory did not consistently result when the suffering was personal.

3. The third modality, reparative and repetitive reactions to suffering, discusses examples of 'reparative' and 'repetitive' responses to one's own suffering through the testimonies of two participants

in two different focus groups, who responded differently to being victims of domestic violence. Here is where psychoanalysis is most germane in theorising the unconscious motivations behind participants' responses and attitudes towards human rights violations.

Identity dilemmas

Kristen Monroe (2004; 2003, 2002, 2001, 1996) has made an invaluable contribution to the field of altruism and political psychology, primarily by arguing for the fundamental role played by identity and a particular view of the self in relation to others in influencing moral action through a sense of human connection. She is particularly interested in the impetus behind moral behaviour and is critical of the limitations of findings deriving from experimental work as they fail to capture the complexity of moral life and its interaction with the political world. In contrast with laboratory-based studies, she offers nuanced narrative analysis of interviews with rescuers of Jews in Nazi Europe. Analysis of moral choice during the Holocaust locates the drive toward morality not in traditional explanations – such as religion, duty or reason – but in identity. This empirical anomaly suggests a gap in the literature on ethics which Monroe addresses through her identity-based moral theory which focuses on the human capacity for intersubjective communication and the need to distinguish boundaries via categorisation. Psychological studies on self-esteem and anthropological, linguistic and psychoanalytic work on categorisation suggest people do categorise and that such categorisation is a universal of human nature. Once people create categories, they feel they must accord equal treatment to all members within that class.

Monroe favours a narrative methodology because narratives reveal the self-reflexive aspects of identity in terms of how the participants think about themselves and how they understand their actions in the story of their times. Narratives also tell us about how different participants organise, process and interpret information; they expose participants' views of what is canonical and how they make choices in their everyday life, and provide participants' 'cognitive 'maps' of themselves, in relation to others and in the specific contexts in which their described behaviour has occurred. Finally, narratives, regardless of whether or not they are factually true, tell us how participants organise events to give meaning to them and, according to Monroe, this reveals how the speaker's mind works. Notwithstanding the questionable assumption that accounts and narratives unproblematically 'reveal' something about the speaker's mind, I agree with Monroe that narratives make visible fundamental operations of meaning-making through the explanations given and the temporal organisation of the speakers' narratives. The relational aspect of identity, she argues, is the key element so far missed by moral theory: 'we need to allow for the critical way in which our perspective on self in relation to others explains shifts in ethical action' (Monroe 2003:409). Through the narrative analysis of her data, Monroe points at the complex intertwining aspect of constructing a moral life, and the ongoing nature of this process, which she describes as circular and interconnected in fashion. Identity is formed and reinforced through others (through teaching, role models and example), and in turns affects others' behaviour.

Oliner and Oliner (1988) and Monroe's (2004) interviews with rescuers illustrate convincingly how they experienced their decision to help as being prompted by a sense of who they were, rather than abstract moral considerations, thus successfully demonstrating the pivotal role played by identity in moral decisions. Although fully agreeing with the importance of identity, I am reluctant to adhere to a view of identity as static and stable as is implied by Monroe. A touch of essentialism colours Monroe's theorisation and is in danger of obfuscating the active work that goes into constructing one's identity in a particular way. This is particularly important in moral reasoning and in discussing human rights issues. The relational quality of identity and the role of 'the Other', as Monroe suggests, are crucial in moral decisions, as confirmed by data in the previous chapter. Here I look at how this relationality is displayed in the focus group discussions and how emotional investment in one's own moral identity deeply affects attitudes towards atrocities and human rights in general.

This section also looks at personal investment in terms of how to position the Other in relation to their biography, thus adding a dimension of personal stake in creating particular versions of reality and constructions of the 'Other'. It takes further the issue of personal investment and explores the identity work running in parallel to these Othering processes. Biographies are brought into the picture to identify moments of intersection and choice between socially available narratives and personal histories. This section will therefore also bridge the 'socially based' with inter- and intra-psychic dynamics of denial, which is the focus of the rest of the book.

Frosh, Phoenix and Pattman (2003) have applied psychoanalytic concepts to provide a persuasive account of why, out of many available positions, specific individuals choose one position over another. They argue that through psychoanalytically informed analysis it is possible to return 'authorship' to the subject which 'enables us to ask questions about why and how specific formations of subject-hood come about; that is, what purposes they serve, what anxieties are actively being defended against, what aspirations fulfilled (2003:41). This specific 'authorship' is what I aim to capture in this chapter.

Karen is a middle-aged woman from Pakistan who works as a civil servant. She is a graduate and her father was a school head teacher.

> *[9:89]   Karen: Money is not going to help. We need people, professional peo-*
> *ple from overseas, like trained teachers, trained doctors, you*
> *know people going there, basically educating those people.*
> *Getting it out of them from the dark ages. And then edu-*
> *cate them, educating them about the daily, day-to-day life.*
> *You know those little things which can sort of bring them*
> *out. (B/uhm) Because they have been suppressed and going*
> *back to history what's happening there has been suppressed*
> *for years and years and years if you go back into history they*
> *have always been suppressed by big powers. They have never*
> *had their own freedom.*

> *[9:158] Karen: I think we, we in this country are very privileged because ah,*
> *the system of government is such that we can air our views,*
> *we can report crime to the police and if not hundred, at least*
> *ninety per cent of all crime is attempted and taken to court,*
> *and there is some law in the country. We are privileged to be*
> *in this country, where there is law which is followed, there is*
> *police there's infrastructure, and things are going smoothly.*
> *There is value of human life in this country, whereas in some*
> *countries of this world, I think this day and age, things are*
> *as if there is no civilisation at all.*

We don't know at what age Karen emigrated to the UK from Pakistan, but in the light of this information what she says acquires additional meaning. The overall feeling conveyed by these two extracts, already discussed in the previous chapter, is that Karen has a very positive transference towards Britain. '*We in this country are very privileged*'. And later on: '*We are privileged to be in this country*'. Interestingly and per-haps unsurprisingly, Karen does not overtly position herself as British, but as someone who is in Britain and is lucky to be here. It might be that this is how far her identity as immigrant allows her to go with-out betraying her roots, while conveying the discomfort of perhaps never really feeling entirely British. Of course, these are only speculations, but what is clear is that Karen really thinks Britain is a great place to be. The lack of ambivalence and continued polarisation could be read in many ways, but arguably Karen has a personal stake in passionately believing in 'Mother England'. Yuval-Davies (2006) has argued that identity is a subcategory of belonging and that it is formed through identifications and emotional attachments. In view of this, many things could be read into Karen's words – the pride of being a British citizen, maybe gratitude for the privileges that living in Britain allows her, cross-generational investment and valuing of education – which, as Yuval-Davies argues, speak of identifications and emotional attachments. It is from that personally relevant and emotionally invested position that Karen speaks.

As well as national identity, religious identity also influenced, overtly or by omission, the positions taken by participants. It is interesting to compare, for example, how religion is absent from Karen's account, despite religious identity being extremely strong in Pakistan,[2] and its centrality in Roy's account, who is also Muslim.

Similar to Karen's, Roy's account presents an 'invested' position. What he offers is not abstract or theoretical arguing. On the contrary, it is clear that it matters enormously to Roy to be able to establish a positive identity for himself as a Muslim within the localised context of the topic of the focus group and the information discussed.

[7:23] *Roy: Overall what I think of these people are, I mean, most of these here are Saudi Arabia, erm Syria, or Afghanistan. Most of the countries that are here follow the Islamic regime. But overall I mean what, 'cause I'm a Muslim and the overall feelings I have of these countries are basically I believe my religion is a religion of peace. These people take certain aspects over the limit fanatically which erm and some of them is, how should I say, total rubbish, some of the things they follow, for example.*

Roy is a 21-year-old undergraduate, lower-middle-class student from Bangladesh. He also focuses on the perpetrators and constructs them as Islamic fanatics who follow '*rubbish*'. The extract above makes clear that Roy is very keen to distance himself from Islamic fundamentalism. His definition of Islam, as '*a religion of peace*' is essential to counteract a negative view of Islam. The discussion that follows illustrates the importance of constructions of the other for the self, and that these are not abstract discussions but are bursting with emotional investment and urgency revealed in the passionate identity work that is being done.

Roy: *It's not it's not only that, it's like any, I mean, for example, the place I'm from er, they follow a stupid regime really whatever, whatever the leader says follow the leader.*

Leila: *Yeah but I'm sure the leader didn't say* Q<*alright twenty two of you go and rape her repeatedly for three days and leave her children starving*>Q[3]

Roy: [*yeah, yeah but then again these, these guards themselves they have a so-called leader no matter what (L/uhm) within them, their sub units, if you get what I mean?*

Leila: *Yeah but I think American armies go out and do that and rape women wherever they go and things like that, don't they, so I think it's not just the leaders that, you know, because it's erm a militant[4] regime.*

Harriet: [*er but it's not like American leaders are saints. Like every American leader er since the Second World War, could be judged as a war criminal. That's why*

Leila: [*yeah yeah I believe so, so I don't think that*

Roy: [*At the end of the day this is what I believe, I mean, Americans er America generally America and a bit of UK are a bunch of manipulators. They manipulate wars. (Leila: uhm yeah) No matter what, they manipulate suffering, so this is this is what I think, personally. And this is what's happening here. I mean for example er this Saudi thing[5] (Leila: uhm) erm they're again taking it over way over the top with these executions (Bruna: who, Saudi Arabia?) yeah Saudi Arabia. They're taking it too [far], going way over the top with chopping hands off whatever. But er basic er I mean er a few years ago, let's say a few years back, let's say a hundred years back when we did have er when there was, how should I say, a so called Islamic state. You know like in Turkey er and way before that there used to be less executions and less erm amputations and whatever since, erm, than what there is right now. 'Cause at that time people, who should I say, people (.) had the knowledge and people were actually properly scared and you know at that time they had the right leaders, you know, erm who had the right knowledge who knew the inside out of the Islamic law. (B/uhm) But in this day basically these leaders, for example the king of Saudi Arabia, he's been, I reckon, manipulated by the US or the so-called Western world to do these things, to basically er go over the top with these executions. Right, that's it really.*

It is not immediately clear what Roy is arguing, and his point is very complicated. It appears that the debate is twofold: for Roy, what is at stake is being able to differentiate between conformity to a leader (whether this is the head of state or a militia leader) and adherence to religious principles. However, Leila is keen to put the responsibility back on to the individuals and the two end up talking at cross purposes to each other. What Roy seems to be attempting is an extremely precise and subtle carving off of a space where his identity as Muslim can be safe. As stated earlier, the length of his speech and the passion with which he speaks tell us that it really matters to Roy to be able to put his point across. Rather than a 'stock answer', Roy's account conveys that what he is trying to do is deeply personal and affectively charged.

He starts with a disclaimer by using his own country as an example of blind conformity to dubious leadership.[6] This automatically positions Roy as able of self-reflection and independent thinking, and different from his compatriots who blindly *'follow a stupid regime'*. That blind conformity is the key to his argument is revealed in his answer to Leila. She does not engage with the specificity of Roy's point, but returns to the Afghani appeal to question that conformity is the point. Roy doesn't give up and, as the ground shifts, he shifts with it. Now he is no longer talking about the Bangladesh president, but any leadership and its followers, regardless of the size of the group. Leila nevertheless persists, and argues that it is about militant (or military) regimes[7] and gives America as an example. Harriet interjects in Leila's support and also incriminates America. This gives Roy the opening he seems to have been waiting for – it is a crucial point for his argument that, yes, the problem with human rights is blind conformity and manipulation by leaders, but no, the problem is not Islam, it is America and the UK. Roy shows awareness that this point might be untactful considering the British location of the meeting, and uses mitigation to mollify the indictment by adding *'a bit'*. His opinion is nevertheless clear: the superpowers manipulate wars and suffering. This is the cause of the human rights violations in Saudi Arabia, as is clearly reiterated at the end: *'the king of Saudi Arabia is manipulated by the US or the so called Western world to do these things, to go over the top with these executions'*. Of course Roy is still left with the thorny issue of Saudi Arabia being a Muslim fundamentalist country – the squaring of this circle is what takes up most of this speech. For our purposes, what matters here is the identity work that is taking place and the emotional investment in having to find a good and moral position for himself and his religion. This is not an easy task – Roy comes from a country with an elected government, from a Muslim majority, with a dubious human rights track record; he is surrounded by a pervasive social representation of Islam as fundamentalist fanaticism and has been asked to comment on the abusive application of Sharia law in Saudi Arabia. I suspect that, precisely because of these factors, his good and moral identity cannot be automatically assumed, but has to be established forcefully through a narrow and perilous path of 'us–them' differentiations.

Roy's stake in producing a convincing account of himself and Islam as morally good cannot be separated from his attitudes towards human rights violations; rather, it is inextricably embedded in it.

Paths to engagement

What transpires from the data above is that narratives of personal connection are varied, complex and ambivalent. This is further illustrated by narratives charting the paths through which participants have engaged with particular charitable causes, prosocial behaviour in general and human rights issues, and how these connections are established and managed. Personal vignettes abounded in participants' accounts – too many to list them all. Tracy, for example, who gives to RSPCA, NSPCC and cancer research, describes how she became involved in fundraising.

Tracy: Fundraising is different. Somebody I worked with, her son died and he had a heart condition, and we had a huge fundraising event for that. They built a unit for him in [London hospital] and I made over a thousand pounds for that. But I think that was because that was something, because I worked with her, I didn't know her son that well, but I knew the woman well and she's still a friend. I think because I felt so involved and so, I was, I was just like a demon and I wanted to get as much money as possible. My friends all gave and I think because like [friend's name] gave and my mum gave, and I think because they could see that this was something that affected me. I guess, but I don't know, I wanted to, you know this was like, Q< I'm doing this.>Q But then it was a shock thing because I would say Q<my friend has lost a son, they couldn't have children, these were IVF babies, this is so sad. >Q. So at the same time I was still using these shock tactics because that was what worked. There's no good me just saying Q<oh just raising money for heart disease.>Q But it is, because that's still *valid charity so I also know that if you can also say as well what the, you know, the reasons behind it.*

I have selected Tracy's account for several reasons. First, it illustrates the different levels of Tracy's emotional engagement in different prosocial activities. Although Tracy makes monthly donations to the three charities, she appeared detached when listing the charities. But when she talked about her fundraising activities, her narrative was emotionally charged and she described herself as '*I was just like a demon*': that is, emotionally 'possessed'. It's the level of emotional intensity that is important here and how the communication of this intensity convinced her friends and family to donate. The second reason for my selection, also relates to emotional connections. When faced with the challenge of raising money for a cause she felt really strongly about, she did not hesitate to apply exactly the same tactics she had been so critical about when used by NGOs. Her formula captures precisely that used by Amnesty's format for life stories: *my friend has lost a son, they couldn't have children, these were IVF babies, this is so sad.* She is perfectly aware of using the previously disapproved of 'shock tactics', but she knew that emotionally laden 'pulling at the heartstrings' is what works. In order to do that she had to make the communication personal; she could not just unemotionally mention the cause she was fundraising for, but had to provide a personal life story. What I think she wanted and managed to convey was the immensity of the loss for her friend who had gone through intense hardship to have the baby who was then snatched away by heart disease. The cruel unfairness of it all. Tracy wanted donors not just to relate rationally to heart disease; she wanted them to imagine what it was like to be her friend – *that* particular human being having to bear *that* unbearable loss. It is the affective charge that matters here. What drove Tracy was intensely personal and emotional. Interestingly for campaigners, it was her capacity to feel so strongly about the cause she was fundraising for and her capacity to put her emotional investment across to others that made her campaign a success.

It is the move from the general human capacity for suffering to the unique specificity of individual suffering that is so crucial. While the former can be rationalised, the latter makes that particular human being and their suffering stand out and get under our skin. Nobody knows why and how one story, similar to many others we have heard before, suddenly gets through the layers of defensiveness in a way that makes us respond differently. Cohen's anecdotes at the beginning of *States of Denial* illustrate how complex and unpredictable that dynamic is.

An emotional connection with the suffering of the Other seems to play a key role, in particular when the connection is mediated through one's own suffering as described in the dialogue between Dahlia and Lilly about the ritual of fasting once a year:

Dahlia: *[…] But I do think that uhm, if we had never experienced any kind of pain or suffering that we wouldn't be able to er feel empathy […]*
Lilly: *[Because it helps, it helps relate. I'm just, I'm not saying that, you can never obviously never know what they're feeling (when) it's just complete hunger. But I'm just saying like, I can relate to, when I see a hungry child I can, that slight bit, you know you have that little connection there.*

What is suggested here is that one's own experience of suffering is a necessary condition for the capacity to put oneself into the sufferer's shoes and imagine what it is like to be them (empathy). Thus one's suffering creates the essential 'little connection' Lilly refers to. But this is a perilous and uncertain path because, while personal experience of suffering – direct or vicarious – seems to be essential in enabling a connection, too much suffering disables people's capacity for responsiveness by engendering a self-protective turning away. For example, Fred argued:

Fred:[8] *For instance, many Holocaust survivors the way they've actually survived up to now is by building a comfortable life round them, having only nice things round them, and they will not talk about, many I'm not, this is not them all by any manner, but many of them will not talk about human rights abuses at all. Because they've suffered so, so many horrors they just don't want to see anymore.*

Fred is describing a familiar defensive response to trauma: avoidance and emotional cocooning in the form of wealth and comfortable living. Implied in this rendition is that too much suffering might make the sufferer reluctant to engage with anybody else's pain. There was agreement in the group that extreme suffering exempted people from being socially responsible for others because as Dahlia put it: *'they probably have enough to just survive and get through life'*. On the other hand, people who have not been touched directly by trauma, as Yvonne argued, *'are extremely hard to target because when I read this I get, I feel very sad, I feel very upset but also in a way I can't relate to it in any way. Like it's never happened to my family to my background and therefore it doesn't really touch me as deep as it should. And they, people like me are the people who should help. But we're also really hard to target, so how we're gonna make them feel responsible or to take action?*

This dichotomy hinges on the elusive notion of an 'optimal' amount of suffering. Yet, it's simply absurd to try to quantify prescriptively the 'right' amount of suffering necessary for people to respond to that of others. We know that what is crushing for one person can barely leave a mark on another. People respond differently even to intrinsically and unquestionably traumatic events depending on the individual capacity for resilience and the circumstances surrounding the event. Similar to earlier discussions about the optimal amount of information necessary to spur the public into action, in this case too I argue that the issue is not simply and straightforwardly one of quantity, rather of the contextualisation and embedded trajectory of the suffering and its relational function. Put simply, the question is not how much suffering people have to experience to become concerned and act about the suffering of others, but how is the suffering used and processed. Does it act, as Lilly says, as a connector or, as Fred argues, to distance oneself from the other and from parts of oneself? The key dynamic described here is the capacity to identify with the suffering through an emotional, rather than cerebral, recognition of a shared human vulnerability. Turner (1993:506) calls it 'collective sympathy', according to which 'human beings will want their rights to be recognised because they see in the plight of others their own (possible) misery'.

However, the data suggest that collective sympathy is a necessary but not sufficient condition, and that while a 'lived' knowledge of suffering is essential, it is no guarantee that it will lead linearly to action. The mechanistic quality of the way in which participants tended to refer to the role of suffering in generating empathy and prosocial action implied that some experiences are simply too crushing and lead to avoidance, while others are beneficial and foster connections between self and other. What is left out of this rendition is individuals' differential capacities to psychically manage their own emotions, and how biography is pivotal both in such emotional management and in people's responses to human rights violations.

Reparative and repetitive reactions to suffering

The theme of personal suffering and its outcomes is continued in this section, which discusses accounts from two particular participants from separate groups, Colin and Tamar, both of whom have experienced domestic violence. My purpose here is, first, to observe the emotional states accompanying and ensuing from ostensibly similar traumatic experiences, but resulting in different trajectories and, second, to see how this informs Colin's and Tamar's individual stance in relation to human rights issues and prosocial attitudes.

Before we can begin to compare and reflect on the emotional states expressed in these two sets of accounts it is important to recognise material differences 'out there', the most important being that while Colin is referring to traumatic events in his past, Tamar is still a victim of domestic violence.[9] It is not therefore surprising to find differences. It is not just that Colin has acquired some distance and had time and opportunity to process his experience; it is also that one would expect Tamar to be in a more defended position because of her need to find ways of surviving and making tolerable what is clearly an abusive and very dangerous situation.

Far from personalising these trajectories into personality traits, Colin's and Tamar's words are used purposefully as exemplars of how painful personal experiences can be managed through reparation or rationalisation of repetition. Rather than suggesting that what they are saying represents what Colin and Tamar have always done and will always tend to do, I am using their words to capture the affective quality of their thinking and how it colours their attitude towards Others' suffering.

1. [10]*Colin:* *Yeah, I sort of feel a mix here because I don't feel shocked because, because like you say you just see it everywhere and you know that this stuff has happened in the past and is happening and yet I do feel depressed and if I think about it, horrified. I mean I think, and actually the depression is more I think and that's I think because I suppose there's like a feeling of powerlessness, you know what I mean?*

2. *Colin:* *Yeah, I don't think you can restrict what you care about 'cause I read this and care about it intensely but it is practically restricted what, how much you can do anything about, so maybe there's a sense in which you have to distance yourself in some way or other because you can't do anything about it, you know?*

What now follows from Colin is in response to another group member questioning whether what Amnesty was describing had actually happened or not.

3. *Colin:* No because whether that's true or not, that is going on all around the world. You know, I mean, you know, whatever you can I imagine awful things that one human being can do to another it's either being done or it's been done very recently somewhere in the world. And there's no great leap of the imagination taking place.

4. *Colin:* I worked for erm, I give to a domestic violence charity and it's a conscious decision I've made which is I'll give as much as I can to that and that the rest the rest of it, I just let go, 'cause that's the sort of form of protection (xxx) I think, I need to feel that in some way or another I'm working to affect a change in something.

The next contribution is in response to my question of whether it was by chance he became involved in issues of domestic violence.

5. *Colin:* No no. It wasn't chance for me. (B/it wasn't?) No, my father was violent, that's why I chose it. I just looked at it like that.

6. *Colin:* It can. I think. But it also gives you a drive, gives, you know, it might pick something a proximity to domestic violence for instance. Sometimes it's difficult, and yet erm also it gives me the drive to do it and the personal drive to do it.

7. *Colin:* But you can do what you can do. It's not true there's nothing you can do. You can do what you can, yeah. If it was true, there's nothing you could do then uhm there'd be no point in democracy, there'd be no point in social action. And there is a point and they are effective and they've been shown to be effective, yeah.

The following was in response to whether people thought human rights should be universal or culturally specific.

8. *Colin:* I used to think that this is relative erm and now I don't, I think they are universal. Yeah, certain basic human rights are. I don't think human rights exist actually. I think they're things that you can fight for and can be taken away in a snap at any time. They're like ground gained in battle, you know, I don't think they are anywhere, they don't hang around in space or in god's (xxx) book or something. You know, they're something that you fight for.

The first thing to strike me when reading these two accounts is how Colin's speech is full of open and acknowledged mixed emotions. This is how he starts the first extract: he talks of having mixed feelings, not shocked but depressed, horrified and powerless. Colin's emotional vocabulary is rich and nuanced suggesting that he is familiar with his emotions and able to differentiate and express them. Importantly, this list of emotions indicates that he is emotionally open to being affected by Others' suffering, not defended. Paul Hoggett (2009) claims that one condition for compassion is that the self is affected by the Other's suffering in some way – touched by it, moved by it, pained by it, perhaps even shocked by it. He believes that compassion is a more reliable and important dynamic than pity or empathy. He says 'when empathizing, I project myself imaginatively into the position of the other. Here all the mental activity is with me; the other is the recipient' (Hoggett 2009:147). Hoggett contrasts the active function of the self involved in empathising with Bion's (1962) concept of *containment* – the capacity for the self to contain the unprocessed mental material of the other, to bear it, and to some extent make sense of it, whatever it is – grief, hatred or suffering. Hoggett says: 'Here the issue is not so much the self's capacity to actively and imaginatively project into the other but rather its capacity to be disturbed by the other, to be affected by the other. In his or her suffering, the other seeks to get through the self, the other is active and the disposition needed in the self resembles a kind of receptive passivity that Benjamin (2004) terms *surrender*. Lacking this capacity, the other can never leave his or her imprint or impression upon the self. ' (Hoggett, 2009:147).

Colin's words suggest the kind of emotional openness described by Hoggett: '*I read this and care about it intensely*'. He is also aware of the toll it takes to 'care intensely' and how it cannot be sustained as a full-time activity. That's where his biography comes in; he has elected to focus on domestic violence because his father was violent. He also acknowledges that not shutting down, but staying connected with his history, is troubling and produces ambivalence: he knows that staying open is what drives him, but '*sometimes it's difficult*'. His reasons for staying engaged are clearly stated: '*I need to feel that in some way or another I'm working to affect a change in something.*' Thus Colin's language continues to be emotionally laden. He does not talk of rational reasons or normative imperative; he is fully in touch with the personal investment in what he does and how he needs to feel he can make a difference somehow. We can immediately see the conflict between the dreaded helplessness and a hard-fought-for sense of hope and agency. His speech in extract 7 is passionate when he disputes the widespread belief that '*there is nothing you can do*'. Colin's use of warfare metaphors – '*human rights are things you can fight for, but are like ground gained in battle'* – conveys that he is not talking about human rights theoretically or abstractly, but as something very alive and meaningful in his life *because* of his own painful experiences. Psychoanalytically, it could be suggested that Colin is also referring to his own private emotional battle and the ambivalence in staying connected with the vulnerability, terror, helplessness and anger he is likely to have experienced. The 'suffering Other', then, beneficiary of his charitable behaviour, is someone he not only can identify with (thus recognising their vulnerability), but can also help, thus symbolically helping himself as a child, projected onto the suffering other. In this sense, Colin's relation with human rights and social responsibility is one of reparation.

Many authors (Clarke and Hoggett, 2009; Hoggett, 2009; Froggett, 2002; Rustin, 1991) have referred to Klein's concept of reparation and the achievement of the depressive position as the foundation of morality. This entails emotional openness and tolerance of the painful and ambivalent feelings that are provoked. As Butler (1998) argues, the basis for moral concern lies in our primary ambivalence in relation to others.

The paradox of infancy and adulthood is that, as a consequence of the child having to attempt to destroy his or her mother in order to test out the existence of an object that is separate from himself or herself and move from dependence towards interdependence, as adults we are haunted by the real and imaginary injuries we inflict on others in our life, others who are still a part of our internal world and in that sense part of ourselves. The reparative drive is therefore ultimately a drive to make amends for our hatred, to atone for our own violence (Hoggett, 2009:125). The attainment of subjectivity – that is, the realisation of interdependence – ultimately depends upon our conviction that we have inside something good enough to overcome our destructiveness. And while, according to Klein, this may in part be the outcome of constitutional factors, it is also contingent upon the impact of a benign environment.

The child starts with the universal experience of utter helplessness and vulnerability, constantly on the brink of being potentially overwhelmed by a world she can't control. Klein is particularly interested in how the infant manages the oscillation between the good experiences of being fed and cared for and the overwhelming anxieties generated by feelings of cold, hunger and pain. She suggests two fundamental states of mind which start in infancy but continue to govern human life throughout the paranoid-schizoid and the depressive positions. The paranoid-schizoid state of mind allows the infant to protect the 'good object', which provides the child with the good experiences of love and care and is loved in return, by separating ('splitting') it from the 'bad object', which is experienced as withholding and persecutory and is hated and attacked by the infant. As the child develops and begins to take her survival more for granted, she begins to recognise that the 'objects' she has been dealing with – the good and bad mother, father, self – are complex, whole people about whom she has mixed feelings (Gomez, 1997: 42). It is during this time that the infant realises that, as the good and bad object are one and the same, she has attacked her good object and she begins to feel guilt and grief.

> The pain of guilt gives rise to the new capacity for reparation. The baby comes to realise that even though anger can damage, love can mend. It is belief in reparation that prevents us getting quagmired in depression, a continuing danger for those who have not yet discovered or do not trust their ability to make amends. [...] These early forms of reparation develop into helpfulness and individual interests and talents, all ways of contributing to society. The capacity for reparation is thus a vital emotional achievement which Klein viewed as the basis of constructive living and creative power
>
> (Gomez, 1997:43)

This suggests that, as well as being constructive for society, helpfulness and prosocial behaviour are also internally and personally reparative. Maybe, then, the vulnerability of the suffering other – for Colin, the victim of domestic abuse taps into his own experience of vulnerability and helplessness, a helplessness that can only be counteracted with the reparative power of action.

Thus, as Hoggett (2000) argues, in seeking to help others, in offering our concern, in endeavouring to make things better we are also seeking to repair our own internal world, to mend the rents and tears within the fabric of the self which are the inevitable outcome of the struggle to be our own person. From this perspective the desire to preserve the environment from despoliation, the desire to help rebuild communities in Africa or in our own cities which have been crushed and demoralised, all of these can be considered expressions of the reparative drive. In this sense the nature of the other, the extent to which it objectively embodies strangeness or familiarity, is irrelevant for, considered internally, we know the other intimately. What is crucial is not so much the objective qualities of this Other but its capacity to represent something internally for us. For this the reparative drive can be considered as *a generalised capacity to feel concern*. Clearly, the particular way in which this reparative drive finds expression will be socially constructed. It may be expressed in the philanthropism of the rich towards the poor, in the struggle to establish animal rights, to preserve the National Health Service or help out the elderly neighbour. Because the reparative drive is always socially mediated, it does not in itself give support to any particular social or political project – what is considered 'benign' as opposed to malign will vary according to cultural expectations and political values.

What we see in the scenario provided by Tamar is starkly different.

Bruna: *Do you think domestic violence is an abuse of human rights?*[11]
Tamar: *Yeah*
Seb: *Definitely*
Adrian: *Yeah*
Seb: *That's the worst thing*
Adrian: *Yeah*
Bruna: *And um, say your next door neighbour um was beaten up, constantly, and broken limbs and things like that, um how would you feel then, what would you do?*
Tamar: *You don't get involved (.)*
Seb[12]*:*   *[Don't get involved that's right]*
Bruna: *Why?*
Tamar: *Because you get scared of xxx*[13] *people are scared, I used to get beaten up (.) and you could hear it from, neighbours could hear it but they don't get involved because they're scared.*
Bruna: *How did you feel when they didn't get involved?*
Tamar: *You wouldn't want them to get involved, it's nothing to do with them, you don't want people knowing that your old man beats you up and tries to strangle you.*
Bruna: *But surely you would like him to stop?*
Tamar: *Obviously, yeah, but (.)*
Bruna: *And if the neighbours called the police he would stop?*
Tamar: *Until the next day and the next day (Adrian: Yeah) and the next day. How many times can the police come round. The only person that can stop it is you*
Seb: *[Police]*
Adrian: *Funny, I see, yeah, the situation, you know, you, for want, you go poking your nose in and the old man comes round and says Q< look stop it> Q and you know starts hitting you around, you know, and*

> *it's nothing, none of your business, don't poke your nose. So it's, it works both ways, sort of the backlash*

Tamar: And then you get it back for

Adrian: [Yes

Tamar: [their poking their nose

Seb: [Yeah

Adrian: [Yes.

Seb: [It's nothing that you can do, like I say you don't get involved, you'll just get hit back, you know, what's the point you're just getting involved in somebody else's matter which is nothing to do with you.

Tamar: I recently got beat up and four of my friends got involved, one of them had his nose bit off, one of them ended up nearly losing the sight in his eye and um and one of my mates got beaten up by a bloke because they got involved, and it didn't solve anything.

Adrian: If anything it probably makes it worse

Tamar: [And it made it worse

Seb: [Made it worse.

Froggett (2002) argues that the move to the depressive position, and the love, knowledge of the other and tolerance of ambivalent feelings are the basis of a sense of connection with the other. She says: 'the development of a capacity to recognise others as whole and separate is fundamental to the *desire* to know. It signifies the ability to tolerate frustration and overcome fearfulness at things outside of the self. [...] The depressive position thus establishes a connection between love, knowledge and morality' (Froggett 2002:38).

Whatever her childhood experiences might have been, this is certainly an impossibility for Tamar who, one gets the impression, lives in constant fear for her life. It is in this light that I read her unemotional, and ostensibly calm and detached, justification of non-intervention. Tamar comes across as deeply defended, unable to own up to her fear which is projected onto the neighbours or potential rescuers (line 13–15). In explaining why she would not want anybody to intervene, she hints at fear of exposure and the shame deriving from her abuse being known: '*you don't want people knowing that your old man beat you up and tries to strangle you*'. The shame, it could be argued, is doubled by her realisation that she should be doing something about her situation but she doesn't despite believing '*the only person that can stop it is you*'. In this dreadful situation of fear, shame, pain and paralysis, all that is left to Tamar is rationalisation. Thus, non-intervention has to be rationalised as the best thing for all concerned. As Adrian puts it, '*it works both ways*' and non-intervention is construed as better for the victim, who following intervention would be beaten double, and for those who intervene, who also get injured. Boundaries are drawn literally at neighbours' doorsteps and the idea that you should not 'poke your nose' when it's not your business is elevated to an acceptable principle of moral conduct. Helplessness in this case is also essential in sustaining everybody's position; paradoxically, it is the most comfortable and easiest alternative, or maybe the only one that seems possible. Tamar's bleak account is void of hope. A fatalistic, matter-of-fact attitude towards suffering and help is the most consonant with such unspoken despair.

Biography adds complexity and meaning to Tamar's position towards human rights in general; without biographical knowledge Tamar's attitude could be taken to be one- dimensional indifference. For example, when somebody says that homelessness is a human rights issue and explains what he thinks causes it, this is what she says:

Adrian: [*Um what I call abuse at home, um, just trying to get away from an abusive father, abusive mother a drunken father, mother, whatever um stepfather xxx, um anything like that just to get away from it um*
Tamar: *But then there is help out there isn't there (.)*
Adrian: [*Yeah.*
Tamar: [*But people don't (.) um people need to help themselves before anybody else can help them. You see a lot of these kids wandering the streets and they don't bother looking for help.*
Bruna: *So do you feel responsible for them?*
Tamar: *No, [...] Life is what you make it isn't it (.)*

Or later when discussing the Afghani woman in the Amnesty appeal:

Tamar: *You can't help walking down the road and not getting raped, I mean, you, she's obviously trying to help herself and her kids isn't she (.) but if there's twenty-one men outside going to rape you, um not a lot you can do about it.*

And when I asked her if she continued reading, her answer was:

Tamar: *No.*
Bruna: *No, you turn the page?*
Tamar: *Mmmm (.)*
Adrian: *Yep.*

Seb: [*Yeah (.)*
Bruna: *And then what?*
Tamar: *You just forget about it don't you.*
Bruna: *You forget about it?*
Seb: *You don't want to read it (.)*
Tamar: [*No.*
Bruna: [*Why not? (.)*
Tamar: *Because it's sick and (.) sad (.)*

I detected self-reproach in Tamar's comments and wonder whether her comment 'there is help out there, isn't there?' and 'people need to help themselves before anybody else can help them' obliquely refers to herself too and her knowledge that there is help out there for her too. If there is self-reproach then it is likely that the shame of being a victim of domestic violence is compounded by the shame of others also knowing and her inability to help herself. Far from offering a mono-causal or individualistic explanation of how Tamar arrived at the position she is taking, I am trying to illustrate that emotional states of mind and people's past experiences always colour their moral standing. Furthermore, that it is indeed crucial to regard public attitudes as in context and in transition. Strategically, Colin's approach could be taken to exemplify a 'reparative' attitude – that is, attempts to repair one's suffering by helping to prevent others from experiencing the same suffering – and Tamar's a 'repetitive' one – stemming from hopelessness and despair, that rationalises and, to some extent, legitimises the status quo. Tamar's attitude to human rights violations might come across as callousness and indifference, but it is far from that.

The two examples above show how embroiled affective states, beliefs and attitudes towards human rights are in people's attempts to maintain some kind of coherence in their life and sense of self. The next and final section will illustrate this further.

Identity and emotionally charged positionings

This final section brings together identity, biography and psychodynamic defences in the following contributions by Neil as he displays two completely different attitudes and responses towards human rights abuses. Neil is 19 years old, a white European undergraduate who defines himself as not having a social class. I have numbered the extracts and respected the order in which they appeared in the discussion.

1. *Neil: I was surprisingly undisturbed by it because I've heard it so many times before erm from Amnesty International 'cause it's like I think erm, but I mean I know that I ought to feel really really shocked that somebody has been raped while they're trying to buy food for their starving children, but, and part of me really is disgusted that that can still happen but it's so remote and because I've never, I don't hear about Afghanistan or anything so because it's so remote from me, I, it just doesn't shock me I feel guilty in a way that I'm not upset, but I think I should be.*

2. *Neil: It tries [the appeal] they try to make you feel guilty and that, nobody likes to feel guilty when you don't want to, when you're not expecting it.*

3. *Neil: One, one thing that I noticed when I was going through it when you were saying about shock tactics, I think, the function of the use of shock tactics was that I actually started to go very clinical because I study psychology and at the moment I'm reading some stuff on evolutionary psychology and I was thinking well is there, is the rape the function of the male in a group with armies and things like that. And I started to think about it in abstract, clinical terms.*

Bruna: Uhm. So in fact it made you distance yourself more?

Neil: [I think perhaps that's a]

Bruna: is that what you're saying?

Neil: Yeah, perhaps it's a, perhaps it's a function of shock tactics that it forces people, they can't cope with the overswell of emotions so they completely rationalise everything. (B/uhm)

4. *Neil: Apart from deconstructing it. Sometimes in fact I actually keep these, I actually put them in files somewhere for me to actually use when I deconstruct them properly. But [some laugh] which is really really nasty, but, I, I actually used to be a member of Amnesty until they started pestering me for more money at which point I decided that I wouldn't bother because I'm a student and the last thing I need is people badgering me for money when I haven't got any. Erm, so nowadays I, I just, I mean I know that if I do open it and I do read it I might get, I might feel something too much and if I, I don't want that so I just bin it unopened most of the time. And like you say, it's extra paperwork. I get ten or twelve of these everyday from a variety of organisations or people asking for credit cards or pizzas or whatever [people laugh] it goes in the same thing though, it's junk mail you didn't ask for.*

Throughout this book, Neil's comments have deserved plenty of attention because of their sophistication and often for being provocative.

Most of his interventions were lucid, articulate, analytical and clearly influenced by his studies in psychology at a prestigious London University. However, at the point when I ask which human rights the participants found meaningful, a sudden change in the emotional tone takes place and Neil begins to talk in a very different voice. Two things jump out of the text. First, the change of tone marks the end of referential ambiguity. Neil abandons the general 'you' and 'some people' and begins to speak in the first person. Second, the emotional register changes dramatically and suddenly Neil appears less defended and begins to speak with emotions. The dramatic change is marked by the following statement where he shares with the group that he is gay and his suffering:

5. *Neil:* *I'm a supporter, I'm an ardent supporter of gay rights because I'm gay and I've suffered quite a lot in schools so I'm particularly focused on that sort of issue.*

6. *Neil:* *One thing one thing that I relate to quite quite strongly was the erm bombing of the Admiral Duncan[14] in Soho last year, because obviously that shocked my community quite a lot. Erm and today because I'm not at [London University] at the moment of course, it's summer, so I'm unfortunately temping in an office. Erm and the people I work I work with are quite conservative and were all they were reading through the paper, the morning papers today and tutting and saying how horrible it was and this guy was a Nazi and it was evil and he was really really horrible and terrible. And then half an hour later, if that, they were talking about how terrible gay people were and how awful that was and how disgusting it all was and how we've all got to be killed. And you just, you can't help getting cynical about human nature. People you see every single day just close around you and then you just think Q< well, why should all these people thousands of miles away be any different from the people I know?>Q*

7. *Neil:* *[...] I could never rape anybody, I mean I've been raped and I personally could never do it to somebody else because I know how horrendous it is and I know exactly how horrible it makes you feel and it makes you want to, it makes you makes you feel guilty, it makes you want to hurt yourself. And it's a guilt that you cannot get rid of. And like I said, I've already said I think guilt has a large part to play in problems and all sorts of things. [...] somebody being raped in a park in [affluent London area] I would describe that as a human rights abuse just as much as I would*

mass genocide or the concentration camps in the Second World War. Erm, 'cause everybody is human, everyone has a right to be themselves.

Extracts 5, 6, 7 tell a very different story from what we heard up to that point and allow crucial insight into what preceded it. It might also explain why Neil originally presented himself as so guarded and detached.

Being gay makes him part of a threatened, prejudiced-against and persecuted social group. Additionally, Neil suffered trauma and had his human and civil rights violated. As a member of a persecuted minority, he has learnt not to trust others and to be wary of the fleeting nature of human loyalties. Unlike previous interventions, his tone in describing his colleagues' comments is bursting with emotions. He conveys pain and rage when he reports how some people think of him as disgusting and that he should be killed. The last statement of extract 6, where he, in turns, rejects and turns his back on humanity, is the most chilling and reveals the emotional complexity behind his original unresponsiveness. What follows is a psychoanalytically informed analysis of Neil's words. This is not intended as a privileged insight into his psyche, but as an attempt to allow the multiplicity of Neil's voices to be heard. In revisiting the earlier statements in light of Neil having revealed his identity as persecuted and traumatised, I am approaching Neil as a psychosocial subject 'whose inner worlds cannot be understood without knowledge of their experiences in the world, and whose experiences of the world cannot be understood without knowledge of the way in which their inner worlds allow them to experience the outer world' (Hollway and Jefferson, 2000:4). In particular, a psychoanalytically informed reading recognises that unconscious dynamics, alongside other factors already listed in this book, also play a role in people's responses and narratives.

Going back to extract 1, with which Neil opened the group discussion, he claims not to be shocked by the information. In light of what comes later, it is unsurprising that Neil, out of all the information provided, goes immediately for the rape and declares that he *'ought to feel really really shocked'*, but he doesn't because, he claims, it is *'so remote'*. He subsequently qualifies the remoteness as resulting from his ignorance about Afghanistan, thus attempting to construe it as simply physical and intellectual remoteness. That notwithstanding, an additional reading is possible according to which Neil is describing a psychological remoteness resulting from psychodynamic processes of defence. If the remoteness is taken to be defensive, then the information, far from being unemotive, would have initially evoked an excessive amount of emotions. As a victim of trauma, Neil might be defensively disassociating. At the end of extract 3 Neil describes the dynamic very accurately, but attributes it to other people: *'perhaps it's a function of shock tactics that it forces people, they can't cope with the overswell of emotions so they completely rationalise everything'*. His reflexivity is not completely asleep, however, and allows him to recognise this process in himself: *One, one thing that I noticed when I was going through it when you were saying about shock tactics, I think, the function of the use of shock tactics was that I actually started to go very clinical'*. The emotional disconnection thus leaves a colder and distant speaking subject who observes from afar. From the emotional distance Neil can use his psychological knowledge to distance himself by analysing the text as an abstract exercise, rather than bringing him nearer to human suffering.

That the content of the information creates conflict and emotional disturbance is demonstrated throughout his speech. Neil says openly in extract 4 that he approaches human rights information defensively; he is afraid of the emotions they might evoke in him and this is why he throws them in the bin unopened: *I mean I know that if I do open it and I do read it I might get, I might feel something too much and if I, I don't want that so I just bin it unopened most of the time*. Yet, this gem of self-disclosure is buried under mountains of denial of that vulnerability. He starts and finishes extract 4 from a position of, I would say, detached contempt where he is strong and able to deconstruct, fed up with 'pest Amnesty' and all the others who try to get something out of him, and able to put them in their place: the bin, with the rest of the junk mail.

His vulnerability and commitment to Amnesty is revealed in the 'cracks' of his narratives; in extract 4 where he reveals his fear of getting too upset and in extract 1 and 2 where he mentions guilt, Neil's Achilles heel, and the anxiety that guilt might creep up on him if he is not careful and *'nobody likes to feel guilty when you don't want to, when you're not expecting it …'*.

That guilt only begins to make sense after Neil's dramatic revelations that he is gay and he has been raped. From that moment, marked by extract 5, we have a very different Neil. His speech is saturated with emotions. He passionately describes himself as an *ardent supporter of gay rights*, and as being shocked by the bombing of the Admiral Duncan. The most poignant and emotional account is when he describes how he felt after the rape: *'I know how horrendous it is and I know exactly how horrible it makes you feel and it makes you want to, it makes you makes you feel guilty, it makes you want to hurt yourself. And it's a guilt that you cannot get rid of'*. Neil is describing the familiar and toxic damage experienced by victims of abuse. All these are spoken in first person, as Neil takes up the identity of gay and victim of human rights violation.

In the midst of such turns and contradictions, who is Neil? Is he the cold, detached and indifferent Neil of the first set of extracts or the conflicted, troubled, bursting-with-emotions Neil of the second set? He is both and many others.

The complexity displayed by Neil teaches an important lesson about the dangers of a de-contextualised assessment of public response to human rights information. It also illustrates the problems with making hasty causal correlations between action and identity. Moral reasoning is far too complex to abide linear connections. It demands multiple, multi-layered reflections on the varied ways in which people construct their moral stances. Neil's personal investment in distancing himself from the traumatic impact of rape illustrates poignantly the interplay of emotional investments and personal biographies in the selection of particular accounts of denial available and socially accepted at that time.

Summary and reflections

This chapter has discussed and illustrated that cultural, religious and national identities deeply coloured participants' moral positioning and how attitudes and reactions to human rights violations are filtered and experienced through them. We have also seen how human rights information can be highly evocative and tap into personal meanings which are often highly charged emotionally. This suggests the need to unpack the idea of public indifference, at least in the descriptive sense of the term, as a myth.

Lived experience of suffering appears to play a necessary role in sensitising members of the public to distant suffering, but this is not a sufficient condition for action. Thus personal suffering has a crucial but not predictive role in connecting self and other. The role of personal experience and biography in general suggests that people don't arrive at moral decisions through abstract normative or simplistic linear decision-making processes, thus illustrating the negotiated nature of moral decisions which are never linear or pristine.

Reactions to information regarding human rights violations are deeply personal and affectively charged, but quantity, quality of emotions and personal capacity for managing emotional states are pivotal in determining proactive responses. Mechanistic 'stimulus–response' models of emotions are simplistic, unrealistically linear and fail to engage with the complex nature of emotions.

Psychodynamics are totally absent in existing literature, yet, as the next chapter will illustrate, they are a key component in issues of moral reasoning and responsiveness to human rights violations. Connected to this is also the crucial role played by agency and personal capacity to manage emotions. This chapter has provided some examples of the determining function of the latter; the next chapter explores further the affective content of participants' reactions to human rights information. It also continues to use a psychodynamic lens to explore how members of the public react emotionally as well as how they use socially constructed resources to make sense of their emotional responses.

7
A Plea for Emotional Complexity: Conflicts and (Psycho)Dynamic Equilibria

Roy: *Well as I was reading the rest it all makes me, a part of me just like switched off slightly before I could go on. But I still kept feeling then hopelessness anger erm and I was erm reading more I was feeling more erm shame I think. Shame at myself for wanting to switch off I think and not wanting to. Erm just not wanting to know anymore. But I think a part of that is just feeling so help hopeless and helpless.*

Bruna: *Right. Is that why you want to switch off?*

Roy: *Yeah, 'cause it just seems like it's just so much and it feels like there's so much that needs to be done and I think it's the it's so many different things like education would be one part but I think it's so so many other things that need to be done that it just feels like it's it's an almost impossible task . . . .*

This chapter continues the engagement with the affective impact of human rights information on members of the public. The previous chapter has concentrated on the role of emotions at the intersection between information of human rights violations and private lives. In that context the focus was on how through personal experience and biography the information acquires specific emotional meanings which deeply affect the subject's overall response to and understanding of human rights issues.

Here the focus is slightly different. Although meaning is still at its core, this chapter explores how the information impacts affectively on members of the public, how they react and understand this affective impact, and how individuals' understandings of this emotional loop inform their actions in response to appeals and human rights information in general. Although previous chapters have also viewed participants in dynamic interaction with the information, the producers of information and the socio-cultural meanings of it, here the focus is more on the affective impact and psycho-dynamics of that interaction.

The psychosocial model of emotions offered in this chapter is attentive to both individual affective responses and emotions, and socially constructed justifications based on emotions. Particular attention is paid to the phenomenon and the public's understanding of not engaging emotionally or initially engaging then disengaging emotionally – what has often, and in my view erroneously, been described as 'compassion fatigue' or 'psychophysical numbing'. The model I present takes into account both the psychodynamic (particularly in terms of intra-psychic conflicts that might get evoked in the process) and the social aspect of such processes (in the form of psychologically informed vocabularies of denial). Hence psychoanalysis is considered and used in two different ways. When looking at participants as affectively troubled by the information, psychoanalysis is used as a theoretical frame providing a 'lens' to grapple with the psychodynamics of participants' affective responses to human rights information. When participants position themselves as reflexive consumers, however, psychoanalytically and psychologically informed accounts will be considered as sophisticated vocabularies of denial.

Consequently, in this chapter, more than anywhere else in the book, language and how it is used is at its most ambiguous and, as a consequence, so is the status of participants' accounts. At times accounts will be read at face value; at others, they will be interpreted either psychodynamically or discursively. Psychoanalysis will play a different role depending on the reading. In the first instance, and in order to engage with the psychodynamics of the affective impact of human rights violation on the public, psychoanalysis is used as a theoretical frame engaging with the dynamic unconscious processes of the mind. This is not a claim to direct and privileged access to the participants' minds, but an attempt to reflect on the possible unconscious psychodynamic aspects of the processes described by participants, in order to provide a 'thicker' and more nuanced understanding that does not stop at a cognitive reading. In this sense, the analysis of extracts will attempt to 'translate' what participants say through a model of human subjects as conflicted and influenced by intra-psychic dynamics. In this usage psychoanalysis is a theoretical frame that can capture and make sense of participants' emotional responses and their affective contents in a very different way from the discursive analyses provided so far.

Although, later in the chapter, I return to the discursive and consider psychoanalysis as a discursive resource offering a sophisticated and powerful vocabulary of denial, there is clear preponderance in this chapter of psychoanalysis as a theoretical frame. My intention is not to privilege one use of psychoanalysis over the other, but to put forward all these readings as equivalent in order to capture the psychosocially complex, conflictual and multi-faceted nature of moral reasoning and emotional responses to human rights violations. Like spinning plates, all these levels should be kept going as it is in the different meanings they offer and in the tensions between them that we can observe the dynamism and liveliness of the interlacing processes generating passivity. To foster this multi-level approach and to capture the messy complexity of the phenomena, the discussion intentionally moves back and forth between these readings. The 'hall of mirrors' effect is the nearest metaphor for what I am trying to evoke, with the exception that in our case no object is considered as 'real' in opposition to mere illusion. Instead, all the readings stand as 'real', side by side, throwing light and shadows onto each other (Figure 7.1).

According to this psychosocial model the members of the public should be understood simultaneously as psychological subjects as well as morally agentic, which makes psychology and psychoanalysis both explanatory paradigms and rhetorical resources for morally acceptable justifications of apathy.

The three modalities offer three different explanations of the role played by emotions, and in particular emotional disconnection in the generation of passivity. As described above, these modalities attribute different status to how participants talk about their emotional reactions, namely they are taken at face value as foreshadowing psychodynamic conflict, and as rhetorical moves.

The first modality, 'troubled identities' looks at members of the public as 'defended' (Hollway and Jefferson, 2000) and emotionally conflicted subjects. As such, accounts capture how a subject becomes a site of emotional conflict. Unlike the relatively more accessible aspects of emotional reactions described in the next two categories, this modality looks at instances in which participants hint at psychodynamic and intra-psychic conflicts evoked by information on human rights abuses. A psychoanalytically informed analysis of audiences' talk illustrates how human rights information and appeals may tap into and stir up internal conflicts, such as feeling guilty and ashamed of one's own selfishness or discovering troubling reactions to the information. Particularly crucial is the passionate response to feeling emotionally manipulated by

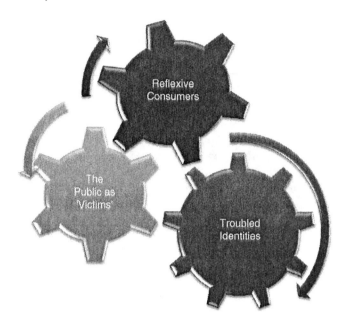

Figure 7.1 The three modalities in which emotional reactions can be understood: 'troubled identities', 'victims' and 'reflexive consumers', portrayed here as interlocking cogs

campaigners and the complex and often counterproductive response to appeals eliciting guilt. It is argued that resistance to and defensiveness against these conflictual emotional states may contribute to emotional disconnection and active turning away from human rights issues.

The second modality views members of the public as 'emotional victims', suffering from 'secondary trauma' resulting from the frequent exposure to disturbing information about human rights violations. Taken at face value, the main concern when analysing the extracts in this modality is to consider the impact of mediated messages and campaigning on the public. It engages with the frequent and familiar claim that the information affects the public so adversely that they must protect themselves. In analysing this type of account, I will critically explore ideas of compassion fatigue, defence mechanisms, switching off, desensitisation and numbing. In terms of better informing the public and campaigning, the question is: how can the public be equipped and helped to deal with shocking information in a way that enables them to stay engaged rather than disconnect?

The third modality views members of the public as 'reflexive con-sumers'. Contrary to the previous modality in which participants posi-tioned themselves as passive recipients of shocking information, it views participants as agentic and emotions as a powerful rhetoric. That is, they use a particularly common and effective vocabulary of denial. Reconnecting to the concept of denial that runs through the whole book, this dimension looks at how 'emotion talk' is a powerful account-ing strategy. This section argues for the importance of understanding the vocabularies of emotional denial currently available and from which it gets its discursive power. Particular attention is paid to 'psychobabble' and psychological discourse in enabling audiences to take the position of emotional consumers.

These analyses of the three modalities attempt several things at once. First, they offer three possible readings of ways in which emotions oper-ate and how affects are activated by appeals and information on human rights violations. In this sense they offer an empirically based mapping of emotional responses. Second they critically interrogate accounts to tease out if and when participants actively 'turn away' as a 'real' psy-chological response, or when 'turning away' is a sophisticated rhetorical strategy. This is not a 'truth-finding mission', but rather an effort to illustrate how reactions and meanings in each of these modalities over-lap and are in constant dynamic equilibrium both within the modality and between them.

It is not simply that passivity is psychologically and ideologically over-determined, but that holding the tension between different read-ings makes visible the intricate relationship between psychodynamic conflicts, psychological insights and discourse, and emotional vocab-ularies of denial. Different tools and theoretical frames are needed to make sense of each and the relationship between them.

In the concluding section of this chapter I consider both positive and negative impacts of these uses and experiences of emotions on the ability to respond proactively to information regarding human rights abuses.

Troubled identities and emotional conflicts

The modernist assumption underlying appeals is 'if only people knew, they would do something about it': that is, it focuses on the cogni-tive aspect of informing the public. Yet most appeals contain forceful emotional messages, and the ways in which emotions are implicitly or explicitly evoked or mobilised varies enormously. From a direct and active attempt to evoke guilt, moral obligation and other self-referential emotions, to other-oriented feelings such as pity, empathy, sympathy and compassion, most appeals aim to connect the viewer emotionally with the victim.

Despite differences in formulation, there seems to be agreement that guilt and social responsibility facilitate helping and that guilt spurs people into prosocial action, an assumption also underlying NGOs' communications with the public. As Stan Cohen (2001:182) points out, the 'not-so-hidden-subtext of many appeals is that if you don't comply with the appeal's request, you will feel guilty'. However, there is very little empirical knowledge about how guilt affects responses to human rights appeals. In particular, although it is easy to see how guilt may be evoked by some appeals, nobody has explored how audiences understand the guilt they experience and what kind of actions and reactions the evoked guilt produces.

Indeed, the majority of participants in this study mentioned guilt as an emotion that prompts people into action. For example, Amy: '*I think guilt and compassion wants to make you do something*'. Overall statements of guilt were expressed calmly and reflectively, but there were other instances in which participants referred to their experience of guilt with intense animosity. In these cases, although guilt was experienced, it seemed to backfire and have the opposite effect from that wished for by NGOs.

Cohen astutely pointed out that, in fact, ostensibly simple, pragmatic and unemotional messages such as 'skip lunch, save a child' present in matter-of-fact ways the grotesque disparity between the required cost-free gesture and literally saving a human life. These simple guilt-inducing messages make them particularly intrusive for the viewer and are likely to provoke resentment towards the sender. 'They in turn indict you for your selfish refusal to make a sacrifice for others. Your refusal is even more reprehensible when no sacrifice at all is required. Indeed, the easier the effort (sign a petition, buy ethically grown coffee), the smaller the unit sum (£1, the price of a cup of tea), the more you feel guilty for not making it' (Cohen, 2001:182).

What Cohen is describing is a familiar emotional loop, often passionately referred to by participants, in which viewers strongly react to their own emotional reaction. We have looked in detail at the troubled relationship between audiences and human rights agencies' communications in terms of operations of denial. But a discursive analysis of vocabularies of denial cannot account for the passion and intensity of affect expressed by some participants. Here I will explore dynamics of guilt in relational terms through psychoanalytic concepts.

Beside the recognition that guilt should motivate action, the most frequent way in which guilt was mentioned was in relation to the manipulative intention attributed to campaigners. Importantly, even when participants did not mention guilt as an emotion directly evoked by the appeals, nonetheless they recognised that this was the emotion the appeal was aiming to evoke. There seems to be widespread alertness to the reasons why emotions were evoked, to the point that, overall, emotions towards campaigners' attributed intentions seemed stronger than emotions towards the victim. That members of the public seem to have a much more powerful emotional engagement with the 'messenger' than with the message is a finding with potentially important implications for campaigners.

The following quotes are examples of the strength of feelings provoked by the appeals, which do not involve the victims or the causes of human right.

[P2]: Ian: *They were trying to make you feel guilty to fill in their form, you know. The second one, definitely makes, I felt it was trying to make you feel guilty about something. Uhm, the first one said, Q< if you can't think of anything to write then please fill in this coupon >Q. with a few lines. I FELT ABSOLUTELY INSULTED by that point. The coupons they want us to xxx is a big coupon, lots of boxes to fill in Q< who are you>Q, the one the Q<if you can't think of>Q section [shows] that they are not actually serious about, doesn't even have their address on. And that didn't do any favours to me at all, to read it.*

Leila: *Q< let's shock you a bit and say that if you don't wanna read this what more can I say?, how wicked must you be if you're not moved by these stories (B/uhm) then give us the money we'll just, you know, accept that you're a you know, you're cold-hearted or something>Q.*

Both Ian and Leila refer to guilt in their accounts. Ian openly accuses Amnesty of attempting to manipulate his emotions by provoking guilt in order to make him fill in the form. This makes him feel insulted, partly because, he seems to imply, he feels that Amnesty's communication is disingenuous. He does not think Amnesty is at all interested in who he is and his views; all they want is his donation. I have already discussed the 'all they want is my money' repertoire as a denial operation, but what we see here is quite different. In the vast majority of cases, when participants used vocabularies of denial they came across as calm, reflexive and reasonable. Indeed, as I have repeatedly argued, being seen as a reasonable person and being able to produce an ostensibly objective and rational explanation of one's behaviour was key to the dynamics of denial. The rhetorical power of repertoires depended heavily on the factuality and objectivity of their presentation. The speaker often appeared almost detached while rehearsing 'what everybody knows'.

What we are seeing here is a different emotional register altogether. Ian comes across as angry and feeling personally insulted. That his speech is affectively charged is illustrated by his behaviour in the group when he furiously spat out '*I FELT ABSOLUTELY INSULTED*'. The personal nature of the exchange is important as it speaks of a passionate, defensive and antagonistic engagement with the appeal-makers. A similar personal and passionate tone is also present in Leila's account, in which she describes what she perceives Amnesty is saying to her. There is a strong judgemental quality to the account. As in Ian's reported experience, Leila attributes manipulative intentions to Amnesty: '*let's shock you a little bit*'. What is described is not a neutral and disinterested exchange: the '*what more can I say?*' is the kind of exasperated comment one might use at the end of an argument. As with Ian's account, Leila's too conveys passion and emotional engagement. Finally, the moral judgement expected is harsh: not responding would make Leila '*wicked*' and '*coldhearted*'. These are strong words, which Leila feels are personally directed at her. There is something chillingly sadistic in the way she describes Amnesty toying with her emotions – '*let's shock you a bit*' – which clearly Leila finds very upsetting.

There was something excessive in these emotional reactions which erupted suddenly and violently as if pent up for a long time. This was particularly surprising when compared to the relative absence of affective response in relation to the victims of the abuses. Where does the affective charge come from? How can we make sense of such passion coming from such unexpected places? I will start by employing a psychoanalytic reading of guilt and then move on to an exploration of possible psychodynamics of guilt in the case of human rights violations.

The Jiminy Cricket of humanitarianism

Among English dictionary definitions of guilt (which comes from a Teutonic root, '*schuld*', meaning debt), we find: a failure of duty, delinquency, offence, crime; the fact of having committed, or of being guilty of, some specified or implied offence; guiltiness; the state of having wilfully committed a crime or heinous moral offence; criminality, great culpability. Thus, the definition of guilt relies on an implied moral code which is socially shared, codified in law or social norms and internalised. In relation to these moral codes, guilt implies an action or an omission of action. The widespread consensus in the focus groups that appeals provoked guilt confirms that apathy does not stem from a lack of normative duty to help which, on the contrary, appears to be recognised and strongly felt. Participants overall agreed that they ought to help, and experiencing guilt for failing to do so suggests that this norm is also emotionally integrated.

However, in terms of the causative line between emotions and actions, there is ample evidence in the data of a stage in between eliciting guilt and acting on that guilt, which is occupied by a reflection on why this guilt was elicited, but also by powerful and unprocessed emotions. For example:

Neil: I actually used to be a member of Amnesty until they started pestering me for more money at which point I decided that I wouldn't bother because I'm a student and the last thing I need is people badgering me for money when I haven't got any. Erm, so nowadays I, I just, I mean I know that if I do open it and I do read it I might get, I might feel something too much and if I, I don't want that so I just bin it unopened most of the time. And like you say, it's extra paperwork. I get ten or twelve of these every day from a variety of organisations or people asking for credit cards or pizzas or whatever [people laugh] it goes in the same thing though, it's junk mail you didn't ask for.

We have discussed Neil's quote in the previous chapter, so I won't analyse it in detail here. But in this context it is important to note Neil's annoyance at Amnesty which he experiences as *'pestering'* and *'badgering'*. Again, this is strong language, portraying Neil and Amnesty as engaged in an emotional tug of war: Neil is aware of Amnesty's attempt to evoke strong emotions in him and he refuses to feel these emotions. We know from what we learnt about Neil's biography why it is essential for him to protect himself from having too strong emotions and that, as noted in the previous chapter, taking the cool position of the joker, who contemptuously throws the appeals in the bin, protects him from dangerous emotions.

In terms of passivity generation, reflecting on why their emotions might be evoked not only allows audiences to distance themselves from the other's suffering, but also presents them with the opportunity of occupying the position of the critical consumer, which will be discussed later in this chapter. That position is familiar and gives them more solid and less exposing ground to stand on (compared to having their raw emotions exposed and manipulated). This reading adds an extra layer of meaning to Neil's comparing human rights appeals to pizza flyers and other advertising,

The limitation of looking at participants' positioning exclusively discursively is that it doesn't fully explain the animosity towards NGOs expressed by so many participants, nor the emotional intensity of their feelings. It might simply be that these participants were engaged in self-referential pity (Chouliaraki, 2008), but these accounts do not entirely reflect the narcissistic states described by Chouliaraki. Rather, they point at the role of emotional conflict and unprocessed affective contents that get played out between members of the public and NGOs. At the simplest level, having a conscience is uncomfortable, and moral action and reasoning cannot be fully understood without recognition that people might want to resist difficult emotional states. Can the derailment of emotions onto NGOs be a simple case of displacement? If so, what is displaced and acted out in these affectively laden experiences? A psychoanalytically informed analysis provides unique insights into the psychodynamics of this resistance, in terms of both content – *what* might be resisted – and the transferential relationship – *who* might be resisted. In terms of content, it is worth exploring further the possibility that taking a detached position and using vocabularies of denial might also be a way of defending against emotional conflicts stirred up by the information of which participants might not be fully aware. This would then compound the resentment towards the agencies for forcing onto the public difficult emotions and conflicts. Psychodynamically, this could be read in terms of the judgemental function of the superego being projected onto the agencies which are then experienced as critical and judgemental, rather than facilitative. Agencies become the nagging voice of audiences' harsh superegos. Shame and guilt play a crucial role in both these aspects of repression.

In 'The Ego and the Id', Freud said: 'as a child grows up, the role of the father is carried on by teachers and others in authority; their injunctions and prohibitions remain powerful in the ego-ideal and continue, in the form of conscience, to exercise moral censorship. The tension between the demands of conscience and the actual performances of the ego is experienced as a sense of guilt' (1923:37). In this model, participants' guilt could be imputed to a feeling of having failed their own internalised norms of social responsibility. In the specificity of public responses to appeals, guilt seems to arise in the moment in which Amnesty, which has been implicitly given moral authority, makes the public aware of its shortcomings. However, moral authority does not have to be experienced as punitive, but could be facilitative. These two aspects of moral authority were conceptualised by Freud as performed by the two unconscious agencies of the super-ego and the ego-ideal.

The superego concept describes the special, internal monitoring agency by means of which people evaluate themselves and their behaviour, while the term ego-ideal was first introduced by Freud in 'On Narcissism' (1914), in which the ideal is the substitute for the lost narcissism of childhood and was clearly differentiated from the conscience, which had a more censoring function.

Generally speaking, the ego-ideal, as the 'loving function of the superego' (Schafer, 1960), contains the ideals towards which the individual strives, whether they come from identification with previous narcissistic states, identification with idealised parents or from society. The superego, on the other hand, tends to have a more critical, punitive and censoring function (Schafer, 1960).

Generally speaking, guilt tends to be considered as resulting from a superego judgement, while shame focuses more on self-consciousness and self-imaging than on guilt. Lewis (1971:30) describes the difference: 'the experience of shame is directly about the *Self*, which is the focus of evaluation. In guilt, the self is not the central object of negative evaluation, but rather the *thing* done or undone is the focus.' Because both shame and guilt can result from a moral transgression, the emotions can occur together, which is one of the reasons why they are often confused (Pines, 1987; Miller, 1985; Lewis, 1971; Jacobson, 1965). Of particular relevance in terms of guilt and shame, and their role in human rights issues through the mediating role of NGOs, is the form of self-representation that is the ideal self most desirable at any one time: 'the-self-I-want-to-be' (Sandler et al., 1963) and what happens when 'the self I want to be ' is compared to 'the self I am'.

Geras (1999) and Levi (1989) have attributed a crucial role to shame in bystanders' passivity. Levi talks of the vaster shame, 'the shame of the world', and how the majority of Germans under Hitler deluded themselves that not seeing was a way of not knowing, and that not knowing relieved them of their share of complicity (Levi, 1989:65–6). Geras is clear in defining shame as the emotional expression of 'seeing and not acting', thus linking shame to knowing and not intervening

(Geras, 1999). But, as we have seen 'knowing' is not a straightforward state of affairs.

Geras refers to Holocaust survivors' accounts as 'testimony to the scarcely thinkable that must nevertheless be thought' (Geras, 1999:47), thus obliquely hinting at tensions and conflicts taking place in the 'twilight zone' between thinking and unthinking. Cohen claims that in that 'twilight zone' denial breeds. Psychodynamically, denial of unbearable knowledge could be conceptualised as an attempt to 'unthink' a thought. Some psychoanalytic concepts are helpful in teasing out what might happen in that space. The idea of a 'thought un-thought', proposed here, borrows from Bollas's (1987) 'unthought known', which refers to experiences and contents of one's mind that we unconsciously 'know' but haven't been able to think properly. My formulation is also influenced by Bion's concept of 'beta-elements' as 'undigested facts' (Bléandonu, 1999), or psychic experiences which cannot yet be processed by the mind. Thus the 'thought un-thought' refers to the defensive process of dealing with deeply troubling and difficult knowledge that makes their thinking hard and resisted against. The 'un-thinking' part thus on the one hand acknowledges the struggle and the traumatic component involved in knowing, but also retains an element of agency that *actively* does the 'un-thinking' as an undoing of what is known.

Geras identifies shame as the emotional expression of this 'unthinking'. He refers to Primo Levi's description of what he saw in the Russian soldiers' faces at the moment they entered Auschwitz:

> It was the same shame we knew so well, which submerged us after the selections, and every time we had to witness or undergo an outrage: the shame that the Germans never knew, the shame which the just man experiences when confronted by a crime committed by another, and he feels remorse because of its existence, because of its having been irrevocably introduced into the world of existing things, and because his will has proven non-existent or feeble and was incapable of putting up a good defence.
>
> (Levi, 1987:154–6)

Levi's words are important, especially when he describes knowing about the atrocities and their horror as ' having been irrevocably introduced into the world of existing things'. The power of knowledge lies in its irrevocable nature. This is why Holocaust deniers have to be so zealous and active: a known fact takes residence in people's minds forever. A century of psychoanalysis has taught us that however covered, distorted or disguised, traumatic experiences and troubling knowledge never go away; but also that knowledge can be worked on, nibbled at the edges, made nebulous or undermined. In short, it can be, but only to some extent, 'un-thought'.

Geras focuses on the act of witnessing and how the shame is physically expressed in the face, the primary point of interchange between the world and the self. He expresses it thus: 'To see such a thing. To have to face it. And to be unable to look another in the eyes. Seeing, a mode of and a common metaphor for knowing' (Geras, 1999:51).

These reflections help make sense of participants' expressed shame and guilt in response to knowledge of human rights violations. Applying a psychoanalytic lens enables a 'thicker understanding' of what might be 'unthinkable' and unbearable in that knowledge, and of the full emotional implications of trying to 'un-know' the knowledge of human rights violations. On similar lines, Weintrobe (2013) applies a psychoanalytic lens to the exploration of public denial of climate change, to try to understand the psychodynamic bases of such denial, but also ways for counteracting the affective blockages to a different engagement.

Chasseguet-Smirgel (1985) suggests a link between the ego-ideal and self-esteem which depends greatly on other people's responses to us. She considers the 'loss of society love' as a narcissistic injury and shame as the product of the discrepancy between ego and ego-ideal. She, like Sandler et al. (1963), stresses the importance of peers in the 'checking out' of our ideals in the external world and the impossibility of doing so in isolation, thus recognising the impact of superego and ego-ideal on the Self and its interaction with societal norms. Of particular importance in this dynamic is the concept of self-representation, particularly in Sandler's formulation (1986). Earlier this was described as 'the self-representation can assume a wide variety of shapes and forms, depending on the pressures of the id, the requirements of the external world and the demand and standards of the introjects' (Sandler and Rosenblatt, 1962:152). This highly dynamic model, consonant with that adopted in this book, views self-representation as the constantly changing result of a negotiation of external and internal forces. The great emphasis placed on experience suggests that if a certain behaviour or response has been reinforced by the outside world, it is likely to become part of the ideal states with which the individual can identify.

Failure to live up to one's ideal damages self-esteem and provokes the traumatic and incapacitating feelings of shame and inferiority (Sandler et al. 1963) Thus low self-esteem derives from a discrepancy between self-representations – that is, between wishful self-images, the self we would like to be – and the self we really are (Sandler, 1986; Wumser, 1981). Sandler et al. (1963) argue that the relationship between the real and the ideal self is important for our sense of self-worth. The experience that we are approximating our ideal self provides us with 'narcissistic supplies' and a sense of well-being and self-worth. The extracts below seem to describe similar dynamics:

Fred: *I think that this kind of adverts are counterproductive. Not because I don't think people should know this but just because I don't think that the average person can deal with this. You read this, you push it right out of your mind because because it's, it's just so hard to acknowledge that you're part of the same species. That if another, if another person can do this, then you can do it. And that's a, that's a horrible, it's unacceptable, it's unabsorbable.*

Tina: *Amnesty used to have a campaign where they used the torture equipment [general agreement] as a photograph, to leave it up to your imagination and in a way that was kind of more shocking, you know . . .*

Bruna: *why?*

Tina: *your, your imagination was just like, your, you worked out what was going on..*

Bruna: *so we become the torturer?*

Ian: *EXACTLY, because we can actually come up with the image of what someone's done, you've just done it.*

Fred is describing a defence against information that is traumatic for 'the average person' and their self-assessment and self-image, suddenly challenged by the appeal. Fred argues that the information forces a re-assessment which is intolerable to the 'ordinary person', which I take to mean a benign and moral human nature. And yet if we don't chose to distance ourselves from the message or from the perpetrators of abuses as monsters, we are then confronted by the 'unabsorbable' truth that, as Tina puts it, '*if another person can do this, then you can do it*'. This, then, according to Fred, is what is defended against: '*you push it right out of your mind because, it's just so hard to acknowledge that you're part of the same species*'.

The same point is pursued by Tina and Ian. By discovering their capacity to imagine how to torture a person, the illusion of distance, of a fundamental difference between them and the torturer, is taken away. Arguably, the realisation of that similarity is the shock factor, rather than the torture itself as it connects the reader in an inescapable way to the event and to parts of oneself one would rather forget about.

Hence the threat is twofold. First, there is the horrifying descriptive content of the information. Second, there is the threat to the image of ourselves as good people and the idea of our world as orderly and safe. By threatening what is our good view of ourselves, it threatens our ideal self and self-esteem. By threatening our image or fantasy of what the world is like, it also endangers our sense of safety.

A further threat might lie in the repressed sadism that images of horrors confront the viewer with. Susan Sontag (2003) has commented on the allure of repulsive images: 'Everyone knows that what slows down highway traffic going past a horrendous car crash is not only curiosity. It is also, for many, the wish to see something gruesome. Calling such wishes "morbid" suggests a rare aberration, but the attraction to such sights is not rare, and is a perennial source of inner torment' (Sontag, 2003:96). Sontag cites several sources which support this view. Plato in *The Republic* took for granted that we also have an appetite for sights of degradation and pain and mutilation. Sontag labels this appetite a 'despised impulse' and argues that it must also be taken into account when discussing the effect of atrocity pictures. She cites Edmund Burke[1] who, in the 18th century, claimed: 'we have a degree of delight, and that no small one, in the real misfortunes and pains of others. There is no spectacle we so eagerly pursue, as that of some uncommon and grievous calamity' (*A philosophical enquiry (1757)* quoted in Sontag, 2003:97). Finally, Sontag (2003:98) cites Bataille who, referring to a photograph he kept on his desk portraying the horrific image of a Chinese prisoner undergoing 'the death of a hundred cuts', said 'to contemplate this image, is both a mortification of the feelings and a liberation of tabooed erotic knowledge – a complex response that many people must find hard to credit'.

If people resist acknowledgement of such responses even to themselves, they are hardly likely to want to discuss them voluntarily in a focus group, where everybody is eager to appear as a nice and moral person. Yet Rachel was brave enough to hint at it:

[2:279]: Rachel: *In a way it's too much in a way, I don't understand why people and sometimes myself, I mean. I usually turn off there but there are moments in which I look at them. So in a way we are kind of fascinated by this kind of problems. Er as a kind of, er sometimes I I thought it as a kind of er erm*

Bruna: *titillation?*

Rachel:	*yes, So it's a kindof a erm (.) erm*
Bruna:	*distancing?*
Rachel:	*No. Not distancing, erm no it it will come up. [laugh] But in any case it seems like if you want to see that all the bad happens to somebody else, and in a way it relives you.*

Rachel is struggling to find words; this is the challenge of acknowledgement. It is impossible to analyse discursively what cannot be said in words. Equally, it is in many ways problematic to attempt to read unconscious material in the participants' words or, as in this case, the lack of them. Yet it would seem odd not to at least consider that sadism and aggression might be evoked by images and information of human rights violations.

As Froggett (2002:35) reminds us, Klein is notorious for her grim view of the centrality of hate and aggression in mental development. However, out of the recognition of the hateful and destructive attacks emerges the need for reparation. Indeed, it is the reparative impulse born of guilt and gratitude that forms the basis of ethical life. The basis for moral concern lies in our primary ambivalence in relations to others.

Accounts acknowledging unconscious or morally troubling reactions to the witnessing of others' suffering were indeed very few. Thus we can only speculate, as the repressed is by definition inaccessible to consciousness. Yet, the psychoanalytic concept of reaction formation adds an interesting facet to the complex emotional relationship human beings have with the suffering of others. A reaction-formation has been defined as a psychological attitude or habitus diametrically opposing a repressed wish and constituted as a reaction against it, for example, bashfulness countering exhibitionistic tendencies (Laplanche and Pontalis, 1985). Further, shame and disgust, have been considered to be a reaction formation to voyeurism (Abrahams, 1913). I wonder whether this is also what Bob is hinting at when he says: '*you see this sort of posters and a lot of the time [...] they make you repulse against it.*' In psychoanalytic terms, if repulsion is taken to function as a reaction formation, what might also be defended against, is the voyeuristic and sadistic pleasures in being told a story about rape, torture and abuse. For Anna Freud (1936) the super-ego anxiety – that is, fear of the superego reaction – has to be added to the list of powerful motives for defence. The implications of what she argued are highly relevant to this study: that the source of danger is our reaction to a particular situation or desire rather than the situation itself. In this view our reaction and its implication for our sense of self would definitely be too unacceptable and incompatible with our sense of being 'good moral people'.

Despite the paucity of empirical evidence, it is still worth engaging intellectually with the possibility that these unconscious dynamics might indeed play some role in audience passivity. It is also worth exploring the possibility of extending the idea of defence against unpleasurable affects and freedom from disturbance, from the individual level to the social arena. What is defended then could be the shared need and belief that one belongs to a democratic, progressive nation and to the benign West. One could identify several defence mechanisms in operation at a social level: for example, collective denial of how the West is not only involved but directly implicated in human rights violations and rationalisation of how neoliberalism promotes and prioritises individualistic well-being over social responsibility. There might also be a process of sublimation of Western interference into Third World affairs, for example 'we are helping them, we are investing in them, we are protecting their freedom', as also suggested in the recurrent trope 'in countries like that', discussed in Chapter 5. But there might also be a profound guilt about how the West benefits from the plight of others: '*Colin: we are in Western society and we feel guilty for the fact that we walk around you know, in decent air using washing machines.*'

Essentially, what we defend against might be the implication that we are involved, but that we don't want to know. What is appalling, then, is that we are made aware of our connection to these brutal events, of our social responsibility and the acknowledgement that even though we know about them, nevertheless we are allowing the atrocities to carry on. I am suggesting that what is defended against is the *moment of contact between us and the atrocities* – the realisation that our social responsibility and human compassion, for whatever reason, do not stretch far enough to getting us involved. It is, in this sense, an internal battle between conscience and apathy: in psychoanalytic terms a defence against superego anxieties; in ordinary terms, 'the shutting down of the needling of the conscience'. Going full circle, then, donations might play a perverse function, beautifully verbalised by Colin.

Colin: *We are in Western society and we feel guilty for the fact that we walk around you know, in decent air using washing machines, and it's like so you know a couple of standing orders and it's all alright then. You know, you've squared up your moral responsibilities, you know.*

Looking at donations in this way gives them a completely different meaning. They are not necessarily an expression of compassion, empathy and a connection with the suffering other but, on the contrary, a way of distancing oneself – a quick glancing and shutting down, an easy, convenient and effective distancing oneself without properly engaging first.

According to Colin, human rights and humanitarian agencies are fully aware of this mechanism and use it to their advantage:

Colin: *I think a lot of charities tend to kind of play on that I think you know in a sense it's like Q< sign here, sign here then you can sort of walk the street you know being a happy man> Q, you know, going down the wine bar or whatever. That's a cynical way of looking at it but that's what worries me I think about a lot of charity advertising.*

Everyday morality is messy and presents us with terrible dilemmas. Perhaps it is easier to construct a view of oneself that excludes morality and choice. It might be easier to think of these decisions being out of our control. Equally, it might bring relief to be angry and resentful towards those who force us to look at what we want to avoid. If we could only silence those voices and turn away … But uncomfortable emotions and unpalatable truths cannot be permanently repressed without leaving a trace. They come back to haunt us in many and unpredictable ways.

[7:29]: Roy: *Well as I was reading the rest it all makes me, a part of me just like switched off slightly before I could go on. But I still kept feeling then hopelessness anger erm and I was erm reading more I was feeling more erm shame I think. Shame at myself for wanting to switch off I think and not wanting to. Erm just not wanting to know anymore. But I think a part of that is just feeling so help hopeless and helpless.*

Bruna: *Right. Is that why you want to switch off?*

Roy: *Yeah, 'cause it just seems like it's just so much and it feels like there's so much that needs to be done and I think it's the it's so many different things like education would be one part but I think it's so so many other things that need to be done that it just feels like it's it's an almost impossible task.*

The next section looks in detail at the phenomenon of switching off, but the quote from Roy is an important reminder of the impossibility of ever fully switching off and that repression always leaves traces of the repressed behind. Roy also gives a very good illustration of the circularity of emotions and of the emotional loop through which members of the public react to their own emotional reactions.

Members of the public as emotional victims

... and if the perception of reality entails unpleasure, that perception, that is, the truth, must be sacrificed.

(Sigmund Freud, 1937:237)

The extract below from Tina captures one of the most frequent narratives offered by participants to explain how they respond emotionally and cognitively to information of atrocities. It also continues the investigation of what is emotionally intolerable in information about human rights violations that cannot be totally understood through discursive analyses.

[7] Tina: *It's all right. Uhm, yeah I think it was similar to what [Leila] was saying. I was kind of reading it and reading it and then it came to the rape and because it kind of, got worse, it was she was raped then it was, you know, twenty two men and then it was three day. There was a point at which I, not quite switched off but, the horror sort of subsided and, I don't know.*

Bruna: *How did that happen?*

Tina: *I think it's, in a way it's because it's like a defence mechanism. We hear this so much that, you were saying that, 'is it covered in the media?' but I think it is covered a lot in the media, the same with the stories like this. And the problem is that we do now switch off. I think, or some of us do. And so I can be horrified, immediately horrified by the stories but then, there's a way of thinking Q < well >Q, telling yourself Q<you can't do anything about it>Q. So then going off and sort of making yourself a cup of coffee or something. And switching off and getting on with your life.*

In her account, Tina identifies the moment when she read about the particularly shocking details of rape as the point at which she kind of switched off and the *'the horror sort of subsided'*. Although she is very precise in identifying the moment, she claims not to know what happened – or so I understood her *'I don't know'*. When pressed, she gives the standard explanation involving the familiar jumble of defence mechanism, desensitisation, switching off and altogether disconnecting from the issue. As this bricolage of affective states and emotional processes was repeatedly presented as the emotional chain responsible for disconnection from the violations, it seems important to try to untangle the components. This section engages with each one of the listed concepts in the attempt to understand both the original and technical meaning of these discrete but interconnected emotional states, and what participants might mean by using them in their everyday connotations. In doing so, I want to remain open to the face value of what participants claim to be feeling when talking to switching off, desensitisation and defence mechanism, and simultaneously as powerful cultural tropes, as Dean (2004) defines them in her study on the Holocaust. She suggests that numbness may be becoming a conventional framework within which we think about our connections to others and argues that the narrative on numbing is far more complex. Echoing Susan Sontag, she explores why numbness remains such a powerful cultural trope, stating that '*numbness is not only a psychological form of self-protective dissociation; it is arguably a new, highly self-conscious narrative about the collective constriction of moral availability, if not empathy, and may thus constrain humanist aspirations in ways we do not yet recognize*' (Dean, 2004:5). Similar to the multiple readings proposed in this chapter, Dean also regards as important the holding open of the possibility of overlapping, albeit potentially contradictory, meanings in emotional accounting of passivity.

Among the many emotional reactions mentioned by participants, I found desensitisation the most intriguing, particularly when compared to the strength of emotions expressed in relation to agencies. Most participants referred to an 'emotionless' state as the 'end point' in their reaction to the suffering of victims of human rights violations, in particular when accounting for why people are not more responsive to the knowledge of the suffering of others. This was presented as a given; participants did not seem to feel they had to explain what they meant nor ask questions. It was never disputed.

There is something intriguing in the idea that profoundly emotional messages end up generating an absence of emotions. What happens to, as a participant put it, the 'over-swell of emotions'? How do audiences make sense of what happens to them? The descriptive and the rhetorical inevitably get mixed up and can easily be mistaken for the same thing.

This section uses a psychoanalytic lens to understand psychodynamically participants' experiences of being exposed to disturbing information.

The following two extracts are representative of the fairly common trend in the groups to talk about desensitisation when referring to two separate but connected phenomena. One relates to ideas of desensitisation resulting from overexposure, habituation and adaptation, and the other suggests that desensitisation is the effect of a defence mechanism. In the group discussions the two were intertwined, as is clearly illustrated in the first example where the speaker moves from one to the other and back. However for analytic purposes I will discuss them separately.

Bruna: [...]*so, the first and I think the most immediate question is how did you feel? What, what kind of reactions did you have reading all of this?*

[P2] Bob: *Well you tend to shut yourself off from it because it's so, um, appalling. And, um, you sort of feel sick, your stomach makes you feel that it's really, you don't want to know anything about it,(.) um, so, it's like, if you see a lot of it you then becomes, it doesn't become anything, [...] You desensitise yourself. And if you only see little bits of it, you get the opposite effect, where it's repulsion alright, so, you see these sort of posters, and a lot of the time they're just, you know, make you repulse against it and you just want to run away from it, you don't want to look at it*

[P1] Jack: *There is, there is, I mean, one of the first words that were mentioned was desensitisation, you see, you're hearing everyday about something of horror happening in this country, whether it be a child disappearing, somebody being raped, somebody being knifed at the side of the road, or whatever, it does happen in this country, the more people watch television, the more people read newspapers, it's constantly being shuffled at you and it's becoming almost more acceptable to hear about these things.*

Desensitisation as defence mechanism

In recent times social sciences and humanities have seen a 'return to affect' (Wetherell, 2012; Leys, 2011) and an increased interest in the role of affect in social phenomena (e.g. Weintrobe, 2013). There is a long tradition in psychoanalytic thinking (Sandler, 1985) that argues that affect is the main motivating force in human existence. At a basic level, we seek pleasure and avoid discomfort. We have sophisticated ways of doing this. For example, we unconsciously elaborate strategies, 'defence mechanisms', to protect ourselves from uncomfortable truths.

We repress, sublimate, rationalise, project, and displace our difficult feelings.

Throughout Freud's work, the mental apparatus is conceived as functioning as a regulator for adaptation to demands from both internal and external sources. It maintains a 'steady state' (homeostasis) in the face of constant disturbance. The emphasis on defence is really the beginning of psychoanalysis and one of the elements making psychoanalysis a *dynamic* theory of the mind (Wolheilm, 1991:32) – so much so that it could be argued that the different phases in Freud's metapsychology are based on the answer given to fundamental questions: What are defences? What are defences defending against? What are the consequences of defences? These questions are also fundamental to this discussion.

A defence mechanism functions as a protective shield. 'Reizschutz', literally protection against excitation, was to denote the particular function of protecting the organism against excitations deriving from the outer or inner world. The concept of defence is elaborated both by Freud, in 'Inhibitions, symptoms and anxiety' (1926), and by his daughter Anna Freud, in her work 'The Ego and the mechanisms of defence', as described by Laplanche and Pontalis (1985). Anna Freud shows how defence mechanisms can be directed not only against instinctual claims but also against anything liable to give rise to the development of anxiety: emotions, situations, super-ego demands.

This is very relevant to our topic in that the participants, as discussed in the previous section, seem to feel threatened at many levels. They are threatened by the information *per se* (situation), the upsetting emotions evoked by the information (horror, disgust, empathy, helplessness, guilt), and by the demands of their super-ego and ego-ideal (to be good and morally responsible people). Therefore, in the sense in which desensitisation is evoked in relation to ideas of trauma and self-protection, the participants are invoking desensitisation as a defence mechanism. The information coming from outside is traumatic and defence mechanisms come into action to stop the upset.

This seems exactly what Neil, Tina and Jane are describing:

Neil: *yeah, perhaps it's a, perhaps it's a function of shock tactics that it forces people, they can't cope with the overswell of emotions so they completely rationalise everything*

Leila: *After the first bit after I got to erm where her children ah no after erm Q< one by one the men raped her. She is raped by twenty-two men, it took three days >Q after that I wanted to switch off. Well I did*

> *slightly switch off. I read it but er, you know you just feel like it's kind of, like a kind of shield I've got up.*

Tina: *It's all right. Uhm, yeah I think it was similar to what [Leila] was saying. I was kind of reading it and reading it and then it came to the rape and because it kind of, got worse, it was she was raped then it was, you know, twenty-two men and then it was three day. There was a point at which I, not quite switched off but, the horror sort of subsided and, I don't know.*

Bruna: *How did that happen?*

Tina: *I think it's, in a way it's because it's like a defence mechanism. We hear this so much that, you were saying that, 'is it covered in the media?' but I think it is covered a lot in the media the same with the stories like this. And the problem is that we do now switch off. I think, or some of us do. And so I can be horrified, immediately horrified by the stories but then, there's a way of thinking well, telling yourself you can't do anything about it. So then going off and sort of making yourself a cup of coffee or something. And and switching off and getting on with your life and.*

Jane: *I think the, the start of page one, actually, probably works a bit better, because it's segmented, almost like separate issues, whereas the other one just gives a catalogue of, of events and you almost kind of think O.K. well that's enough now. Whereas with the other one, you know, you have time for a breather*

Leila refers to a 'shield' that went up when she read about the horrific details of rape. Neil describes in more details the trigger (the overswell of emotions which audiences cannot cope with) and the reaction (the defence of rationalisation). Paraphrasing these explanations for a moment, the participants are explaining their reactions as due to the action of some kind of homeostatic mechanism that breaks the circuit, as it were, when the stimuli become too intense and too disturbing. Jane juxtaposes this to a situation that is more manageable, where she can recover – *'you have time for a breather'* – before facing the next trauma. This suggests the existence of an equilibrium that has to be restored over and over again, which, according to psychoanalysis, is exactly what defences are employed to do. They reduce and eliminate any change or situation liable to threaten the integrity and equilibrium of the bio-psychological individual.

Mixed in there is a very different emotional state which Tina moves to seamlessly when explaining why, after a certain point, she experienced less horror. She says: *'I think it is covered a lot in the media the same with the stories like this. And the problem is that we do now switch off.'* What she is claiming here is quite different from the scenario in the first part of her account. While before the switching off was as a defence from stimuli that were too strong, here she is claiming that the power of the stimulus to produce a lasting impact is lessened by its repetition. The first is a defence mechanism, and the second is what psychologists call 'habituation'.

A systematic engagement with the confusion between these two cognitive-emotional states is important for several reasons. First, the confusion speaks of processes of hybridisation undergone by what were originally technical and highly specialist terms, when they enter everyday parlance. It is in their ordinary, un-technical use that these terms acquire ideological and moral value.

Second, the ideas of apathy because of defensive desensitisation and apathy as habituation imply opposite courses of actions for campaigners. Defensive desensitisation suggests that sheltering audiences from excessively traumatic information in appeals and campaigns would be beneficial in enabling audiences to become involved in human rights issues. Processes of habituation, however, suggest that if the information is too bland or fails to make an impression because it is too similar to what is already known, audiences find it difficult to hold it in their mind long enough to do anything about it. We will come back to these dilemmas later in the book.

Third, this confusion allows us to understand better an extremely powerful concept consistently used by scholars to explain audience passivity: compassion fatigue. It refers to a lowering of audiences' response to traumatic information due to familiarity. This type of explanation was used in all groups, often explicitly defined as 'compassion fatigue', thus suggesting that the term hase become acceptable in everyday speech, as also illustrated in Chapter 2. Tester's (2001:13) defines compassion fatigue as 'becoming so used to the spectacle of dreadful events, misery or suffering that we stop noticing them' The concept of compassion fatigue originated in the clinical domain and was originally known as Secondary Traumatic Stress disorder (STS). Figley (1995 describes STS as follows:

> the natural consequent behaviours and emotions resulting from knowing about a traumatising event experienced by a significant other. The stress resulting from helping or wanting to help a traumatised or suffering other. The professional work centred on the relief of the emotional suffering of clients automatically includes absorbing

information that is about suffering as well. Although I now refer to it as compassion fatigue, I first called it a form of burnout, a kind of 'secondary victimisation'.

(Figley, 1995:7)

STS was first diagnosed in nurses in the 1950s. Sufferers can exhibit several symptoms including hopelessness, a decrease in experiences of pleasure, constant stress and anxiety, and a pervasive negative attitude. What is made clear by early studies is not that health professionals' capacity for compassion lessens over time, but that some of the patients' emotional reactions to trauma are absorbed by the clinicians as a cumulative effect of their being exposed to stories of trauma. So we have two parallel processes here: 1) *repetition* having a damaging cumulative effect; 2) *numbing* as 'emotional contagion' (Miller et al., 1988), whereby mental health practitioners exhibit similar symptoms to PTSD (Post Traumatic Stress Disorder) patients. Crucially, the numbing is not the effect of lesser compassion due to habituation, but the contagion of defensive numbness (symptomatic of PTSD) from patient to clinician. To put it simply, compassion fatigue originally referred to a side effect of exercising empathy towards traumatised people on a daily basis, not a reduction of empathy.

The term 'compassion fatigue' has recently been picked up in Media and Communications. Journalism analysts argue that the media has caused widespread compassion fatigue in society by saturating newspapers and news shows with often de-contextualised images and stories of suffering. This has caused the public to become cynical, or become resistant to helping people who are suffering. Journalism analysts cite research which shows that visual images affect brain activity in demonstrable and measurable ways.

Particularly noticeable in this line of argument is Susan Moeller's work (1999) which makes a direct connection between the constant flow of horrific imagery originated by the media and audiences' lessening ability to feel. She argues that compassion fatigue is a modern syndrome, resulting from formulaic media coverage, sensationalised language and overly Americanised metaphors. Moeller asks important questions on the politics behind such media operations and seems to suggest that the media might be creating an audience that has seen too much – or too little – to care and might be thus abdicating their special responsibility to the public.

Compassion fatigue has also been called a form of burnout, which is how the term was originally used in Media and Communications to describe journalists' secondary trauma in being routinely exposed to atrocities. Yet the term has been used to explain quite a different kind of phenomenon that elsewhere has been called 'demand fatigue' (Cohen and Seu, 2002; Cohen, 2001). For example, the term 'compassion fatigue' was used after the 2004 Indian Ocean earthquake to explain an apparent decrease in donations for other natural disasters. This apparently also occurred during the 2005 hurricane season. Thus compassion fatigue has mutated into an explanation for the resistance of the general public to give money to charity or what is clearly perceived (see Chapters 3 and 4) as repeated solicitations by charitable organisations, as testified by the *Oxford Dictionary*'s definition: 'indifference to charitable appeals on behalf of suffering people, experienced as a result of the frequency or number of such appeals'. This illustrates how the concept has been used erroneously (in terms of its original technical meaning) and misleadingly. It is one thing to say that viewing a traumatic event is upsetting; quite another that the viewing is traumatic itself.

As Cohen (2001) points out, the populist psychology thesis of 'compassion fatigue' is used as a composite of several psychological concepts. One is the cognitive concept of information overload denoting a quantity and intensity of stimuli that exceed our mental capacity to pay attention: that is, we reach 'audience saturation'. 'An audience watches a TV documentary showing children with legs blown off by land-mines; by the sixth child, they feel themselves running out of psychic diskette space; their mind can't cope anymore; they change to another channel' (Cohen, 2001:188).

Reference to these psychological processes of habituation and normalisation were a frequent occurrence in the focus groups. For example:

[7:75]: Peter: *Now you see so many (Tina: yeah, in agreement) films with these types of horrors in them. You see such dramatisation, so it's almost like normal thing. It's like you're saying, you could almost break down a few years ago if you were to see something like this maybe I don't know, fifties or something, if you were to hear this in those days maybe there wasn't so much, but now.*

Images once seen as intolerable eventually become accepted as normal. Hence the potential impact of an image is lost because of its familiarity. As Paula said: *'you see it night after night, and sort of in two weeks time you're looking at it, it doesn't really mean anything does it?'* Neil feels the same: *'I was surprisingly undisturbed by (reading the information) because I've heard it so many times before'*; and so does Carol: *'and that's why we did become very desensitised because we've seen that much of it on the television on the news'.*

All these participants are describing the psychic numbing allegedly occurring when images of brutality and horror become too familiar to retain any visceral power. Cohen (2001) is not convinced by this mechanical explanation. He argues that compassion fatigue is 'vague as a description and even vaguer as an explanation, is simply a 'urban myth', with no supporting evidence in personal biography or cultural history' (Cohen, 2001:191). The problem is not audiences' psychological compassion fatigue, but political issues of the media's framework of reporting. Cohen claims that 'wanting to do something' to stop the suffering, to help others, is a universal human response. The reason why audiences' responses have become dimmer has little to do with fatigue or the sheer repetition of images. 'The reason is that any dimming of compassion, any decreased concern about distant others, is just what the individual spirit of the global market wants to encourage' (Cohen, 2001:195). He agrees with Moeller (1999) that compassion fatigue is not an unavoidable consequence of covering the news, but an unavoidable consequence of the way news is now covered.

Similarly, Tester's (2002) analysis of compassion fatigue hints at the ideological operation involved in adopting compassion fatigue, desensitisation and defence mechanisms as explanatory concepts of moral apathy and the way atrocities are reported in the media. As an example he refers to Janine di Giovanni (1994), who claims that compassion fatigue emerges as a defence mechanism on the part of journalists and thereafter audiences too. Her explanation also combines the psychoanalytic idea of defence mechanism and the psychological reactions of habituation and desensitisation due to information overload. She claims that journalists (and consequently audiences) cannot respond emotionally to so much dreadful news without falling into neurosis. Therefore the psychological 'switching off' is a way of protecting themselves from the overwhelmingly terrible world. Tester rightly argues that the concept takes for granted much more than it manages to explain and that it makes some questionable assumptions. First, it assumes some kind of golden age in the past when 'switching off was not the dominant response'. In other words, compassion fatigue requires the assumption of a personal or historical past in which compassion was not fatigued. There is little or no evidence to support this. Second, it implies a general psychological trait of all journalists (and audiences) everywhere.

Despite these incisive criticisms, the idea of a golden era when audiences, not yet suffering from habituation, responded proactively is active and in circulation as a self-exonerating script, as demonstrated by Peter's and others' statements. Hence, as argued by Cohen (2001) and Moeller (1999), instead of accepting the view of audiences mechanically and automatically switching off we should be focusing on their *active* 'looking away'. Before moving to the next section dealing with the 'active turning away', I want to briefly return to trauma and the 'excessive' affects identified so far in the accounts. It is important not to lose sight of and to maintain an engagement with the affective impact of traumatic information on the public. Compassion fatigue, despite its popular appeal, is neither the only nor the most convincing explanation for the vagaries of the public's affective responses to human rights appeals. Yet, in the absence of alternative explanations or ways of processing emotionally disturbing information, it is not surprising maybe that in a neoliberal society the public might find the position of 'emotional consumers' familiar and reassuring, as the next section will illustrate. An ontological confusion over the nature and function of audience desensitisation as a psychological reaction to traumatic information or a 'cultural construct' seems to permeate debates. Of course it is, to some extent, both. Yet, the differentiation is crucial, particularly when we think about countermeasures. In the first formulation the question is what can be done to enable audiences to tolerate the inevitable upset resulting from viewing horrors and turn the shock into desire for mastery and reparation – that is, action rather than detachment and switching off? The second take, desensitisation as 'cultural construct', poses a very different set of questions. Assuming generalisable psychological traits suggests deterministic inevitability either because people (and audiences at large) are *intrinsically* predisposed to responding in a certain way, or because they are governed by their own self-protective cognitive or unconscious mechanisms of defence. What is left out of this picture is the *active* turning away. This, in my view, is the nub of the problem.

'Emotions' as a vocabulary of denial for reflexive consumers

In this last section I am interested in the ideological and rhetorical effects of how audiences use the term 'compassion fatigue' in the context of human rights practice. Resorting to a past 'golden era' warrants the speaker's disassociation by claiming good faith, and blaming the disconnection to mechanisms beyond their individual control, but recognised as a social and shared phenomenon. This effect is compounded

by positioning oneself as the victim: if audiences are the victim of continuous bombardment, it is not surprising that they protect themselves
by switching off. This section looks at how members of the public, as
reflexive 'emotional' consumers, use emotional explanations as vocabularies of denial, but also how they assess their own emotional responses
as consumers defending against the manipulative intentions of the
messengers.

Engaging with the *active* turning away involves a move from an understanding of talk as an expression of what happens inside people –
that is, an explanation – to seeing it as a part of the process through
which people construct and reconstruct the world and their subjectivity in everyday talk through historically, socially and contextually based
accounts. From this angle, psychoanalytic and psychological theories
which were used in the previous sections to explain what participants
were describing are here considered as a shared resource to make sense
of their behaviour and reactions to themselves and to others.

In this sense, 'compassion fatigue' does not pertain to a claimed
underlying universally shared human reaction, but is a particularly
effective and current cultural construct, resulting from a bricolage of
highly technical concepts. As such, 'compassion fatigue' is lived ideology and, as rhetorical device, an effective way of making accounts
of apathy and desensitisation look reasonable and unavoidable (Potter
and Wetherell, 1995; Edwards and Potter, 1992). In approaching participants' speech as social action, references to internal processes are taken
not as statements about such processes, but as dilemmas of interest
(in this case a desire to maintain a good self-image; to be seen as moral
and compassionate despite the lack of action and involvement). These
dilemmas of interest are hidden by resorting to commonsensical, factual
explanations organised to undermine alternatives (Wood and Kroger,
2000). In this sense then, we are not concerned with the existence (or
not) and nature of compassion fatigue, but with how it functions as a
cultural resource to make particular claims

Let's then revisit what Bob said:

Bob: *Well you tend to shut yourself off from it because it's so, um, appalling.
And, um, you sort of feel sick. Your stomach makes you feel that it's
really, you don't want to know anything about it (B/um). Um, so, it's
like, if you see a lot of it you then become, it doesn't become anything
[…] You desensitise yourself. And if you only see little bits of it, you get
the opposite effect, where it's repulsion (B/ah, ah). Alright, so, you see
these sort of posters and a lot of the time they're just, you know, make*

> *you repulse against it. And you just want to run away from it, you don't*
> *want to look at it (B/um)*

In the first line Bob uses the idea of a defence mechanism: the information is so appalling that it leads to shutting off. That leaves Bob having to justify his action, not terribly commendable from an ethical point of view: he is told of a fellow human being's suffering and he doesn't want to know. But how can we blame him if he feels sick? Bob has a stake in convincing us that it is not that he, Bob, doesn't want to know; it is his stomach that tells him that really he should not know. Agency and responsibility are handed over to the stomach, an involuntary organ. The moral subject is in this way constructed as grappling, struggling with a body or internal dynamics independent of his own will.

Bob is describing something ordinary and familiar. We all recognise the reaction and the cliché: 'I felt sick; it was sickening.' And yet, I suggest, these ordinary commonplaces operate the important ideological function of removing responsibility and blame. They also counter the possibility of alternative action/reaction. The subject is passive, dominated by forces beyond its control. This is simultaneously true and not true. Bob, almost in a 'slip of the tongue' or perhaps in an implied political semi-awareness, at the same time attributes agency to himself. Because, although he says that *'your stomach makes you feel that [...] you don't want to know anything about it'*, at the same time he also acknowledges that *'you shut yourself off'* and that *'you want to run away from it, you don't want to look at it'*

Freud captured the ambiguities and complexities of what happens when we want to run away from a difficult truth, but don't want to be seen as doing that. In his discussion of defence mechanisms in 'Analysis terminable and interminable', Freud makes an analogy with a book containing statements considered undesirable. One way would be for the offending passages to be thickly crossed through. However, if what was desired was not only the disappearance of the passage but also the *intention* of mutilating the book, the best option would be ' if the whole passage would be erased and a new one which said exactly the opposite put in its place [...] and it is highly probable that the corrections had not been made in the direction of the truth' (Freud, 1937:236). He concludes: 'if the perception of reality entails unpleasure, that perception – that is, the truth, – must be sacrificed' (Freud, 1937:237).

On similar lines, I am suggesting that the dilemma of not wanting to know about human rights abuses and at the same time not wanting to be seen to be doing so is resolved by resorting to psychological explanations of being desensitised and experiencing compassion fatigue. Different discourses allow different possibilities for subjectivity. Science as objective and mechanistic is by definition beyond morality. The type of subjectivity made available by a scientific discourse is one governed by physiological autonomous mechanisms. This allows a translation of the participant's response from a moral and social sphere to an individualistic cognitive/physiological domain, where issues of morality and social responsibility become irrelevant. Psychological and psychoanalytic concepts, or psycho-babble, have been incorporated into the vocabulary of valid explanations of human behaviour. At that level they might be stating the obvious, but viewed as rhetorical tools they allow the 'shifting of domains', the re-framing of the problem, the new demarcation of the territory. Furthermore the employment of this reasonable, self evident, commonsensical explanation forecloses further investigation of the mechanics of desensitisation and moral apathy. It also pre-empts the possibility of a closer examination of what exactly is defended against.

The mechanistic view of human functioning sustains the idea of a threshold of information to which we react. News of horrendous human suffering becomes stimuli we get used to, just as our pupils restrict in bright light (defence mechanism) or we don't smell a bad smell after a while (habituation due to overexposure). How can anybody blame our eyes or noses for doing what they are programmed to do – that is, protect us from damage and bad experiences? They can't help it.

In the focus groups the evidence that the problem of desensitisation was constructed not as a moral dilemma, but as a simple physiological stimulus–reaction, is very significant. The participants would like to communicate that they simply can't help it. This involves a process through which the information is reframed and repositioned in a different arena, thus providing justifications and explanations which otherwise would not be possible (Cohen and Seu, 2002). Psychological explanations, absorbed into everyday common-sense talk, allow the reframing in this case. Ideas of an unconscious mind, mixed with some notions of physiologically based autonomous reactions, are used to support this claim.

In short, what I am suggesting is that emotionally based explanations can be used as a powerful vocabulary of denial.

Summary and reflections

Influenced by Boltanski (1999), Hoijer (2004:522-3) identified in her research four forms of compassion to be found in audience reactions to distant suffering: 'tender-hearted compassion, blame-filled compassion, shame-filled compassion and powerlessness-filled compassion'. Tender-hearted compassion denotes a reaction that focuses on the suffering of the victim and expresses feelings of pity and empathy. Blame-filled compassion describes feelings of anger and indignation that are prompted by witnessing suffering. This anger is most often directed at those seen as responsible 'for the excesses'; in political conflicts this is most likely viewed as a person in power rather than the individual perpetrators of violent acts. Shame-filled compassion 'brings in the ambivalence connected with witnessing the suffering of others in our own comfortable lives and the cosiness of our living room'. Hoijer states that shame is an emotional state that stems from the knowledge that we have behaved dishonourably. In relation to distant suffering, respondents feel shame due to the knowledge that they have dishonoured their moral responsibility to help the victim. In these cases shame may also be accompanied by feelings of anger and indignation directed towards oneself for having failed to act/prevent suffering. Finally, powerlessness-filled compassion indicates the respondents' awareness of the limited powers they have to effectively alleviate the suffering of distant others.

It is possible to recognise some of Hoijer's emotional states in the accounts analysed in this book. However, Hoijer's categorisation doesn't go beyond the descriptive and has primarily focused on the role of the media in determining these reactions in audiences. In this chapter I have engaged with the complex and multi-layered constellation of phenomena surrounding emotional responses to human rights violations.

The main argument put forward by this chapter is that the 'desensitised subject' should be understood as a psychological subject as well as morally agentic and that psychology and psychoanalysis should be considered simultaneously as explanatory paradigms and rhetorical resources for morally acceptable justifications of apathy.

In the first instance I have applied a psychoanalytic reading drawing on a dynamic understanding of the mind to investigate the participants' affectively charged responses to human rights violations and their communication by NGOs, in particular those evoking shame and guilt. Applied to the relationship between NGOs and the public, the psychodynamics of shame and guilt can provide an important explanation for the acrimony towards agencies so often displayed by participants. I have paid particular attention to the detrimental emotional impact of what audiences might experience as being 'manipulated', 'used' and 'set up' in terms of shame and 'ideal self'.

In the first and second section of this chapter, that knowledge of human rights violations as traumatic is taken at face value. The shutting off, closing down, turning away, not wanting to know, are understood as defence mechanisms – either because audiences find the shock tactics through which the information is disseminated and the content of the information itself traumatic, or because they have become indifferent due to overexposure to news of horror, people end up in a state of self-defensive desensitisation. This is explained by drawing upon classical psychoanalytic explanations of how defence mechanisms work and mainstream psychological concepts such as habituation and normalisation. The concept of 'compassion fatigue' is also critiqued in this context.

On the other hand, extracts from focus groups also illustrated how psychological and psychoanalytic explanations can be employed rhetorically to justify indifference and lack of action in that they are part of a vocabulary of denial.

In concluding this chapter, I suggest that it is worth exploring what these findings tell us about what could be done to empower audiences to act or at least to feel able to act when confronted with distant and overwhelming problems. It might be worth thinking in relational terms of the emotional role played, or that could be played, by agencies. I want to return briefly to Bion and his idea of the container and the contained and how a parental figure's fundamental role is to hold and contain emotions the child cannot contain or understand themselves. The unfortunate comparison of members of the public with children is not intended as patronising and infantilising but rather to point at the difficulties in managing and containing the complex and powerful emotions evoked by knowing about atrocities and unspeakable suffering. It might be controversial to suggest that human rights agencies should take up the 'container' role and communicate horrific information to the public in a way that enables them to process it. This is not just a matter of of providing the viewers with a contextualisation of the information to enable them to make sense of both what is happening, as well as why and what can be done to remedy the problem. Agencies might also want to consider that, in the moment in which they engage the public, they are in a relationship with them. An awareness on the part of agencies that audiences experience them and perhaps expect them to play a kind of parental role might help improve communication

8
Conclusions

> Could one feasibly entertain the vision of a global human community in which an obligation to come to the assistance of others in danger or distress was widely felt as amongst the most powerful of imperatives, moving people to action when the risks of acting were small to non-existent, making a serious demand on their consciences – on their day-to-day practical deliberations – even when the risks were greater than that, and making of shame something more than a 'metaphysical' shadow, more than a post hoc individual sentiment following failure to act; making shame, and of the foretaste of it, an effective, mobilizing norm of social life?
>
> (Geras, 1998:57)

Passivity Generation has investigated what happens when the public is informed about human rights violations, and the actions (or inaction) resulting from this knowledge. What happens between knowledge and action has usually been conceptualised as a single gap, but I contend (Seu, 2010) that such conceptualisation is over-simplistic and misleading. Rather, several gaps can be identified between knowledge and action. The first is between the actual human rights violation and its communication to the public (through media or NGOs' communications). Another is between this communication and its reception by the public (this includes the public's understanding of the communication and their cognitive and emotional reactions) and a further gap is between public reception of the information and their (in)action.

Figure 8.1 is an attempt to provide a visual representation of how public passivity has been theorised in *Passivity Generation*. The key argument is that public passivity is generated by a mixture of factors and

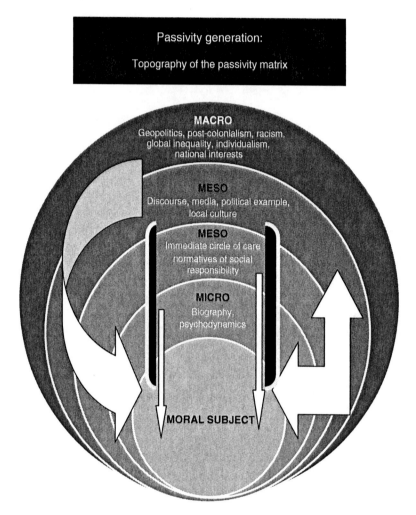

Figure 8.1   Passivity generation: Topography of the passivity matrix

that it can only be properly understood if all the factors and forces in operation, with their different modalities and levels of influence, are taken into consideration. The factors can be roughly grouped as macro – social, political and ideological factors; meso – immediate circles of care and discourses, scripts and cultural norms of social responsibility; and micro – psychodynamic and biographical factors. Unfortunately, one-dimensional graphs are static and only capture the topography of the forces, rather than their dynamic interactions. They fail to capture how these factors never interact in a unilateral, one-directional, linear, top-down process. Rather, the public is actively, responsively, ambivalently in interaction with these forces.

In the Introduction I attempted to convey the dynamism of these relations through the metaphor of the tray of buzzing bees which represents what physicists call a 'dynamic equilibrium': the condition of a system that has its total energy distributed among its component parts. The unchanging condition of its parts results from the balance or cancelling out of the influences or processes. The resulting stillness, which might be mistaken for inaction, is in fact the equilibrium resulting from the convergence of the influence of contrasting and opposing forces. I am suggesting that this systemic dynamic equilibrium can be helpfully applied to understand public passivity. Hence the title, *Passivity Generation*, which has attempted to grasp the paradoxically lively and generative potential of what ostensibly appears as inertia. The crucial point about a model of dynamic equilibrium is that it describes a precarious stability which, by definition, is constantly under threat of disruption. As subjects are made of, and out of, power they are in a dialectical and agentic interaction with the different forces in operation. Thus, this book has argued and illustrated how what might appear as a static equilibrium or overall passivity is, on the contrary, very unstable and open to shifting either way – towards further passivity, but also towards active engagement. It is precisely the inherent dynamism theorised in this book that opens up possibility for intervention and change.

Passivity Generation has closely investigated the factors involved in the dynamic equilibrium of passivity, how these factors interact with each other and the extremely complex way in which the public responds to them. It is essential to hold and appreciate the complexity, tensions and contradictions.

The first part of this chapter examines the findings from the data discussed in the book, to elucidate the complex dynamics involved in the three key stages of the 'knowledge–reaction–action' continuum.

Knowledge

What has become clear from the way participants talk about human rights violations is that human rights information is heavily mediated. I am not referring exclusively to the inevitable translation of the raw events into narratives and sound bites depending on the medium used (newspapers, televised news, documentary or NGOs' campaigns and appeals), but also to the filtering of the information through pre-existing social scripts which bear heavily on the ways in which the public can think and make sense of human rights issues. Chapter 2 offered an abbreviated mapping of the range of scripts through which the human rights information is filtered. These scripts provide a ready-made understanding of human rights and their violations. Importantly, they also provide exoneration from responsibility for the public through a varied range of discourses, ranging from socially recognisable platitudes about life, to psychologically informed justifications based on feelings of helplessness and being overwhelmed; from familiar debates on cultural relativism to legalistic rejections of moral responsibility, and so on. The common feature of this otherwise disparate list of scripts is their banal, everyday quality. We have heard them all, in some form or another. This not only means that these represent the cultural boundaries of how human rights are talked about by 'ordinary' members of the public; it also means, in line with Lakoff (2008), that as they circulate, these frames, metaphors and images are strengthened, thus stabilising and perpetuating the possible responses available to the public. I am suggesting that it is *to* and *through* these cultural scripts that the public responds, rather than to the pristine information per se. The first finding is that in order to understand how the public responds to the Universal Declaration of Human Rights – which was forcefully and unanimously supported by each participant – we need to know how they intersect with these ready-made scripts. This is supported by the regular and unquestioned use of these scripts across focus groups, which I have explained in terms of 'allusions' that depend on shared knowledge. The person who alludes to something counts on preparedness for resonance: that is, on the preparedness of the recipients consciously to call to mind the facts that are alluded to. Knowing about these moral scripts is essential in order both to gain insight into how the public actually understand human rights and their violations, and to counteract scripts that foster and justify passivity.

Many other social and cultural factors mediate the public's reaction. Of particular relevance is the climate of distrust of the media as manipulators of truth in terms of both content (media's ideological bias) and techniques (e.g. use of Photoshop). The data suggest a problematic assimilation between NGOs and media logics which strongly affects the public's reception of the mediated knowledge. This finding is supported by some research in the field of Media and Communications. Cottle and Nolan (2007), for example, claim that as humanitarian agencies' communication strategies have increasingly assimilated to 'media logic', they have become embroiled in the practices and predilections of the global media. As a result, they reflexively expend time and resources in warding off increased risks of mediated scandals and are compromising their organisational integrity. This suggests that more attention should be paid to the growing alignment of humanitarian appeal practices with the operation and style of the media. Calhoun (2007) also argues that, even though in the media the power of visual images and immediacy are key to what makes human suffering ethically compelling to strangers, the role of the media in relation to humanitarianism has not been systematically and seriously considered. Similarly, Sliwinski (2009) claims that it is not the legal discourse of human rights (which constructs human dignity and freedom as being inalienable), but the visual discourse (which mediates suffering and asks individuals to exercise their faculty of judgement) that has the power to make audiences respond to distant suffering as deserving pity and moral action. All this suggests that more attention should be paid to how the public responses to distant suffering are influenced by the public relations to the media in general, even though this is in direct contrast to current thinking in humanitarian discourse where humanitarianism is seen as separate from media.

Reaction

It is evident from the extracts discussed in this book that human rights information is not passively and unreflexively absorbed, but is processed through pre-existing schemas and worldviews. Equally evident is audiences' resistance to being drawn in sympathetically, as shown by the widespread use of distancing rather than empathic processes of meaning-making. This is important in many respects, not least when considering how the distancing militates against NGOs' attempts to bridge the gap between the public and suffering others. I have identified three distinct ways and possible reasons used by the public to distance themselves from human rights abuses.

The first involves ideological processes of denial and symbolic delineation of moral boundaries, both considered human rights practices. Second, we have idiosyncratic and self-protective mechanisms of distancing that are rooted in biography. Third, participants referred to defensiveness caused by the traumatic nature of the information.

In terms of ideological processes, in Chapter 4 I identified three specific denial repertoires or *topoi* used by participants to explain their reactions to human rights appeals and information and justify their passivity in response to them. The 'medium is the message', 'shoot the messenger' and 'babies and bathwater' were taken as examples of implicatory denial in that they justify the speaker's passivity on the basis of the way in which the communication is constructed and used by NGOs, the credibility, trustworthiness and efficacy of NGOs, and the action proposed to alleviate the problem of human rights violations. They are implicatory denial because, paraphrasing Cohen (2001), they not only provide a familiar and 'good' story – in this case 'this is why the public respond the way it does' – but also the reason why this response is morally right. In other words, they use easily recognisable explanations while preserving the speaker's moral stance. I will return to the importance of this later on when discussing the complexity of moral reasoning involved in these operations.

I have argued that public denial is an operation of power and production of knowledge because it enables the replacement of the moral, compassionate subject by the 'consumer-savvy bystander', equipped with sophisticated analytical tools to assess and critique the style, function and effects of the appeal, and the trustworthiness of the appeal-maker, like a consumer debating whether to 'buy' a product. This is a power operation in so far as it plays a role in sustaining and colluding with more systemic and official operations of passivity and denial, such as those described by Cohen (2001) and van Dijk (1992). This is not denial in the common sense of the term (i.e. unconscious and automatic), however; it is sophisticated, reflexive, and a powerful means of distancing.

Another ideological distancing operation is the symbolic drawing of moral boundaries through which countries in which human rights are violated are considered outside the participants' moral concern and duty of care. These operations were discussed in detail in Chapter 5, which focused on the ideological effects of the trope '*in countries like that*' in audiences' discussions of human rights abuses. First of all, by referring to countries where human rights are abused as '*countries like that*', participants implied the existence of a group of, otherwise unnamed, countries defined by shared characteristics. Those using this trope expected other, previously unknown members of their focus group to understand what they meant without further explanations. Indeed, not once were such allusions challenged or further particulars asked. This suggests an unspoken and shared assumption that such a category does indeed exist and that, despite the heterogeneity of the group membership, the participants agreed on which countries belonged in this category. Crucial to this implicit agreement is the assumption that these are *physical* and identifiable places. Second, participants went to a lot of effort to make explicit the characteristics of these alleged countries. The attributed characteristics were always negative, and they were regularly contrasted with the positive characteristics of '*this country*' (Britain). Third, this type of account regularly appeared in connection with explanations of why the participant did not actively respond to human rights appeals, based on reasons of either the physical distance of '*these countries*' (hence the importance of defining them as separate and physically far away) or their profound differences from the speaker's country (in terms of education, culture, lawfulness, development and so on.).

I have disputed the concrete nature of this categorisation and suggested instead that the trope is an ideological operation constructing suffering Others as distant, different and beyond the participants' sphere of moral responsibility. In other words, this type of account's function is to define the symbolic boundaries of the participants' moral community, determining who they are, and are not, morally responsible for. This symbolic moral exclusion, like the ones discussed above, is a form of implicatory denial used to justify audiences' passivity and disconnection from human rights issues. It is also a powerful mechanism of distancing in so far as it ideologically delegitimises (Bar-Tal et al., 1989) and dehumanises the other into being faceless, distant, different and, crucially, morally beyond the pale. This process of dehumanisation is in total opposition to human rights campaigners' attempts to re-humanise and individualise the suffering Other which it underpins: for example, the use of specific victims' personal stories in order to elicit identification, but also to inform audiences of the historical and political causes of their suffering. Through their attempts at re-humanising populations suffering from human rights abuses, campaigners seek to evoke empathy and compassion to spur audiences into action. The use of the trope '*in countries like that*', however, operates as a mechanism of disassociation between audiences and the suffering Other and ultimately militates against these attempts. It is not only that placing such populations beyond the speaker's moral order exonerates audiences from their moral responsibilities; it also blocks empathy, which requires imagining how it is to be someone else, to step inside their world and glimpse their concerns, cognitively and emotionally, as if from their perspective (Halpern and Weinstein, 2004).

By determining who is within and who is without a 'moral order', using this trope when thinking about human rights issues has serious implications in terms of how large sections of humanity are understood, related to and treated, both on the geopolitical scale – for example, in terms of foreign aid and openness or closedness to asylum seekers – and in the micro scale of neighbourly relations. It certainly militates against campaigners' attempts to bridge the 'us–them' divide through principles of shared humanity, universal compassion and international solidarity.

Chapter 5 also discusses the geopolitical context of this ideological operation, in particular against the background of post-colonialism and the use of racist discourse, and how this is manifested in the employment by participants of three distinct but overlapping constructions of the other as barbaric, underdeveloped and esoteric. I have illustrated how specific representations of the 'Other' are used strategically by focus group participants when talking about human rights abuses and how pejorative and 'reflexively' racist constructions of victims and perpetrators of human rights abuses are used in the process of Othering for specific purposes: for example, to construct specific views of human rights abuses as overall attributable to intrinsic characteristics of non-Western nations, such as barbarism, inferiority and fanaticism; to bolster the speaker's subjectivity and moral stance by differentiating the Self from the Other; to justify speakers' passivity through differentiating and distancing of the Self from the Other; and by constructing human rights abuses as a non-Western problem. These carefully crafted accounts, which were interspersed with disclaimers and ostensibly benign qualifiers, are considered examples of 'modern' racism, in other words discursive strategies that present negative views of a particular social group, while safeguarding the speaker from accusations of racism or prejudice (Augoustinos and Every, 2007; Van Dijk, 2000). The relation with racism is twofold. On the one hand racist and racialised discourses, which are in circulation in society, are used as a resource to give substance to the 'self–other' construction which is essential to drawing moral boundaries and justify passivity. On the other, through this operation racist discourse is given legitimacy and further strengthened through its circulation, contributing to the normalisation of racist constructions.

These denial operations provide precious information on audiences' reactions to appeals and the subtle and sophisticated ways in which participants distance themselves from human rights abuses. It is crucial to recognise that these operations have real impact and consequences. They don't just promote a particular construction of what human rights are about and why abuses take place, which in itself is important in terms of how the public understand human rights and their abuses. Racist constructions of perpetrators (and by extension victims) as barbaric, inferior or esoteric are essential to a de-politicised view of human rights. They are also essential in distancing audiences from the Other and the human rights they violated because of their shortcomings.

These processes bear resemblance to those described by criminologists studying techniques of neutralisation employed by the socially deviant to justify their actions. Among them, normalisation ('this is how things are') rationalisation ('this is how it came to be like this'), essentialising ('this is how they are – it's inbuilt in their nature, history, culture') have featured particularly strongly in the accounts described in this book. In terms of their rhetorical and ideological function they all implicitly justify passivity as 'there is nothing we can do about it', thus distancing and exonerating the speaker.

This goes some way towards explaining the focus groups' deafening silence around the victims of human rights violations. The vast majority of focus groups' time was taken up by discussions of causal explanations and accountability in human rights, and participants in all the groups spent a large amount of time debating why, and because of whom, atrocities were committed. While perpetrators were discussed at length, very little was said about the victims of atrocities. Indeed, very often in the focus groups I was left wondering who the sufferer/victim was, as frequently participants positioned themselves as the sufferer and as potential victims of manipulation, exploitation and shock tactics (see e.g. the 'shoot the messenger' repertoire). This could be explained by Chouliaraki's concern (2008) about the danger of Western audiences becoming increasingly preoccupied with their own mediated self-pity rather than the suffering of distant people (Chouliaraki, 2008).

This is only part of the story, however, and the third part of this section on public responses will argue that there might be important psychological dynamics preventing too close a connection with the victim of atrocities. Before that, to conclude the discussion of factors that distance the public or bring it closer to human rights issues, I will discuss self-defensive, idiosyncratic mechanisms rooted in biography and issues of identity.

First of all, it is worth considering that if the speaker's moral positioning is so dependent on pejorative constructions of the Other, then perhaps these *have* to be negative and damning, not only to bolster speakers' subjectivity in general, but also to warrant their moral stance. As Frosh argues, 'the outside Other is primary, built into the structures of a society premised on difference and division; and it is in relation to this primary Otherness that each individual subject emerges' (Frosh, 2005:205). The racism expressed here, then, could be considered highly functional. Speakers *need* the other to be barbaric, underdeveloped, belligerent, brainwashed and religious fanatics in order to distance themselves, to avoid being implicated globally, historically and individually, while preserving their own benign and moral identity. The role of this allegedly universal process is particularly troubling in the context of reactions to appeals that are meant precisely to do the opposite and bring the distant suffering Other closer to audiences, by bridging the 'us–them' divide through principles of shared humanity, universal compassion and international solidarity. Yet, these Universalist principles don't account for positions being always invested emotionally and embroiled in identity. How much this is the case was illustrated in Chapter 6, which made visible the ways in which, however much the speakers worked hard at trying to construct their opinions as objective and rational, the moral positions taken by them were never neutral or pristine. Rather, they were saturated with passionate investment in one's identity and the need to establish a good sense of self, particularly in terms of religious identity. The consistent juxtaposition of negative Other and positive self-presentation tells us that this type of account also performs important identity work: it not only avoids guilt for their passivity, but by warranting their moral stance it bolsters the speaker's self-perception and overall confirms their positive identity. Participants' stake in producing a convincing account of themselves as morally good cannot be separated from their attitudes towards human rights violations; the two are inextricably entangled in complex ways. Participants showed great awareness of how they might be perceived in the local and wider social context and their accounts showed the strength of their reflexive and self-referential thinking when approaching human rights issues. This was particularly evident with Muslim participants.

Biographical factors also played an important, albeit complex and non-linear, role in distancing participants or bringing them closer to human rights issues. For example, being touched by suffering seemed a necessary first step, while in some cases vicariously or directly experienced suffering made people responsive and proactive; in other cases it distanced them through self-protective avoidance. This suggests that an 'optimal' amount of suffering is necessary to empathise and respond – what I have called the first step in the 'path to engagement' and participants have defined as 'that little connection' with the suffering other – but an excessive amount is counterproductive. What constitutes the 'optimal' suffering varies on individual circumstances and life stages. Particularly important in this fluctuation is whether the sufferer is able to process their own suffering through reparation or rationalisation of repetition. While the latter fosters defensive rationalisation and blocks empathy towards themselves and others, reparation can be a formidable force in humanitarian responses and prosocial behaviour in general. Crucially, reparation involves the members of the public's capacity to identify empathically with sufferers and their being driven to help them.

The subject's experience of Others' responses to their own suffering, and generally of being cared and respected, also plays an important role in their responsiveness, or lack of responsiveness, to Others' suffering. The participants' accounts illustrated how all these biographical factors were pivotal in the way they related to human rights issues and whether they responded empathically or defensively, proactively or by self-distancing. One particularly striking example, given by Neil, illustrated the dangers of reaching conclusions about public responses without taking into consideration people's states of mind and feelings.

The role of emotions in (un)responsiveness to human rights issues is particularly intricate and complex. That human rights issues are 'emotive' in themselves is self-evident. In addition, most human rights communications and appeals contain forceful emotional messages. The ways in which emotions and affects are implicitly or explicitly evoked or mobilised varies enormously, from a direct and active attempt to evoke guilt, moral obligation and other self-referential emotions, to other-oriented feelings that aim to connect the viewer with the victim through the witnessing of their plight: for example, pity, empathy, sympathy and compassion.

Data from the focus groups have evidenced the large role played by emotional conflict, resistance and 'troubled' reactions to human rights issues and the inadequacy of mono-causal, simplistic or linear explanations in capturing the complexity of emotional reactions. As well as participants being users of vocabularies of denial, their accounts showed that there are affective and intra-psychic aspects to members of the public's reactions to appeals that are crucial in determining responses. There was evidence of emotional stumbling blocks to higher responsiveness which related to personal sensitivities and specific personal and biographical experiences. Specifically, appeals clearly provoke emotions and emotional conflicts; they evoke memories and connections to past traumas. Personal experiences of being cared for, or not, in times of need might be evoked and/or denied in response to information about human rights appeals and information.

The psychosocial model in this book is attentive to both personal emotions and socially constructed justifications based on emotions. Particular attention was paid to the phenomenon of not engaging, or initially engaging then disengaging emotionally, which has often, and in my view erroneously, been defined as compassion fatigue or psychophysical numbing.

The model emerging from the data illustrates the importance of two interrelated ways in which emotional processes play a role in responses to human rights abuses: the psychodynamic (particularly in terms of intra-psychic conflicts and defences that are evoked in the process) and the social aspect of such processes (in the form of socially acceptable narratives used by participants).

Emotional reactions are understood differently on the basis of these two aspects. Both play an important part in the public reactions to human rights abuses. Considering at face value members of the public's accounts of their experiences of receiving disturbing information about atrocities has serious implications for the use of shock tactics in communicating to the public. There is plenty of evidence in the data that disturbing information affects audiences in an adverse way and prompts them to protect themselves through defence mechanisms, switching off, desensitisation and numbing. I will discuss the implication of these findings for agencies later in the chapter, but clearly this raises the question of how the public can be equipped and helped to deal with shocking information in a way that enables them to stay engaged rather than disconnect.

Appeals eliciting guilt seem to generate particularly counterproductive responses. A recurrent feature in participants' accounts was the passionate animosity towards campaigners. I suggested considering the role of a potential superego transference in the relation between NGOs and the public. I will come back to this later, but I suggest that this transferential relationship might explain to some extent why participants often experience persecutory rather than reparative guilt, which brings paralysis and resentment.

Emotions also play an important role in public responses in the unconscious ways in which human rights information taps into and stirs up internal conflict in individual members of the public. The resistance and defensiveness generated by this kind of 'internal trouble' of conflictual emotional states may contribute to emotional disconnection and active turning away from human rights issues.

Such defensiveness and resistance against emotional connection might make identification with the victim simply too threatening. Participants almost never allowed even a fleeting identification with the victim – maybe it is just too scary and anxiety-provoking to even briefly put oneself into the shoes of the Afghani woman of the appeal, or being forced to watch one's mother being stoned to death. Imagining oneself even for a moment being tortured is bound to provoke anxiety. Resistance to identification with extreme helplessness and neediness (which we all experience as children to some extent), and the overwhelming anxiety these provoke, seems perfectly justifiable.

Yet that moment of recognition of shared vulnerability is essential in many ways. Turner (1993) in fact puts it at the heart of the very possibility of human rights. Additionally, if disconnecting from disturbing identification might be a relief, it is bound to provoke shame, a powerful emotion stirred up both by the knowledge of atrocities and by not doing anything about it. Geras (1999) refers to this as the 'shame of the world'. While reparative guilt prompts action, unfortunately shame leads to hiding.

Dean's eloquent statement is particularly relevant here:

> Numbness, that is, manifests an important challenge to the liberal ideal that we can empathically project ourselves into others with whom we share a common humanity, whether strangers or neighbours. For numbness is not only a psychological form of self-protective dissociation; it is arguably a new, highly self-conscious narrative about the collective constriction of moral availability, if not empathy, and may thus constrain humanist aspirations in ways we do not yet recognize.
>
> (Dean, 2004:5)

Indeed, we have seen how justifications for inaction based on emotions are also a powerful and effective vocabulary of denial. Popular versions of psychological discourses appear to be commonly used resources when justifying inaction because of the emotional impact on the public. The public showed impressive levels of sophistication when assessing emotional communications from NGOs. As 'emotional consumers', participants are fully aware of having their emotions stirred by campaigners and react particularly strongly to what they perceive as being emotionally manipulative. It is important to note that at this level the public does not differentiate between human rights, humanitarian or other charity appeals, but classifies them all as 'pulling at their heart strings to get donations'. This is counterproductive at many levels but certainly in terms of the specificity of human rights communication aiming at informing the public and 'bearing witness' to atrocities.

Thus, and in agreement with Dean, I would also argue that the intriguing phenomenon of emotional numbness is both a psychological form of self-protective disassociation *and* a powerful vocabulary of denial. It is paramount that campaigners and scholars studying and combating public passivity engage and understand both.

Action

The two preceding sections on knowledge and reactions foreshadow this last one on action by identifying factors that prevent the public from getting to the point of acting, by neutralising the appeals and information, and by distancing. The grim picture presented so far seems to leave little room for hope yet, amazingly, the public does respond and human rights causes continue to be supported in many ways including public donations. This last section, therefore, concentrates on lessons that can be drawn from the data about what can help counteract passivity generation. As it will become clear, I don't see the problem of action only pertaining to individual members of the public – a well-established but very problematic tendency in literature – but to other actors too, operating in society with considerable more power than the individuals.

What seems to be conveyed repeatedly by the very insistence, sophistication and wide variety of justifications used by participants is that the Universal Declaration of Human Rights (UDHR) has become universally normative and fully accepted and respected, at least in its principles. This, in itself, is a positive sign and supports Ignatieff's optimistic view that human rights have become accepted into ordinary parlance. But it does not necessarily mean that human rights principles are understood or integrated into people's everyday lives, despite UDHR having acquired some kind of normative status.

Equally normative seems to be the imperative to help others in need. People overall tend to help others and are responsive to their suffering in proactive ways. It is clear that the first step in most cases takes place in the most immediate circle of care involving the nearest and dearest. It is indeed true that 'charity starts at home'. The challenge is in how to get the public to go beyond that immediate circle of responsibility, which is particularly difficult in relation to the need to feel able to help. Predicted efficacy is a factor well identified in research, from bystander phenomena (Latane and Darley, 1976, 1970) to the identifiable victim effect (Jenni and Loewenstein, 1997). It is clear that people need to feel they can 'make a difference', but this is a challenge in human rights issues. As Geras points out:

> Given the nature of the evils under consideration, evils that are very great, often locked into institutional networks or social and political systems difficult to transform or overturn, and sometimes also geographically distant from the people who come to know about them as evils, there is nothing effective they can do to oppose them. The view that they do too little is therefore misconceived. However, they *can* do *something*. It is a merely banal point that many small responses can add up to a great response, and the observation is also common that responses of protest against injustice and needless suffering tend to encourage other similar responses, while conversely silence, unconcern, complicity and the like feed upon themselves, they feed the same disposition in others. So people can certainly do something.
>
> (Geras, 1999:30)

Some people have a sense that this is true, or at least possible. We have seen in Chapter 2 that, for some, political scripts go some way towards counteracting the widespread sense of helplessness and powerlessness experienced by the public. But for many, political scripts are counteracted by disillusionment with politics in general and widespread distrust in political leaders.

A recent Oxfam report (2008) talks about public giving in terms of money, but also giving in terms of time, voice and product. Darnton and Kirk (2011:14) add to this list the

> impact associated with the public's actions and conversations in the public sphere (including those in the media, responding to public concerns). These interventions open up space for the kind of political, socio-economic and pro-environmental change that is necessary to tackle global poverty. The public's role here is more than pressuring the government to accede to campaigning demands, it is about opening up the political and wider societal space to the possibility of deeper change. It is only with deeper change that we can build new institutions and societal norms, which in turn will enable different models of development, and more effective results.

Although fully agreeing with this sentiment and despite the pitfalls of monetary donations, in the short term often the public's first connection with a campaign is through money. Notwithstanding the potential for donations to be a shortcut to guilt-free disconnection, with human rights issues it is harder to use that path to engagement. Human rights violations do not lend themselves to practical and quick solutions – what is the correspondent of 'give £10, buy a goat' for human rights? – nor to engagement through immediate circles of care: while it is highly likely that someone within that circle might have been affected, say, by cancer, it is less likely that, having lived in a stable democracy for decades, they have had first-person experience of the horrors of military dictatorship. Unlike humanitarian appeals, which overall offer a recognisable line of connection between individual action (particularly donations) and benefits for the victim, human rights appeals offer a less identifiable line. With perhaps the exception of letter-writing and putting pressure on the government, it is hard for those who are not already so inclined to see how, for example, a donation could make a difference to victims of human rights abuses.

These two factors, intrinsic to human rights issues, might contribute to not knowing how to help and to the idea that human rights violations only happen in 'countries like that'. Here is the space where important work can be done. First it is crucial that the public is informed about human rights violations constructively and in ways that enable them, both cognitively and emotionally, rather than through sensationalist, shocking and de-contextualised media bites that leave the public traumatised and unequipped for dealing with the information and the emotions stirred by it. Human Rights agencies have a pivotal role to play in this, to which I will return later.

Considering the amount of work participants put into disconnecting themselves, it seems that making links is an essential stage towards action, and that the way the information is provided is key in making meaningful links.

The data suggest that human rights information per se is not intrinsically or directly conducive to action. In fact, in operations of moral exclusion it can become a means of indirect blame and normalisation and can contribute to psychological and moral distancing. Of course, informing audiences is essential, but there is no evidence in these extracts that the old refrain 'if only people knew they would do something' holds true. The relationship between knowledge and action is indeed much more complicated than that. *How* the information is used by the audiences and what is culturally acceptable seems a more crucial factor than what kind, what amount and in what form the information is given, as argued by some (see Chouliaraki, 2006). The socio-political habitus in which the public operates is crucial in providing modalities for understanding both the violations and their expected response to them. A late capitalist society that fosters individualism and narcissistic self-gratification is likely to provide a rich and sophisticated 'vocabulary of denial' to justify disengagement with human rights issues. If, as the data suggest, socially acceptable scripts filter the information in ways that preclude action, then it is essential to know as much as possible about existing scripts to counteract their toxic effect. For example, starting from the discourses and ideological operations identified in this book, active effort has to go into fighting racist discourses and attribution of atrocities' causation to inherent qualities of populations and countries where violations take place.

Many actors can contribute to this necessary operation. The government has a fundamental role to play, through anti-racist education and with just and progressive legislation and policies, but also and foremost through example. As Darnton and Kirk (2011) have pointed out, and has been supported by my data, the perception of governmental corruption is a major stumbling block to public socially responsible responsiveness in humanitarian causes. Conversely, we have seen striking examples in the data (e.g. Dahlia and Jill) of how government initiatives that approach foreign aid as an unquestionable duty and foster a sense of responsible connectedness to distant others promote the internalisation and practice of those progressive principles in the public. After all, research has repeatedly provided evidence showing that leading by example is the most effective way through which we learn, and that when a society values prosocial behaviour and actively fosters social responsibility this makes a difference in terms of individual attitudes, responses and behaviour. For example, Handy et al. (2000), who collected survey data from 12 countries, found that while utilitarian motivations did not foster volunteering,[1] in countries with a positive signalling value for volunteering, volunteering rates were significantly higher. As Hoggett (2000:209) puts it:

> The idea of the gift and the desire to give, the capacity for concern, the idea of the gift that seeks no return, the process of gift exchange and the affirmation and celebration of social relationships as an end in themselves rather than a means to an end. All these are central to the idea of society as an interdependent community of friends and strangers. I would argue that it is this that brings out the best within us.

I have already made repeated reference to the media as a powerful instrument in both the perpetuation and the fight against prejudiced representations of suffering Others and human rights. The third actor, with a specific and pivotal role to play, is NGOs.

The 'in-between': The crucial role of NGOs

Social psychological studies have focused on the distance or closeness of the victim, on whether audiences engage with the appeals primarily on an emotional or rational level as factors which foster or prevent prosocial behaviour. In these studies, the appeal itself is considered as a neutral stimulus, often imaginary, and artificially disconnected from the supposed source of the information or appeal (see Zagefka et al., 2008), and with few exceptions (Supphellen and Nelson, 2001) very little attention has been paid to the appeal-makers.

I am guilty of internalising this approach myself, as demonstrated by the lack of questions about the appeal and the appeal-makers in the interview schedule which I designed for the focus groups. It is a major finding from the data, therefore, that the appeal itself is very significant, in terms of how it is put together, who the appeal-makers are and what action is being requested. I have already discussed the importance of this finding for the light it throws on the strategic and rhetorical use of these factors and because they re-contextualise audiences' responses and re-position participants in the cultural and ideological contexts to which they belong.

Furthermore, these findings suggest that treating appeals as straightforwardly and neutrally conveying a message is indeed problematic and point to a lacuna in current research. The analysis has illustrated the importance of examining in detail audiences' perceptions, and attitudes towards and reactions to the appeal-makers, as well as how these reactions are meaningful, both culturally and ideologically. What is suggested here is that the focus on how the victim is portrayed in the appeal should be matched with an interest in how the appeal-maker is perceived, as this can play an important role in the neutralisation of the appeal and in the resistance to collective action and participation. These factors are crucial to the understanding of audiences' moral apathy and how members of the public may, in principle, be supportive of the overall principles of human rights, but decide not to act in response to appeals.

By producing and disseminating representations of social suffering, human rights and humanitarian agencies generate moral concerns and conducts, thus engaging in what Becker (1991 [1963]:145) called the process of 'the creation of a new fragment of the moral constitution of society'. Is this how human rights are perceived by the public? And, crucially, are NGOs successful in their 'moral entrepreneur' activities?

I start from the assumption that Amnesty International's mandate is twofold:[2] as a campaigner for human rights (striving to inform the public and to raise awareness of human rights abuses) and as a maker of appeals (aiming to raise funds by focusing attention on the specific current issues they are working on). In both instances, they address audiences as moral agents. Although the two are vitally interconnected, when it comes to NGOs' relationships with the public it is important to discuss the two separately.

Plucking at the public's heartstrings

Data discussed in Chapters 4 and 7 tell us of a passionate, but often antagonistic, relationship between the public and NGOs. Particularly in 'the medium is the message' and 'shoot the messenger' repertoires, participants unanimously attributed manipulative intentions to NGOs, often feeling that the appeal was strategically constructed to 'pull at their heartstrings' in order to get them to donate money. In Chapter 4 I have considered this a denial narrative. That the repertoire lends itself to being used rhetorically doesn't exclude that it might also be an accurate representation of NGOs' activities in intentionally using information to pull at the public's heartstrings. This is what Darnton and Kirk (2011) claim in their *Finding Frames* report:

> the current reality of NGOs as big businesses, with business models built around aggressive revenue targets, is reflected both in the content of communications and in the techniques used. Research conducted by the sector has shown that the most effective messages for securing donations are those that pluck at the public's heartstrings (see Mango 2008). More precisely, work commissioned by Comic Relief on *The Psychology of Giving* found that giving money involves both the heart and the head, with the initial trigger usually an emotional appeal (Leapfrog 2004). Communications that reveal the shocking truth of suffering among poor people, and then cause us to consider the good fortune of our own position, are seen as the most effective in triggering giving.
>
> (Darnton and Kirk, 2011:30)

We need to unpack the definition of a message being 'effective'. Stirring the public's emotion might be effective in fundraising terms, but it is also the most resented and often the most counterproductive strategy in the long run. Audiences are far too sophisticated and reflexive for this mechanistic and simplistic model of appeal. They might still respond in the immediate aftermath of receiving the information, but they build resistance and resentment. Because of the rich vocabulary of denial at hand, messages of this kind are easily dismissed through the 'all they want is my money' script, as it is largely documented in this book. Audiences' skill and rhetorical cleverness can be seen in the participants' ability to use this kind of repertoire for different ideological effects, thus the appeal for donations is rejected on both consumerist and moral grounds. Participants are able to position themselves as the victim of a marketing ploy and at the same time declaim a lack of moral consideration on Amnesty's part. The negative reaction to appeals is bound to have a knock-on effect on the public engagement with agencies and human rights issues too, in so far as human rights agencies play a pivotal part in raising public awareness. Approaching the public in this instrumental fashion seems to introduce defensiveness right from the start, at the delicate point of the public first getting to know about something traumatic and unjust.

The counterproductive nature of this type of communication has also been identified by others, in both academic and voluntary sectors. Darnton and Kirk (2011), for example, have argued that the practices of the development sector are strongly implicated in the state of public engagement. Data on voluntary income suggest that increasing incomes have been gained by changing the nature of engagement by turning members into supporters, and setting them at arm's length. In the social movement literature, today's NGOs are described as 'protest businesses', and their model of public engagement is called 'cheap participation' (characterised by low barriers to entry, engagement and exit – all of which generate high churn). The sector's engagement models have achieved big numbers and ever-increasing incomes, but with what impact on the quality of public engagement?

These concerns resonate with those expressed in recent work on the dangers of increased commercialisation of non-profit organisations' practices (Vestergaard, 2008) and their 'rebranding' in order to counteract the current 'crisis of pity' (Chouliaraki, 2008). If, as Vestergaard (2008) and Chouliaraki (2008) suggest, humanitarian agencies are being driven by fundraising pressures into moving away from a compassion-based type of campaigning towards a marketised ethical discourse, their efforts may be counterproductive. Such a move might actually increase audiences' moral detachment and, as Chouliaraki (2008) calls it, their 'narcissistic sensibility' by further strengthening the resistance of the 'savvy-consumer' bystander.

There is no question from the focus group data that the 'transactional frame', which reduces public participation to making donations, fosters a 'cheque-book' relationship with NGOs that the public intensely dislikes, but that is functional when wanting to distance themselves. In the long term it does not help NGOs either. An antagonistic relationship with NGOs militates against further engagement with them and is likely to foster a logic of instrumental reason. It is hardly surprising, then, that although Amnesty International addressed the public as moral agents, they responded as consumers. The consumerist mentality further contaminates the mode of relating to human rights issues. The lack of differentiation between human rights communication and humanitarian appeals suggests that relating to human rights communications as humanitarian emergencies has become canonical. Treating human rights violations as if they were the same as the effects of a natural disaster might generate income, but it interferes with the understanding and contextualisation of violations. I am not suggesting that human rights agencies intended this, but that the 'transactional frame' seems to have become the main modality for relating to NGOs transactional and understanding their activities. The lack of differentiation between NGOs' mandates and identities suggests not a problem with branding, but the existence of a model of generalised decoding of their communications that affects all voluntary sectors' interactions with the public and contaminates longer-term and more complex engagement with human rights issues. The data suggest that it also contributes greatly to the fraught relationship with NGOs.

It has been suggested that more effort should be focused on exposing the prevailing (transactional) frame, in order to break it and allow the public to engage differently. I applaud this, but I don't think it will cure the problem entirely, as there are psychological factors also influencing how the public relates to NGOs.

The Jiminy Cricket of social responsibility

> Indeed, this narrative on numbness may represent something quite new in the history of humanitarianism, for it does not simply suggest that most of us won't disrupt our daily routines for the sake of others near or far without a real or imaginary

causal connection to sufferers. It suggests that we are often willing to do so, but to our surprise we feel nothing or are paradoxically immobilized by guilt and even resentful of those who make claims upon us.

(Dean, 2004:5)

Dean's quote captures well the general emotional climate of the public response to NGOs which featured irritation, resentment and, at times, outright anger. We have seen how agencies were characterised as pests and a bother, and how participants at times might give money just to get rid of them. There was then disappointment when, once the agency had their details they would on the contrary continue sending disturbing information and pester people to increase their monthly donations. This seems to have further discouraged the public from longer-term engagement with agencies and to preferring anonymous, one-off donations.

Leaving aside the role of the 'transactional frame' in this scenario, why would the public have such a passionate and antagonistic relationship with NGOs? Chapter 7 has explored the psychology of the relationship. Data suggest that, despite the widespread belief that evoking guilt prompts action, this is not the only and most frequent outcome of making the public feel guilty. It seems that often the method actually backfires, provoking persecutory, rather than reparative, guilt, which militates against cognitive and emotional engagement with human rights issues and fosters inauthentic and compliant behaviour, such as giving a donation to placate the 'nagging'. Key to this problematic version of the 'knowledge–reaction–action' chain is the public's transferential relationship with NGOs whereby Amnesty International, in this case, becomes the harsh superego figure pointing at participants' faults. This is a crucial stumbling block in responsiveness to human rights issues and could further explain why so much energy went into undermining Amnesty's authority and, simultaneously, granting a moral stance for the speaker, despite their inaction. Of course, the most deleterious ideological impact of this 'malignant positioning' (Gilbert and Mulkay, 1982) in terms of collective action and social responsibility is that, by undermining the messenger, it potentially weakens the impact of the message and erodes Amnesty's moral authority. Yet, psychologically, for those members of the public who feel personally attacked by Amnesty as the righteous harsh superego figure, undermining the organisation's moral authority is a reasonable defence manoeuvre.

This also hints at a disjunction between human rights principles as 'high and ideal' and the messiness and imperfection of everyday moral life. I believe NGOs might have a constructive role to play in bringing human rights to a level ordinary people can understand and relate to. Making them feel bad for not doing more is only going to exacerbate the distancing; after all, Jiminy Cricket was squashed by Pinocchio in an attempt to shut him up.[3] Again, I am not saying that Amnesty and NGOs are intentionally taking the higher moral ground, but it is important that they engage with the public's negative reactions described here. Evoking guilt, particularly when the public is confronted with horrors so great and making a donation seems so pitifully inadequate, but with apparently little else to do, is not facilitative and might make the public switch off altogether.

There are alternative models. Psychologically, a shift from a superego to ego ideal might help in presenting avenues to work towards, rather than failures for those not taken. After all, the UDHR prescribe Kantian categorical imperatives for human beings to work towards: ideals which, more often than not, don't currently translate into practice. I also recommended agencies take seriously their duty of care in metabolising horrific contents in ways that are manageable for the public, and take a supportive rather than judgemental stance in doing so. There is ample evidence in this book that the public finds human rights violations highly traumatic, not only for the horrors they contain but also for the impact they have on individuals and their relations with their own internal conflicts and psychic dynamics. It might seem unrealistic, inappropriate and excessive to ask NGOs, in addition to the extremely difficult work they already do, to be containers of chaos, distress and unbearable pain. Yet, by the very nature of their mission, they do unleash terrible information on the public. It is clear from the data discussed here that the public needs help in digesting the disturbing material of atrocities and human rights violations, and in knowing what to do in response. The information needs to be made emotionally manageable and somehow connected to the public everyday life. Otherwise, in a culture of entertainment and mindlessness, it risks coming across as if it were from '*another planet*' and dizzyingly disorienting. The public needs help in making meaningful links. NGOs are ideally placed for providing new ways of framing and understanding the problem that fosters connections and for engagement to remain open.

In conclusion, it is crucial for campaigners to know *both* about the content of denial accounts, to be informed of the range of culturally available responses to their appeals, *and* to be aware of the complexity of self-positioning of members of the public. They need to be familiar with the *cognition* involved in this particular type of social action and the explicit and implicit patterns of *emotions* that are realised in the ways that people act towards others: in this case, both Others who have had their human rights violated and those who appeal on their behalf. To know more about these two psychosocial components could produce more effective campaigning and a better engagement with the public.

Moral dilemmas; individual and collective responsibilities

As a final reflection I want to briefly return to the wider moral issues foreshadowing public passivity towards human rights violations. Brown and Wilson (2008:1) ask a very important question:

> Why have individuals been concerned with the suffering of others, especially distant others who are not members of their own family, race, gender, social class, or religious community, people with whom they share no apparent social connections or moral obligations?

It is important to acknowledge that the idea of a universal humanity and humanitarianism is very recent (late 18th century), and that we should recognise, rather than take for granted, the 'leap of care' involved in moving beyond our most immediate bonds and identification to caring for distant Others. It is clear from the data that people do care and give, but overall to causes that fall within their immediate circle of care. How far our moral obligations should go has been debated at length by moral philosophers and psychologists. Clarkson (1996), for example, takes a very strong stance in relation to ordinary people's disavow of their responsibility. Paraphrasing Perls (1960) for Clarkson, responsability is an existential commitment. It refers to the ability to respond – to react in some way to the events, invitations and provocations of our world. 'Not to respond is, of course, also a response. In the words of Sartre, we are condemned to a freedom from which there is no exit – an inextricable accountability for our existence and the actions and non-actions of our existence in our inevitable relationships with others. Another version of this states that the only thing required for evil to triumph is for good men to do nothing. This indicates the unavoidable complicity of all who do not engage in resisting or fighting or transforming evil' (Clarkson, 1996:12). By positioning it as an existential commitment, Clarkson allocates moral responsibility to individuals.

Others see it differently. For example, Clement (1996:73) argues that care must be prioritised based on personal and societal responsibility:

> To be a morally good person requires, among other things, that a person strives to meet the demands of caring that present themselves in his or her life. For a society to be judged as a morally admirable society, it must, among other things, adequately provide for care of its members and its territory.'

According to Clement, the provision of care has to be institutionalised, not only for effectiveness but also because a right to care, as with positive welfare rights in general, cannot convincingly be linked to individual duty.

These two positions capture the frequent polarisation of individual vs society in the attribution of responsibility and duty to act. This is a false and most unhelpful polarisation. I agree with Clarkson and others who have argued that social responsibility is an existential and moral imperative for all of us as individuals. I also think, as I have repeatedly pointed out, that the State has great responsibilities too and that provision of care has to be institutionalised for it to be effective and internalised by its citizens. One cannot function without the other.

A possible answer as to how these two can be integrated meaningfully and sustained over time comes from recent psychosocial work on the welfare state. According to Hoggett (2000), Klein provides an account of some of the psychological underpinnings of the universal desire to give, a desire which can be mobilised equally through what Sorokin calls 'tribal' or 'in-group' altruism as through 'universal' altruism (1954:189–90). According to New (1996:130), 'to move beyond conditional forms of giving and reciprocity towards social practices which create solidarities across the boundaries of place, gender, culture and ethnicity it is therefore necessary to 'build societies which can contain hostility [...] and in which reparative principles are institutionalised" '. Hoggett (2000) adds that we need a society which can *embody* this impulse in a non-institutionalised way.

The real challenge, then, is how to enable the embodiment of social responsibility towards near and distant others that is integrated in people's everyday life, rather than experienced as alien, forced and persecutory.

Appendix 1: Demographic Details

Group	Pseudonym	Gender	Age	Ethnic background	Occupation	Salary	Parents' occupation	Newspaper	SES	Education
1	Lisa	Female	20	White	Student	None	Teacher/salesman	*New York Times*	Middle	
1	John	Male	25	Black, European	Student	£8,000 per year	Physician (biochemist)/teacher	None	Working	
2	Abi	Female	51	British	Legal cashier				Middle	BSc Psychology
2	Jill	Female	21	Scandinavian	Law student	None	Retired	*Guardian, Independent*; also Scandinavian ones	Middle	A levels, LLB student
2	Vicky	Female	50	Greek	Psychologist	Unpaid	Teacher/bank clerk	*Guardian, Mail*	Middle	MSc Health Psychology
2	Carol	Female	30	Kenyan-Luo	University administrator	£200 per month	Deceased/secretary	*Guardian, Times*; also Kenyan papers	Working	Studying for MA in women in higher ed. management
2	Rachel	Female	55	Italian	Pensioner		Farmers	Italian ones	Middle	A level, degree
3	Stacey	Female	34	White, British	Hotel consultant	£5,500 per year	Van driver/childminder	*News of the World*	Working	CSE Grade 1
3	Paula	Female	52	White	Telephonist	£800 per month	Policeman/dressmaker	*Daily Mail*	Working	None
3	Kate	Female	45	British	Admin assistant	£15,000 per year	Civil servant/tool maker	*Daily Mirror*	Working	GCSE

	Name	Gender	Age	Ethnicity	Occupation	Income	Parents' occupation	Newspaper	Class	Education
3	Tracey	Female	32	White/UK	Administrator/clerical	£16,000 per year	Telephonist	*Express*	Working	O level
3	Carla	Female	33	Indian	Administrator	£18,000 per year	Worsted spinner/textiles	*Guardian/Independent/Observer*	Working	BA Hons and PG Law LPC
4	Joel	Male	66	White British	Retired/failed businessman	State pension	Army warrant officer/housewife	*Times/Sunday Times*	Middle	BA Humanities
4	Adam	Male	39	Caucasian	Student/accountant/mining		Retired probation officer/nurse	*Daily Mail*	Middle	Degree
4	Mike	Male	46	Black African	Student/teacher		Peasant farmers	*Sun*	Working	MA
4	Emma	Female	22	Jewish	Student		Business	*Times*	Middle	Masters
4	Ruth	Female	25	French	Student		Pharmacist/real estate agent	*Guardian*	Middle	Masters
4	Louise	Female	37	Afro-Caribbean	Computer student; formerly telesales		Retired dressmaker	Several tabloids; sometimes *Guardian/Observer*	Middle	Diplomas in periodical journalism and media studies
5	Yvonne	Female	21	Swedish-White	Student		Administrational consultant/retired economist	Any!	Middle	Studying for BSc Psychology
5	Dahlia	Female	20	Swedish-Jewish	Student		University professor/director of department in Swedish cancer society	Any/Swedish left-wing paper	Upper middle	Now a university undergraduate
5	Mary	Female	25	Spanish	Student	£600 per month (scholarship)	Teachers	*PAIS*	Middle	Postgraduate research
5	Amy	Female	27	Indian	Student		Banker/housewife	*Independent/Guardian/Times/Telegraph*	Upper	Double Masters degree

(Continued)

Group	Pseudonym	Gender	Age	Ethnic background	Occupation	Salary	Parents' occupation	Newspaper	SES	Education
5	Fred	Male	55	Jewish	Retired post office counter clerk		Buyer/housewife + sales assistant	Guardian	Working	A levels
5	Lilly	Female	19	Pakistani British	Student		Journalist/at home	Independent	Upper working	BSc Economics
6	Colin	Male	42	White British	Postgraduate student	£15,000	Retired teacher/nurse	Guardian	Middle	PhD
6	Neil	Male	19	White European	Student	About £5k P/A	Teacher/banker	Guardian	Don't have one	BSc
6	Lorna	Female		White British	Management consultant	Varies as independent	Retired solicitor/housewife	None	None or all	PhD/MBA
6	Anna	Female	48	European	Client manager	£24,000		Financial Times/Guardian/Independent	Middle	Degree
6	Mandy	Female	24	British Chinese	Student		Self-made business	Guardian	Middle	PhD
7	Tina	Female	37	White	Graduate, previously secretary	£13,000	Retired instrument assembler/pub worker	Guardian	Working	Degree
7	Leila	Female	28	African	Counsellor	£7,500 per year	Self-employed teachers	Voice/Express	Working	Degree
7	Harriet	Female	20	White	Student/Freelance interviewer	Pro rata	Self-employed makes + sells clothes/real estate services company director	Guardian	None	BA
7	Peter	Male	28	Asian	Administrator		Nurse	Guardian	Lower	MSc

No.	Name	Gender	Age	Ethnicity	Occupation	Income	Parents' occupation	Newspapers	Class	Education
7	Roy	Male	21	Bangladeshi	Student			*Express*	Lower Middle	BSc
8	Richard	Male	21	North European	Student		Solicitor/teacher	*Guardian/ Independent*		Studying BSc
8	Alf	Male	27	Caucasian	Student, previously Canadian government		Professor/librarian + concert violinist	*Guardian* + Canadian papers	Upper Middle	MA
8	Elsa	Female	22	S.E. Asian	Student		Management consultant/housewife	*Independent/ Guardian/ Financial Times*	Middle	Masters (LLM)
8	Terry	Male	56	White British	Social worker	£18,000	Publisher/teacher	*Times/Guardian/ Independent/ International Herald Tribune*	Middle	BSc
9	Sophie	Female	51	Thai	Secretary	£18,000	Teacher	*Mail*	Middle	Diploma
9	Trudy	Female	28	Asian, Pakistani	Recruitment consultant	£19,500	Accountant	*Sun/News of the World*	Middle	BSc Psychology
9	Maya	Female	47	Asian, Pakistani	Accountant	£25,000	Teacher/housewife	*Times, Telegraph*	Middle	BA
9	Karen	Female	53	Asian	Civil servant	£12,000	Headmaster/housewife	HA Not given	Middle	BA
9	Natasha	Female	21	Asian	Student	Nil	Accountant/Housewife, teacher	*Telegraph*	Middle	BSc degree
9	Pip	Female	28	Indian	Administrator	£17,000	Not given	Not given	Working	BA (Hons)
9	Laura	Female	51	Asian	Housewife, previously teacher	Nil	Mechanic/housewife	*Independent*	Middle	HSC teacher training
9	Jason	Male	58	Asian	Motor engineer (retired)	Nil	Plumber	*Guardian, Observer*	Middle	Not stated
9	Betty	Female	50	Pakistani	Administrator	£15,000 approx.	Army/housewife	*Evening Standard/ Times*	Working	BA Political Sciences and Sociology
9	Christina	Female	46	French	Housewife	N/A	Factory executive/housewife	*Sunday Times*	Middle	BA

Appendix 2: An Appeal from an Amnesty International UK (AIUK) Campaign for Afghanistan

Appendix 3: An Appeal from an Amnesty International Campaign against Torture

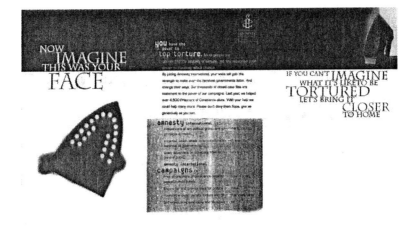

Notes

1 Introduction

1. For further information, see 2010 annual reports from Amnesty International http://thereport.amnesty.org/ or Human Rights Watch (http://www.hrw.org/world-report-2010)
2. For more information see 'Amnesty Against Torture' http://www.amnesty.org.uk/content.asp?CateogoryID= 10228
3. These were also included as a consequence of participants often not differentiating between human rights and humanitarian appeals and campaigns.
4. Dynamic equilibrium describes the condition of a system that has its total energy distributed among its component parts. The unchanging condition of its parts results from the balance or cancelling out of the influences or processes. The resulting stillness, which might be mistaken for inaction, is in fact the equilibrium resulting from the convergence of the influence of contrasting and opposing forces. In chemistry dynamic equilibrium is the state of a reversible reaction where the forward reaction rate is equal to the reverse reaction rate, resulting in no observable net change in the system. Reactions are continuing to proceed in the forward and reverse direction dynamically; however, there is no net change in the amount of product or starting material. Dynamic equilibrium is also called steady state.

2 Between Knowledge and Action: Multidisciplinary Frames and the Psychosocial

1. Boltanski's (1999) formulation of the 'Politics of Pity' draws on Arendt (1990) and characterises it as politics inherently based on spectacle. It is essentially about creating a relationship between the self and a distant stranger.
2. Prosocial behaviour is broadly defined as behaviour that generally benefits other people (Dovidio and Penner, 2004; Penner et al., 2005) and covers a range of behaviours such as helping, cooperating and donating to charity. Authors tend to consider altruism and helping as subcategories of prosocial behaviour or intentional acts that have the outcome of benefiting another person, while research on altruism studies the motivation underlying the behaviour (Dovidio and Penner, 2004).
3. For a more detailed critical review of this field see Orgad and Seu (2013).
4. See Livingstone (1990) and Orgad and Seu (2013) for a detailed discussion.
5. The Transactional Frame will be discussed in the chapters that follow.
6. Out of the 12 focus groups, there were 3 pilots and one main study of 9 focus groups.
7. See Appendix 1 for demographic details.

8. The opening square brackets here indicate that the participants are talking at the same time: all the sentences starting with square brackets refer to overlapping speech in the group discussion.
9. Xxx indicates that a word is inaudible on the tape thus cannot be transcribed accurately.

3 The Web of Passivity: Everyday Morality and the Banality of a Clear Conscience

1. None of the themes were directly prompted by a specific question from the interviewer.
2. Meso level works as an intermediary linking micro-level interactions and macro-level dynamics
3. The number in square brackets before a name denotes the focus group in which the quote originated.
4. *The Big Issue* is a street newspaper published in eight countries; it is written by professional journalists and sold by homeless individuals. *The Big Issue* is one of the UK's leading social businesses and exists to offer homeless people the opportunity to earn a legitimate income, thereby helping them to reintegrate into mainstream society. It is the world's most widely circulated street newspaper
5. These are a few recent examples from the British tabloid the *Daily Mail*: http://www.dailymail.co.uk/news/article-2111180/PJ-Proby-claimed-homeless-5-bank-47-000-benefits-scam.html; http://www.dailymail.co.uk/news/article-2045199/Mother-swindled-40-000-benefits-claiming-homeless.html
6. http://www.dailymail.co.uk/news/article-2140354/Illegal-immigrant-used-fake-UK-passport-claim-30k-benefits-allowed-Chelsea-council-flat.html
7. <Q...Q> denotes attributed speech.
8. In 1970, the world's rich countries agreed to give 0.7 per cent of their GNI (Gross National Income) as official international development aid, annually. Since that time, despite billions given each year, rich nations have rarely met their actual promised targets. For example, the US is often the largest donor in dollar terms, but ranks among the lowest in terms of meeting the stated 0.7 per cent target. See http://www.poverty.com/internationalaid.html for a recent summary of GNI percentage by European countries

4 The Public and NGOs: Neutralisation and Denial in Response to Human Rights Appeals

1. For the sake of accuracy, rather than to doubt the participant's words, to my knowledge Amnesty International never had a 'disarming club' so it is unclear what Alf is referring to.
2. In contrast to 'nurturant' behaviour, which refers to long-term care and support and is generally invisible to those outside the helper–helped dyad.
3. This quote is a good example of the lumping together of appeals from different organisations, including takeaway services.

4. See, for example: http://www.dailymail.co.uk/news/article-1358537/Revealed-Amnesty-Internationals-800-000-pay-offs-bosses.html#ixzz1FXQHpiQZ
5. http://www.amnesty.org.uk/content.asp?categoryID= 12014
6. The conflict in Afghanistan, referred to in the AI appeal in Appendix 2.
7. Public Perception of Poverty research funded by DFiD.

5 Us and Them

1. Sophie is middle-aged secretary from Thailand, living in the UK for over 20 years, self-defined as middle class.
2. Tina is 37, white British graduate.
3. Leila is 28, African and works as counsellor, while Harriet is 20, white and a student.
4. Leila is making reference to the life stories contained in the *Guardian* newspaper's article.
5. Carol is a 30-year-old University administrator, self-defined working class.
6. In this case Karen is voicing a speech allegedly made by the Chinese and the British Government.

6 Identities, Biographies and Invested Narratives

1. I am grateful to Frances Flanagan for coining this term.
2. The ongoing hostilities and tension between India and Pakistan over the disputed territories of Jammu and Kashmir have profound religious roots as discussed in this summary from the BBC: http://news.bbc.co.uk/hi/english/static/in_depth/south_asia/2002/india_pakistan/timeline/default.stm
3. The speakers are referring to the Amnesty appeal on Afghanistan (see Appendix 2).
4. It's unclear whether Leila actually said 'militant' or 'military'; and if she said 'militant', whether she actually and pointedly meant it or whether it was a 'slip of the tongue'.
5. Referring to the *Guardian* article on Saudi Arabia violations of human rights (*The Guardian* (2013a) 'West "turns blind eye" to Saudi torture', http://www.guardian.co.uk/world/2000/mar/29/saudiarabia, date accessed 21 June 2013).
6. At the time of the focus group, Bangladesh parliamentary elected democracy was repeatedly accused of human rights abuses against the Hindu minority, women and children.
7. It in unclear from the recording which word she used.
8. Fred is a 55-year-old retired post office counter clerk who defines himself as Jewish and working class. His highest qualification is A levels. Dahlia is a 20-year-old Swedish undergraduate student from an upper-middle-class background, also Jewish. Lilly is 19 years old, Pakistani British, studying for a BSc in economics. She defines her social class as upper working class.
9. Tamar actually said she had been victim of domestic violence in the past, but the extracts suggest that she was still in that violent relationship at time of speaking.

10. I have numbered these extracts for ease of reference later on. The extracts are in the chronological order in which they were spoken in the focus group.
11. I am still baffled by how I came to ask this question, which I never asked in any other group and which turned out to be so relevant to this group. Did I unconsciously pick up something from the participants? Is this an example of a story that 'had to be told'?
12. [ ] square brackets indicate overtalking
13. Xxx indicates that a word is inaudible on the tape thus cannot be transcribed accurately.
14. The Admiral Duncan is a pub in London's Soho – a nail bomb killed two people and injured 30. The pub is in the heart of the gay community and the incident was seen as homophobic.

7   A Plea for Emotional Complexity: Conflicts and (Psycho)Dynamic Equilibria

1. (1757) *A philosophical enquiry into the origin of our ideas of the sublime and beautiful*.

8   Conclusions

1. Students motivated to volunteer for building their resumés did not volunteer more than students with other motives.
2. I am referring to Amnesty International in particular because two of the prompts were from Amnesty, and the *Guardian* article also contained data from this human rights agency. However, the general principles apply beyond the specificity of Amnesty International.
3. At least in the original version by Collodi, but not in the watered-down Disney rendition.

References

Abraham, K. (1913) 'Restrictions and transformations of scopophilia in Psycho-neurotics.' In Sutherland, J. D. (ed.) *Selected papers on Psychoanalysis*. (pp. 169–234) London: Hogarth Press.

Ailon, G. (2013) 'The psycho-discursive origins of moral panics: Attempting a new theoretical synthesis.' *Psychoanalysis, Culture and Society*, 18(1), 35–55.

Anderson, C. and Keltner, D. (2002) 'The role of empathy in the formation and maintenance of social bonds.' *Behavioral and Brain Sciences*, 25, 21–22.

Anderson, C. J., Regan, P. M. and Ostergard, R. L. (June 2002) 'Political repression and public perceptions of human rights.' *Political Research Quarterly*, 55(2), 439–456.

Aquino, K., McFerran, B. and Laven, M. (2010) 'Moral identity and the experience of moral elevation in response to acts of uncommon goodness.' *Journal of Personality and Social Psychology*, 100(4), 703–718.

Archer R. (1998) 'Universal human rights in the next 50 years.' University of London.

Arendt, H. (1990, 3rd ed. 1963) *On Revolution*. London: Penguin.

Arneson, Richard. (2009) 'What Do We Owe to Distant Needy Strangers?' In Jeffrey A. Schaler (ed.) *Peter Singer Under Fire: The Moral Iconoclast Faces his Critics*. Chicago and La Salle: Open Court.

Arnold, S. (1988) 'Constrained crusaders? British charities and development education.' *Development Policy Review*, 6, 183–209.

Ashford, E. (2011) 'Obligations of Justice and Beneficence to Aid the Severely Poor.' In Illingworth, P., Pogge, T. and Wenar, L. (eds) *Giving Well: The Ethics of Philanthropy*. Oxford: Oxford University Press.

Augoustinos, M. and Every, D. (2007) 'The language of "race" and prejudice: A discourse of denial, reason, and liberal-practical politics.' *Journal of Language and Social Psychology*, 26, 123–141.

Austin, J. L. (1962) *How to Do Things with Words*. Oxford: Oxford University Press.

Bader, V. (1995) 'Citizenship and exclusion: Radical democracy, community, and justice. Or, what is wrong with communitarianism?' *Political Theory*, 23, 211–246.

Baier, A. C. (1987) 'The need for more than justice.' *Canadian Journal of Philosophy*, 13, 41–56.

Ballagan, K. K., Castell, S., Brough, K. and Friemert, H. (2009) *Public Perception of Human Rights*. Equality and Human Rights Commission.

Bandura, A. (1986) *Social Foundations of Thought and Action: A Social Cognitive Theory*. Englewood Cliffs. NJ: Prentice Hall.

———. (1991) 'Social Cognitive Theory or Moral Thought and Action.' In Kurtines, W. M. and Gewirtz, J. L. (eds) *Handbook of Moral Behaviour and Development: Theory, Research and Applications*. (Vol. 1, pp. 71–129) Hillsdale, NJ: Lawrence Erlbaum Associates Inc.

————. (1997) *Self-efficacy: The Exercise of Control.* New York: W. H. Freeman.

————. (1999a) 'Moral disengagement in the perpetuation of inhumanities.' *Personality and Social Psychology Review*, 3, 193–209.

————. (1999b) 'Social cognitive theory: An agentic perspective.' *Asian Journal of Social Psychology*, 2, 21–41.

Barker, M. (1981) *The New Racism.* London: Junction Books.

Barry, B. (1995) *Justice as Impartiality: A Treatise on Social Justice.* (Vol. II). Oxford: Clarendon Press.

Barry, C. M. and Wentzel, K. R. (2006) 'Friend influence on prosocial behavior: The role of motivational factors and friendship characteristics.' *Developmental Psychology*, 42, 153–163.

Bar-Tal, D. (1989) 'Delegitimization: The Extreme Case of Stereotyping and Prejudice.' In D. Bar-Tal, C.Graumann, A.W. Kruglanski, and W. Stroebe (eds) *Stereotyping and Prejudice.* New York: Springer Verlag.

————. (1990) 'Causes and consequences of delegitimization.' *Journal of Social Issues*, 46(1), 65–81.

Bar-Tal, D., Graumann, C., Kruglanski, A. and Stroebe, W. (eds) (1989) *Stereotypes and Prejudice.* New York: Springer-Verlag.

Bartolini, W. F. (2005) ' "Prospective donors" cognitive and emotive processing of charitable gift requests.' *Dissertation Abstracts International.* 66.

Batson, C. D. (1991) *The Altruism Question: Towards a Social-Psychological Answer.* Hillsdale, NY: Erlbaum.

Batson, C. D., Fultz, J. and Schoenrade, P. A. (1987) 'Distress and empathy: Two qualitatively distinct vicarious emotions with different motivational consequences.' *Journal of Personality*, 55(1), 19–39.

Batson, C. D. and Oleson, K. C. (1991) 'Current status of the empathy altruism hypothesis.' In Clark, M. S. (ed.) *Prosocial Behavior: Review of Personality and Social Psychology.* (Vol. 12, pp. 62–85). Newbury Park, CA: Sage.

Baum, R. (1988) 'Holocaust: Moral Indifference as the Form of Modern Evil.' In Rosenberg, A. and Meyers, G. (eds) *Echoes from the Holocaust.* (pp. 53–90) Philadelphia: Temple University Press.

Bauman, Z. (1989) *Modernity and the Holocaust.* Cambridge: Polity Press.

————. (1991) *Modernity and Ambivalence.* Ithaca, NY: Cornell University Press.

————. (1993) *Postmodern Ethics.* Oxford: Blackwell.

Becker, H. S. (1991 [1963]) *Outsiders: Studies in the Sociology of Deviance.* New York: The Free Press.

Becker, L. C. (1992) 'Places for pluralism.' *Ethics*, 102, 707–719.

Belsey, A. (1992) 'World Poverty, Justice and Inequality.' In Attfield, R. and Watkins, B. (eds) *International Justice and the Third World.* (pp. 35–49) London: Routledge.

Benhabib, S. (1992) *Situating the Self: Gender, Community and Postmodernism in Contemporary Ethics.* Oxford: Polity Press.

Benjamin, J. (2004) 'Beyond doer and done to: An intersubjective view of thirdness.' *Psychoanalytic Quarterly*, LXXIII, 5–46.

Benthall, J. (1993) *Disasters, Relief and the Media.* London: I.B. Tauris.

Berkowitz, L. (1972) 'Social Norms, Feelings, and Other Factors Affecting Helping Behaviour and Altruism.' In Berkowitz, L. (ed.) *Advances in Experimental Social Psychology.* (Vol. 6, pp. 63–108) New York: Academic Press.

————. (1978) 'Decreased helpfulness with increased group size through lessening the effects of the needy individual's dependency.' *Journal of Personality,* 46, 299–310.

Berkowitz, L. and Daniels, L. R. (1963) 'Responsibility and dependency.' *The Journal of Abnormal and Social Psychology,* 66(5), 429–436.

Billig, M. (1987) *Arguing and Thinking: A Rhetorical Approach to Social Psychology.* Cambridge: Cambridge University Press.

Billig, M., Condor, S., Edwards, D., Gane, M., Middleton, M. and Radley, A. (1988) *Ideological Dilemmas. A Social Psychology of Everyday Thinking.* London: Sage.

Bion, W. (1962) *Learning from Experience.* London: Heinemann.

Bléandonu, G. (1999) *Wilfred Bion: His Life and Works 1897–1979.* Claire Pajaczkowska (Trans.) London: Free Association Books.

Bobo, L. and Hutchings, V. (1996) 'Perceptions of racial group competition.' *American Sociological Review,* 61, 951–972.

Bollas, C. (1987) *The Shadow of the Object, Psychoanalysis of the Unthought Known.* New York: Columbia University Press.

Boltanski, L. (1999) *Distant Suffering: Morality, Media and Politics.* Cambridge: Cambridge University Press.

Bourdieu, P. (1984) *Distinction: A Social Critique of the Judgment of Taste.* Richard Nice (Trans.) London: Routledge.

Briers, Barbara, Pandelaere, Mario and Luk Warlop. (2007) 'Adding exchange to charity: A reference price explanation.' *Journal of Economic Psychology,* 28(1), 15–30.

Brock, G. (ed.) (1998) *Necessary Goods: Our Responsibility to Meet Others' Needs.* Lanham, MD: Rowman & Littlefield.

Brooks, A. C. (2005) 'Does social capital make you generous?' *Social Science Quarterly,* 86(1) 1–15.

Brown. R. D. and. Wilson, R. A (2008) *Humanitarianism and Suffering: The Mobilization of Empathy.* Cambridge: Cambridge University Press.

Burman, E. and Parker, I. (eds) (1993) *Discourse Analytic Research: Repertoires and Readings of Texts in Action.* London: Routledge.

Burr, V. (2003, 2nd ed.) *An Introduction to Social Constructionism.* London: Routledge.

Butler, J. (1997) *The Psychic Life of Power. Theories in Subjection.* Stanford, CA: Stanford University Press.

————. (2004) *Precarious Life.* London: Verso.

Butterfield, M. (1999, February 14) *To Rejuvenate gun Sales, Critics Say, Industry Started Making More Powerful Pistols.* New York Times: International.

Calhoun, C. (2007) 'Humanitarianism: Progress, Charity, and Emergencies.' 21st annual Sir Robert Birley Memorial Lecture at the City University, London, 2 October.

————. (2010) 'The Idea of Emergency: Humanitarian Action and Global (Dis)Order.' In Fassin, D. and Pandolfi, M. (eds) *States of Emergency.* Cambridge, MA: Zone Books.

Cameron, L. (2011) *Metaphor and Reconciliation: The Discourse Dynamics of Empathy in Post-Conflict Conversations.* New York: Routledge.

Cameron, C. D. and Payne, B. K. (2011) 'Escaping affect: How motivated emotion regulation creates insensitivity to mass suffering.' *Journal of Personality and Social Psychology,* 100, 1–15.

Capdevila, R. and Callaghan, J. (2008) ' "It's not racist. It's common sense". A critical analysis of political discourse around asylum and immigration in the UK.' *Journal of Community & Applied Social Psychology*, 18, 1–16.

Carranza, I. E. (1999) 'Winning the battle in private discourse: Rhetorical-logical operations in storytelling.' *Discourse & Society*, 10(4), 509–542.

Chasseguet-Smirgel, J. (1985) *The Ego Ideal: A Psychoanalytic Essay on the Malady of the Ideal*. Paul Barrows (Trans.) New York: W.W. Norton.

Cherry, F. (1994) *The Stubborn Particulars of Social Psychology*. London: Routledge.

Chouliaraki, L. (2006) *The Spectatorship of Suffering*. London: Sage.

———. (2008) 'Towards a Post-humanitarian Sensibility.' Paper presented at the Humanitarian Communication in the Global Media Age Symposium, Polis, LSE, November.

———. (2010) 'Post-humanitarianism: Humanitarian communication beyond a politics of pity.' *International Journal of Cultural Studies*, 13(2), 107–126.

———. (2012) *The Ironic Spectator: Solidarity in the Age of Post-Humanitarianism*. Cambridge: Polity Press.

Christenson, G. (1997) 'World civil society and the international rule of law.' *Human Rights Quarterly*, 19, 724–737.

Cialdini, R. (1993) *Influence: Science and Practice*. (3rd edn) New York: HarperCollins.

Cialdini, R. B., Brown, S. L., Lewis, B. P., Luce, C. and Neuberg, S. L. (1997) 'Reinterpreting the empathy-altruism relationship: When one into one equals oneness.' *Journal of Personality and Social Psychology*, 73, 481–494.

Cialdini, R. B., Darby, B. L. and Vincent, J. E. (1973) 'Transgression and altruism: A case for hedonism.' *Journal of Personality and Social Psychology*, 9, 502–516.

Cialdini, R. B., Schaller, M., Houlihan, D., Arps, K., Fultz, J. and Beaman, A. L. (1987) 'Empathy-based helping: Is it selflessly or selfishly motivated?' *Journal of Personality and Social Psychology*, 52(4), 749–758.

Clarke, D. (2003) *Pro-Social and Anti-Social Behaviour*. London: Routledge.

Clarke, S. and Hoggett, P. (2009) *Researching Beneath the Surface. Psycho-Social Research Methods in Practice*. London: Karnac.

Clark, R. D. III. and Word, L. E. (1972) 'Why don't bystanders help? Because of ambiguity?' *Journal of Personality and Social Psychology*, 24, 392–400.

Clarkson, P. (1996) *The Bystander: An End to Innocence in Human Relationship*. London: Whurr Publishers Ltd.

Clemence, A., Devos, T. and Doise, W. (2001) 'Social representations of human rights violations: Further evidence.' *Swiss Journal of Psychology*, 60(2), 89–98.

Clement, C. (1996) *Care, Autonomy, and Justice: Feminism and the Ethic of Care*. Oxford: Westview Press.

Cohen, S. (1995) *Denial and Acknowledgement: The Impact of Information about Human Rights Violations*. Jerusalem: Center for Human Rights, the Hebrew University of Jerusalem.

———. (1996) 'Government responses to human rights reports: Claim, denials, and counterclaims.' *Human Rights Quarterly*, 18(3), 517–543.

———. (2001) *States of Denial: Knowing About Atrocities and Suffering*. London: Polity Press.

Cohen, S. and Seu, B. (2002) 'Knowing Enough Not to Feel Too Much: Emotional Thinking About Human Rights Appeals.' In Bradley, M. and Petro, P. (eds) *Truth Claims: Representation and Human Rights.* (pp. 187–201) London: Rutgers University Press.

Cohrs, J. C., Maes, J., Maschener, B. and Keilmann, S. (2007) 'Determinants of human rights attitudes and behaviour: A comparison and integration of psychological perspectives.' *Political Psychology,* 28, 441–470.

Corbridge, S. (1993)' Marxisms, modernities, and moralities: Development praxis and the claims of distant strangers.' *Environment and Planning D: Society and Space,* 11, 449–472.

Cottle, S. (2009) *Global Crisis Reporting: Journalism in the Global Age.* Maidenhead: Open University Press.

Cottle, S. and Nolan, D. (2007) 'Global humanitarianism and the changing aid-media field: "Everyone was dying for coverage".' *Journalism Studies,* 8(6), 862–878.

Cramer, R. E., McMaster, M. R., Bartlett, P. A. and Dragna, M. (1988) 'Subject competence and minimization of the bystander effect.' *Journal of Applied Social Psychology,* 18, 1133–1148.

Creative (2008) 'Segmentation of the General Public in Terms of Attitudes to Global Poverty' – Findings of Preliminary Qualitative Research for DFID/COI.

Creswell, T. (1996) *In Place/Out of Place.* Minneapolis, MN: University of Minnesota Press.

Crompton, T. and Kasser, T. (2010) 'Human identity: A missing link in environmental campaigning.' *Environment,* 52, 23–33.

Cunningham, M. R. (1985/1986) 'Levites and brother's keepers: A sociobiological perspective on prosocial behaviour.' *Humboldt Journal of Social Relations,* 13, 35–67.

Dancy, J. (1993) *Moral Reasons.* Oxford: Blackwell.

Darnton, A. (2007) 'Global Poverty and the Public' desk research. Report 1: Driving Public Engagement in Global Poverty for DFID/COI.

Darnton, A. and Kirk, K. (2011) *Finding Frames: New Ways to Engage the UK Public in Global Poverty.* Oxfam, DFID.

de Waal, F. B. M. (2009) *The Age of Empathy: Nature's Lessons for a Kinder Society.* New York: Harmony Books.

Dean, C. (2004) *The Fragility of Empathy after the Holocaust.* Ithaca, NY: Cornell University Press.

Deutsch, M. and Gerard, H. (1955) 'A study of normative and informational social influence.' *Journal of Abnormal and Social Psychology,* 51, 629–636.

DFID (2000) *Viewing the World – A Study of British Television Coverage of Developing Countries.* http://webarchive.nationalarchives.gov.uk/+/http:/www.dfid. gov.uk/pubs/files/viewworldfull.pdf

Diaz-Veizades, J., Widaman, K., Little, T. and Gibbs, K. (1995) 'The measurement and structure of human rights attitudes.' *The Journal of Social Psychology,* 135(3), 313–328.

di Giovanni, J. (1994) *The Quick and the Dead: Under Siege in Sarajevo.* London: Orion.

Dickert, S., Sagara, N. and Slovic, P. (2010) 'Affective motivations to help others: A two-stage model of donation decisions.' *Journal of Behavioral Decision Making,* 24, 361–376.

Doise, W., Clémence, A. and Lorenzi-Cioldi, F. (1993) *The Quantitative Analysis of Social Representations*. Julian Kaneko (Trans.) Hemel Hempstead: Harvester Wheatsheaf.

Doise, W., Spini, D., Jesuino, J.C., NG, S.H. and Emler, N. (1994) 'Values and perceived conflicts in the social representations of human rights: Feasibility of a cross-national study.' *Swiss Journal of Psychology*, 53, 240–251.

Doise, W., Spini, D. and Clémence, A. (1999) 'Human rights studied as social representations in a cross-national context.' *European Journal of Social Psychology*, 22, 1–29.

Dogra, N. (2006) ' "Reading NGOs visually": Implications of visual images for NGO management.' *Journal of International Development*, 19(2), 161–171.

Douglas, M. (1966) *Purity and Danger: An Analysis of Concepts of Pollution and Taboo*. London: Routledge.

Dovidio, J. F. (1984) 'Helping Behaviour and Altruism: An Empirical and Conceptual Overview.' in Berkowitz, L. (ed.) *Advances in Experimental Social Psychology*. (Vol. 17, pp. 361–427) New York: Academic Press.

Dovidio, J. F. and Gaertner, S. L. (2004) 'Aversive Racism.' In Zanna, M. P. (ed.) *Advances in Experimental Social Psychology*. (pp. 1–52) San Diego, CA: Academic Press.

Dovidio, J. F. and Penner, L. A. (2004) 'Helping and Altruism.' In Brewer, M. B. and Hewstone, M. (eds) *Emotion and Motivation*. (pp. 247–280) Malden, MA: Blackwell.

Doyal, L. and Gough, I. (1991) *A Theory of Human Need*. London: Macmillan.

Dudai, R. (2006) 'Advocacy with footnotes: The human rights report as a literary genre.' *Human Rights Quarterly*, 28(3), 783–795.

Dunn, K. M. (2001) 'Representations of Islam in the politics of mosque development in Sydney.' *Tijdschrift voor Economische en Sociale Geografie*, 92(3), 291–308.

Dunn, Kevin M., Khocker, N. and T. Salabay. (2007) 'Contemporary racism and Islamophobia in Australia.' *Ethnicities*, 7(4), 564–589.

Durkheim, E. (1976, 1912) *The Elementary Forms of Religious Life*. Joseph Ward Swain (Trans). London: Allen & Unwin.

———. (1976) *The Elementary Forms of Religious life*. Joseph Ward Swain (Trans.) London: Allen & Unwin.

Durrheim, K. and Dixon, J. (2005) 'Studying talk and embodied practices: Toward a psychology of materiality of "Race Relations".' *Journal of Community & Applied Social Psychology*, 15, 446–460.

Eagleton, T. (1996) *The Illusions of Postmodernism*. Oxford: Blackwell.

Eagly, A. H. (2009) 'The his and hers of prosocial behavior: An examination of the social psychology of gender.' *American Psychologist*, 64, 644–658.

Eagly, A. and Crowley, M. (1986) 'Gender and helping behavior: A meta-analytic view of the social psychological literature.' *Psychological Bulletin*, 100, 283–308.

Easterly, W. (2006) *The White Man's Burden: Why the West's Efforts to Aid the Rest Have Done So Much Ill and So Little Good*. Oxford: Oxford University Press.

Eckel, C., Grossman, P. and Milano, A. (2007) 'Is more information always better? An experimental study of charitable giving and Hurricane Katrina.' *Southern Economic Journal*, 74(2), 388–411.

Edelman, M. (2006) 'The language of participation and the language of resistance.' *Human Communication Research*, 3(2), 159–170.

Edley, N. (2001) 'Analysing Masculinity: Interpretative Repertoires, Ideological Dilemmas and Subject Positions.' In Wetherell, M. Taylor, S. and Yates, S.J. (eds) *Discourse as Data*. Milton Keynes: Open University Press.

Edwards, D. and Potter, J. (1992) *Discursive Psychology*. London: Sage.

Eisenberg, N. and Fabes, R. A. (1991) 'Prosocial Behavior and Empathy: A Multimethod Developmental Perspective.' In Clark, M. S. (ed.) *Prosocial Behavior*. (pp. 34–61) Newbury Park, CA: Sage.

Eisenberg, N. and Lennon, R. (1983) 'Sex differences in empathy and related capacities.' *Psychological Bulletin*, 94(1), 100–131.

Elias, N. (1982) *The Civilizing Process*. Edmund Jephcott (Trans.) Oxford: Blackwell.

Elliott, A. and Turner, B. (2003) 'Introduction: Towards the ontology of frailty and rights.' *Journal of Human Rights*, 2(2), 129–136.

Epstein, S. (1994) 'Integration of the cognitive and the psychodynamic unconscious.' *American Psychologist*, 49, 709–724.

Etzioni, A. (1995) *The Spirit of Community: Rights, Responsibilities and the Communitarian Agenda*. London: Fontana.

Fabes, R. A., Eisenberg, N. and Eisenbud, L. (1993) 'Behavioral and physiological correlates of children's reactions to others' distress.' *Developmental Psychology*, 29, 655–663.

Fairclough, N. (1989) *Language and Power*. London: Longman.

———. (1992) *Discourse and Social Change*. Cambridge: Polity Press.

———. (1995) *Critical Discourse Analysis: The Critical Study of Language*. London: Longman.

———. (2000) *New Labour, New Language?* London: Routledge.

Feather, N. T. and McKee, I. R. (2008) 'Values and prejudice: Predictors of attitudes towards Australian Aborigines.' *Australian Journal of Psychology*, 60, 80–90.

Figley, C.R. (ed.) (1995) *Compassion Fatigue: Secondary Traumatic Stress Disorders from Treating the Traumatized*. New York: Brunner/Mazel.

Finnemore, M. (1996) Norms, Culture and world politics: insights from sociology's institutionalism. *International Organization*, 50(2): 325–347.

Fiske, A. P. (1991) *Structures of Social Life: The Four Elementary Forms of Human Relations*. New York: Free Press.

Flax, J. (1993) *Disputed Subjects: Essays on Psychoanalysis, Politics, and Philosophy*. New York: Routledge.

Forgas, J. P. (1998) 'On being happy and mistaken? Mood effects on the fundamental attribution error.' *Journal of Personality and Social Psychology*, 75, 318–331.

Freud, S. (1914) 'On Narcissism.' In Freud, S. (ed.) (2003) *Beyond the Pleasure Principle: And Other Writings*. London: Penguin.

———. (1923) 'The Ego and the Id.' In Freud, S. (ed.) (2003) *Beyond the Pleasure Principle: And Other Writings*. London: Penguin.

———. (1937) 'Analysis Terminable and Interminable.' In Freud, S. (ed.) (2002) *Wild Analysis*. London: Penguin.

———. (1926) *Inhibitions, Symptoms and Anxieties*. The Standard Edition of the Complete works of Sigmund Freud. London: Hogarth Press.

Freud, A. (1936) *The Ego and the Mechanisms of Defence*. London: Hogarth Press.

Frey, D. L. and Gaertner, S. L. (1986) 'Helping and the avoidance of inappropriate interracial behavior: A strategy that perpetuates a nonprejudiced self-image.' *Journal of Personality and Social Psychology*, 50, 1083–1090.

Friedman, M. (1991) 'The practice of partiality.' *Ethics*, 101, 818–835.

———. (1993) *What Are Friends For? Feminist Perspectives on Personal Relationships and Moral Theory*. Ithaca, NY, and London: Cornell University Press.

Friedrich, J. and Dood, T. L. (2009) 'How many casualties are too many? Proportional reasoning in the valuation of military and civilian lives.' *Journal of Applied Social Psychology*, 39, 2541–2569.

Friedrich, J. and McGuire, A. (2010) 'Individual differences in reasoning style as a moderator of the identifiable victim effect.' *Social Influence*, 5, 182–201.

Froggett, L. (2002) *Love, Hate and Welfare: Psychosocial Approaches to Policy and Practice*. Bristol: Policy Press.

Frosh, S. (1987) *The Politics of Psychoanalysis: An Introduction to Freudian and Post-Freudian Theory*. Basingstoke: Macmillan.

———. (2003) 'Psychosocial studies and psychology: Is a critical approach emerging?' *Human Relations*, 56, 1547–1567.

———. (2005) *Hate and the Jewish Science: Anti-Semitism, Nazism and Psychoanalysis*. Basingstoke: Palgrave Macmillan.

Gadd, D. (2009) 'Aggravating racism and elusive motivation.' *British Journal of Criminology*, 49, 755–771.

Gaddy, G. and Tanjong, E. (1986) 'Earthquake coverage by the western press.' *Journal of Communications*, 36(2), 105–112.

Gailliot, M.T. (2009) 'The Effortful and Energy-Demanding Nature of Prosocial Behavior.' In Mikulincer, M. and Shaver, P. R. (eds) *Prosocial Motives, Feelings, and Behavior – The Better Angels of Our Nature*. Washington, DC: American Psychological Association.

Geras, N.. (1995) *Solidarity in the Conversation of Humankind: The Ungroundable Liberalism of Richard Rorty*. London: Verso.

———. (1999) *The Contract of Mutual Indifference: Political Philosophy After the Holocaust*. London: Verso.

Gerber, J. (1997) 'Beyond dualism – The social construction of nature and the natural and social construction of human beings.' *Progress in Human Geography*, 21, 1–17.

Gilbert, G. H. and Mulkay, M. (1982) 'Warranting scientific beliefs.' *Social Studies of Science*, 12, 383–408.

Gillespie, W.H. (1971) Aggression and instinct theory. *International Journal of Psycho-analysis*, 52, 155–160.

Gilligan, C. (1982) *In a Different Voice: Psychological Theory and Woman's Development*. Cambridge, MA: Harvard University Press.

———. (1987) 'Moral Orientation and Moral Development.' In Kittay, E. and Meyers, D. (eds) *Women and Moral Theory*. (pp. 19–33) Totowa, NJ: Rowman & Littlefield.

Gilligan, C. and Attanucci, J. (1988) *Two Moral Orientations: Gender Differences and Similarities*. Cambridge, MA: Harvard University Press.

Ginzburg, C. (1994) 'Killing a Chinese mandarin: The moral implications of distance.' *New Left Review*, 208, 107–120.

Gomez, L. (1997) *Introduction to Object Relations*. London: Free Association Books.

Goodin, R. (1985) *Protecting the Vulnerable*. Chicago, IL: University of Chicago Press.

Goodman, M. and Barnes, C. (2011) Star/poverty space: The making of the 'development celebrity.' *Celebrity Studies*, 2(1), 69–85.

Grant, A. M. and Gino, F. (2010) 'A little thanks goes a long way: Explaining why gratitude expressions motivate prosocial behavior.' *Journal of Personality and Social Psychology*, 98, 946–955.

Graziano, W. G., Habashi, M. M., Sheese, B. E. and Tobin, R. M. (2007) 'Agreeableness, empathy, and helping: A person x situation perspective.' *Journal of Personality and Social Psychology*, 93(4), 583–599.

Grouzet, F. M., Kasser T., Ahuvia A., Dols J. M., Kim, Y., Lau, S., Ryan, R. M., Saunders, S., Schmuck, P., Sheldon, K. M. (2005) 'The structure of goal contents across 15 cultures.' *Journal of Personality and Social Psychology*, 89, 800–816.

Grusec, J. E. (1991) 'Socializing concern for others in the home.' *Developmental Psychology*, 27, 338–342.

Habermas, J. (1990) *Moral Consciousness and Communicative Action*. Cambridge: Polity Press.

Haidt, J. (2001) 'The emotional dog and its rational tail: A social intuitionist approach to moral judgement.' *Psychological Review*, 108(4), 814–834.

———.(2002) ' "Dialogue between My Head and My Heart": Affective influences on moral judgment.' *Psychological Inquiry*, 13(1), 54–56.

Hafner-Burton, E. and Ron, J. (2009) 'Seeing double- human rights impact through qualitative and quantitative eyes.' *World Politics*, 61(2), April 2009, 360–401

———. (2010) 'Sociology and human rights: Confrontations, evasions and new engagements.' *The International Journal of Human Rights*, 14(6), 811–832.

Halpern, J. and Weinstein, H. M. (2004) 'Rehumanizing the other: Empathy and reconciliation.' *Human Rights Quarterly*, 26(3), 561–583.

Handy, F., Cnaan, R. A., Brudney, J., Meijs, L., Ascoli, U. and Ranade, S. (2000) 'Public perception of "who is a volunteer": An examination of the net-cost approach from a cross-cultural perspective.' *Voluntas: International Journal of Voluntary & Nonprofit Organizations*, 11(1), 45–65.

Harré, R. and Moghaddam, F. (eds) (2003) *The Self and Others. Positioning Individuals and Groups in Personal, Political and Cultural Context*. London: Prager.

Harré, R., Moghaddam, F., Cairnie, T., Rothbart, D. and Sabat, S. (2009) 'Recent advances in positioning theory.' *Theory & Psychology*, 19(1), 5–31.

Harré, R. and van Langenhove, L. (1999) *Positioning Theory: Moral Contexts of Intentional Action*. Oxford: Blackwell.

Hekman, S. J. (1995) *Moral Voices, Moral Selves: Carol Gilligan and Feminist Moral Theory*. Oxford: Polity Press.

Held, V. (1993) *Feminist Morality: Transforming Culture, Society, and Politics*. Chicago, IL: University of Chicago Press.

Hilton, M., McKay, J., Crowson, N. and Mouhot, J-F. (2010) 'The big society: civic participation and the state in modern Britain.' *History and Policy Policy Paper 103*, Available at http://www.historyandpolicy.org/papers/policy-paper-103.html

Hoffman, M. L. (1990) Empathy and justice motivation. *Motivation and Emotion*, 14, 151–172.

Hoggett, P. (2000) *Emotional Life and the Politics of Welfare*. Basingstoke: Macmillan.

———. (2009) *Politics, Identity and Emotion*. Boulder, COL: Paradigm.

Hoijer, B. (2004) 'The discourse of global compassion: The audience and media reporting of human suffering.' *Media, Culture and Society*, 26(4), 513–531.

Hollway, W. (1984) 'Gender Difference and the Production of Subjectivity.' In Henriquez, J. et al. (eds) *Changing the Subject: Psychology, Social Regulation and Subjectivity*. London: Methuen & Co.

———. (1989) *Subjectivity and Method in Psychology: Gender, Meaning and Science*. London: Sage.

———. (2004) 'Psycho-social research. Editorial introduction to Special Issue on psycho-social research.' *International Journal of Critical Psychology*, 10, 1–5.

———. (2006) *The Capacity to Care: Gender and Ethical Subjectivity*. London: Routledge.

Hollway, W. and Jefferson T. (2000) *Doing Qualitative Research Differently. A Free Association, Narrative and the Interview Method*. London: Sage.

Hoover, C. W., Wood, E. E. and Knowles, E. S. (1983) 'Forms of social awareness and helping.' *Journal of Experimental Social Psychology*, 18, 577–590.

Hopgood, S. (2006) *Keepers of the Flame: Understanding Amnesty International*. Ithaca, NY: Cornell University Press.

Hopkins, P. E. and Smith, S. J. (2008) 'Scaling Segregation: Racialising Fear.' In Pain, R. and Smith, S. J. (ed.) *Fear: Critical Geopolitics and Everyday Life*. Aldershot: Ashgate.

Hornstein, H. A. (1982) 'Promotive Tension: Theory and Research.' in Derlega, V. J. and Grzelak, J. (eds) *Cooperation and Helping Behavior: Theories and Research*. (pp. 229–248) New York: Academic Press.

Hume, D. (1969) *A Treatise of Human Nature*. London: Penguin. (Original work published 1739 & 1740)

Hunt, M. (1990) *The Compassionate Beast*. New York: Morrow.

Hur, M. H. (2006) 'Exploring the motivation factors of charitable giving and their value structure: A case study of Seoul, Korea.' *Social Behavior and Personality*. 34(6), 661–680.

Hynes, P., Lamb, M., Short, D. and Waites, M. (2010) 'Sociology and human rights: Confrontations, evasions and new engagements.' *The International Journal of Human Rights*, 14(6), 810–830.

Hynes, P., Lamb, M., Short, D. and Waites, M. (2011) *Sociology and Human Rights: New Engagements*. London: Routledge.

Ignatieff, M. (2000) *The Rights Revolution*. Toronto: Anansi.

Ingleby, D. (1985) 'Professionals and socialisers: The "psy complex".' *Research in Law, Deviance and Social Control*, 7, 79–109.

Israel, J. and Tajfel, H. (eds) (1972) *The Context of Social Psychology: A Critical Assessment*. London: Academic Press.

Jacobson, E. (1954) *The Self and the Object World: Vicissitudes of their Infantile Cathexes and their Influence on Ideational and Affective Development*. London: The Hogarth Press and the Institute of Psychoanalysis.

Jagger, A. M. (1995) 'Toward a Feminist Conception of Moral Reasoning.' in Sterba, J. P., Machan, T. R., Jagger, A. M., Galston, W. A., Gould, C. C., Fisk, M. and Solomon, R. C. (eds) *Morality and Social Justice: Point/Counterpoint*. (pp. 115–146.) London: Rowman & Littlefield.

James, R. N. (2011) 'Charitable giving and cognitive ability.' *International Journal of Nonprofit and Voluntary Sector Marketing*, 16(1), 70–83.

James, R. N. and Sharpe, D. L. (2007) 'The secteEffect in charitable giving: Distinctive realities of exclusively religious charitable givers.' *American Journal of Economics & Sociology*, 66(4), 697–726.

Jamieson, D. (2005) 'Duties to the Distant: Aid, Assistance, and Intervention in the Developing World.' In Brock, G. and Moellendorf, D. (eds) *Current Debates in Global Justice*. Dordrecht: Springer.

Jenni, K. E and Loewenstein, G. (1997) 'Explaining the "Identifiable victim effect".' *Journal of Risk and Uncertainty*, 14, 235–257.

Joireman, J. and Duell, B. (2005) 'Mother Teresa vs. Ebenezer Scrooge: Mortality salience leads proselfs to endorse self-transcendent values (unless proselfs are reassured).' *Personality and Social Psychology Bulletin*, 31, 307–320.

Jonas, E., Schimel, J., Greenberg, J and Pyszczynski, T. (2002) 'The Scrooge effect: Evidence that mortality salience increases prosocial attitudes and behaviour.' *Personality and Social Psychology Bulletin*, 28(10), 1342–1353.

Jordan, G and Maloney, W. (1997) *The Protest Business? Mobilizing Campaign Groups*. Manchester: Manchester University Press.

Keck, M. and Sikkink, K. (1998) *Activists Beyond Borders*. Ithaca, NY: Cornell University Press.

Kershaw, I. (1983) *Popular Opinion and Political Dissent in the Third Reich, Bavaria 1933–45*. Oxford: Oxford University Press.

Kitwood, T. (1990) 'The dialectics of dementia: With special reference to Alzheimer's disease.' *Aging and Society*, 10, 177–196.

Kogut, T. and Ritov, I. (2005) 'The "Identified Victim" effect: An identified group, or just a single individual?' *Journal of Behavioral Decision Making*, 18, 157–167.

Kohlberg, L. (1963) The development of children's orientations towards a moral order: I sequence in the development of moral thought. *Vita Humana*, 6, 11–33.

———. (1985) *The Psychology of Moral Development*. San Francisco, CA: Harper & Row.

Kohlberg, L. and Hersh, R. H. (1977) 'Moral development: A review of the theory.' *Theory into Practice*, 16(2), 53–59.

Lakoff, G. (1987) *Women, Fire, and Dangerous Things*. Chicago: University of Chicago Press.

———. (2008) *The Political Mind: Why You Can't Understand 21st-Century American Politics with an 18th-Century Brain*. New York: Viking.

———. (2010, 2nd ed.) *Moral Politics: How Liberals and Conservatives Think*. Chicago: University of Chicago Press.

Lamont, M. and Fournier, M. (eds) (1992) *Cultivating Differences: Symbolic Boundaries and the Making of Inequality*. Chicago: University of Chicago Press.

Lamont, M. and Thévenot, L. (eds) (2000) *Rethinking Comparative Cultural Sociology*. Cambridge: Cambridge University Press.

Laplanche, J. and Pontalis, J. B. (1985) *The Language of Psycho-Analysis*. London: The Hogarth Press.

Laquer, T. W. (2009) 'Mourning, Pity and the Work of Narrative in the Making of "Humanity".' In Wilson, R. A. and Brown, R. D. (eds) *Humanitarianism and Suffering*. (p. 31) Cambridge: Cambridge University Press.

Largue, G. A. (1991) 'Ancient Ethics.' in Singer, P. (ed.) *A Companion to Ethics*. (pp. 29–40) Oxford: Blackwell.

Latane, B. and Darley, J. M. (1970) *The Unresponsive Bystander: Why doesn't He Help?* New York: Appleton-Century-Croft.

Latane, B. and Darley, J. M. (1976) *Bystander Response to an Emergency*. Morristown. NJ: General Learning Press.

Latane, B. and Nida, S. (1981) 'Ten years of research on group size and helping.' *Psychological Bulletin*, 89(2), 308–324.

Latane, B., Nida, S. A. and Wilson, D. W. (1981) 'The Effects of Group Size on Helping Behaviour.' in Rushton, J. P. and Sorrentino, R. M. (eds) *Altruism and Helping Behaviour: Social, Personality and Developmental Perspectives*. Hillsdale, NJ: Erlbaum.

Latane, B. and Rodid, J. (1969) 'A lady in distress: Inhibiting effects of friends and strangers in bystander intervention.' *Journal of Experimental Social Psychology*, 5, 189–202.

Laqueur, T. W. (2009) 'Mourning, Pity, and the Work of Narrative in the Making of "Humanity".' In Wilson, R. A. and Brown, R. D. (eds) *Humanitarianism and Suffering: The Mobilization of Empathy*. (pp. 31–57) Cambridge: Cambridge University Press.

Lerner, M. J. (1980) *The Belief in a Just World: A Fundamental Delusion*. New York: Plenum Press.

Levi, P. (1987) *If This is a Man/The Truce*. S. Woolf (trans.) London: Abacus.

———. (1989) *The Drowned and the Saved*. London: Vintage International.

Levine, M. (1999) 'Rethinking bystander nonintervention: Social categorization and evidence of witnesses at the James Bulger murder trial.' *Human Relations*, 52(9) 1133–1155.

Levine, M. and Thompson, K. (2004) 'Identity, place, and bystander intervention: Social categories and helping after natural disasters.' *The Journal of Social Psychology*, 144, 229–245.

Levine, M., Prosser, A., Evans, D., and Reicher, S. (2005) 'Identity and emergency intervention: How social group membership and inclusiveness of group boundaries shape helping behavior.' *Personality and Social Psychology Bulletin*, 31(4), 443–453.

Levine, N. (1976) 'On the metaphysics of social psychology: A critical view.' *Human Relations*, 29(4), 385–400.

Leys, R. (2011) 'The turn to affect: A critique.' *Critical Inquiry*, 37, 434–472.

Lidchi, H. (1993) *All in the Choosing Eye: Charity, Representation and the Developing World*. Unpublished PhD Thesis. Milton Keynes: The Open University.

Lewis, H.B. (1971) *Shame and Guilt in Neurosis*. New York: International University Press.

Lissner, J. (1981) 'Merchants of misery.' *New Internationalist*, 100, 23.

Livingstone, S. (1990) *Making Sense of Television: The Psychology of Audience Interpretation*. London: Routledge.

Loewenstein, G. and Small, D. A. (2007) 'The scarecrow and the tin man: The vicissitudes of human sympathy and caring.' *Review of General Psychology*, 11, 112–126.

Lokman, T. (2010). *A Journalism of Hospitality*. Unpublished PhD Thesis. Philadelphia, PA: University of Pennsylvania.

Macek, P. L., Osecká, L., and Konstroň, L. (1997). 'Social representations of human rights amongst Czech university students.' *Journal of Community and Applied Social Psychology*, 7, 65–76.

MacIntyre, A. (1981) *After Virtue: A Study in Moral Theory* (2nd ed., 1995). London: Duckworth.

Mango Research (2009) 'Child survival attitudes' *Mango Research for Save the Children*. September.

Markovic, M. (1990) 'The Development Vision of Socialist Humanism.' in Engel, J. R. and Engel, J. G. (eds) *Ethics of Environment and Development: Global Challenge, International Response.* (pp. 127–36.) London: Belhaven Press.

Marks, G. and Miller, N. (1987) 'Ten years of research on the false consensus effect: An empirical and theoretical review.' *Psychological Bulletin*, 102, 72–90.

Martin, J. R. (1996) 'Aerial distance, esotericism, and other closely related traps.' *Signs: Journal of Women in Culture and Society*, 21, 584–614.

Matthew, C. and Listhaug, O.(2007) 'Citizens' perceptions of human rights practices: An analysis of 55 countries.' *Journal of Peace Research*, 44(4), Special Issue on Protecting Human Rights (Jul., 2007), 465–483.

Mathews, K. E. and Canon, L. K. (1975) 'Environmental noise level as a determinant of helping behavior.' *Journal of Personality and Social Psychology*, 32, 571–577.

Matza, D. and Sykes (1964) *Delinquency and drift.* Hoboken, NJ: John Wiley & Sons. Inc.

McConahay, J. B. (1986) 'Modem Racism, Ambivalence and the Modem Racism Scale.' In Dovidio, J. F. and Gaertner, S. L. (eds) *Prejudice, Discrimination. and Racism.* (pp. 92–125) San Diego. CA: Academic Press.

McFarland, S and Mathews, M. (2005) 'Who cares about human rights?' *Political Psychology*, 26(3), 365–385.

Mendus, S. (1993) 'Different voices, still lives: Problems in the ethics of care.' *Journal of Applied Philosophy*, 10, 17–27.

Meyer, J., Boli, J., Thomas, G. and Ramirez, F. (1997) 'World society and the nation-state.' *American Journal of Sociology*, 103(1), 144–181.

Miles, R. and Brown, M. (2004) *Racism.* London: Routledge.

Milgram, S. (1974) *Obedience to Authority: An Experimental View.* New York: Harper & Row.

Miller, D. (2004) 'National Responsibility and International Justice.' In Chatterjee, D. (ed.) *The Ethics of Assistance: Morality and the Distant Needy.* Cambridge: Cambridge University Press.

Miller, D. T. and Prentice, D. A. (1994) 'Collective errors and errors about the collective.' *Personality and Social Psychology Bulletin*, 20, 541–550.

Miller, J. Baker. (1978) *Towards a New Psychology of Women.* London: Penguin.

Miller, K. I., Stiff, J. B. and Ellis, B. H. (1988) 'Communication and empathy as precursors to burnout among human service workers.' *Communication Monographs*, 55, 250–265.

Miller, R. (2004) 'Beneficence, duty and distance.' *Philosophy and Public Affairs*, 32(4), 358–383.

Miller, R. W. (1992) *Moral Differences: Truth, Justice and Conscience in a World of Conflict.* Princeton, NJ: Princeton University Press.

Moeller, S. D. (1999) *Compassion Fatigue: How the Media Sell Misery, War, and Death.* New York: Routledge.

———. (2006) 'Regarding the pain of others: Media, bias and the coverage of international disasters.' *Journal of International Affairs*, 59(2), 173–196.

Moghaddam, F. M. (1998) *Social Psychology. Exploring Universals Across Cultures.* NY: WH Freeman and Co.

Monroe, K. (1996) *The Heart of Altruism.* Princeton: Princeton University Press.

———. (2001) 'Morality and a sense of self: The importance of identity and categorization for moral action.' *American Journal of Political Science*, 45(3), 491–507.

———. (2003) 'How identity and perspective constrain moral choice.' *International Political Science Review*, 24(4), 405–425.

———.(2004) *The Hand of Compassion: Portraits of Moral Choice during the Holocaust*. Princeton, NJ: Princeton University Press.

Moyo, D. (2009) *Dead Aid: Why Aid is Not Working and How There is Another Way for Africa*. London: Allen Lane.

Mulhall, S. and Swift, A. (1996) *Liberals and Communitarians*. (2nd edn) Oxford: Blackwell.

Narine, N. (2010) 'Global trauma and the cinematic network society.' *Critical Studies in Media Communication*, 27(3), 209–234.

Nash, K. (2008) 'Global citizenship as show business: The cultural politics of Make Poverty History.' *Media, Culture & Society*, 30(2), 167–181.

Nelson, M. R., Brunel, F., Supphellen, M. and R. V. Manchanda (2006) 'Effects of culture, gender, and moral obligations on responses to charity advertising across masculine and feminine cultures.' *Journal of Consumer Psychology*, 16(1), 45–56.

New, C. (1996) *Agency, Health and Social Survival*. London: Taylor and Francis.

Noddings, N. (1984) *Caring: A Feminine Approach to Ethics and Moral Education*. Berkeley, CA: University of California Press.

Nussbaum, M. C. (1992) 'Human functioning and social justice: In defence of Aristotelian essentialism.' *Political Theory*, 20, 220–246.

Oceja, L., Stocks, E. and Lishner, D. (2010) 'Congruence between the target in need and the recipient of aid: The one-among-others effect.' *Journal of Applied Social Psychology*, 40(11), 2814–2828.

Okin, S. M. (1989) 'Reason and feeling in thinking about justice.' *Ethics*, 99, 229–249.

Oliner, S. P. and Oliner, P. M. (1988) *The Altruistic Personality: Rescuers of Jews in Nazi Europe*. New York: Free Press.

Olivola, C. Y. and Sagara, N. (2009) 'Distributions of observed death tolls govern sensitivity to human fatalities.' *Proceedings of the National Academy of Sciences of the USA*, 106, 22151–22156.

O'Neill, O. (1996) *Toward Justice and Virtue: A Constructive Account of Practical Reasoning*. Cambridge: Cambridge University Press.

Ong, J. C. (2009) 'The cosmopolitan continuum: Locating cosmopolitanism in media and cultural studies.' *Media, Culture and Society*, 31(3), 449–466.

———.(2011) *The Mediation of Suffering: Classed Moralities of Media Audiences in the Philippines*. Unpublished PhD Thesis. Cambridge: Cambridge University.

Olivola, C. Y. and Namika, M. (2009) 'Distributions of observed death tolls govern sensitivity to human fatalities.' *PNAS*, 106(52), 22151–22156.

Opotow, S. (1990) 'Moral exclusion and injustice.' *Journal of Social Issues*, 46(1), 1–20.

———. (2008) ' "Not so much as place to lay our head …": Moral inclusion and exclusion in the American Civil War Reconstruction.' *Social Justice Research*, 21(1), 26–49.

Opotow, S. and Weiss, L. (2000) 'Denial and exclusion in environmental conflict.' *Journal of Social Issues*, 56(3), 475–490.

Orgad, S. (2012) *Media Representation and the Global Imagination*. Cambridge: Polity.

Orgad, S. and Seu, I. B. (2013) 'The mediation of humanitarianism: Towards a research framework.' *Communication, Culture and Critique*. Vol.7, issue 4: 452–470

Oxfam. 2008. 'Mindsets: A New Tool for Understanding our Audiences – Segmentation Overview.' Brainjuicer for Oxfam, December 2008.

Parker, I. (1997) *Psychoanalytic Culture. Psychoanalytic Discourse in Western Society*. London: Sage.

Penner, L. A., Dovidio, J. F., Schroeder, D. A., & Piliavin, J. A. (2005) 'Prosocial behavior: Multilevel perspectives.' *Annual Review of Psychology*, 56, 365–392.

Pettigrew, T. F. and Meertens, R. W. (1995) 'Subtle and blatant prejudice in Western Europe.' *European Journal of Social Psychology*, 25, 57–75.

Perls, F. S. (1960) *Gestalt Therapy Verbatim*. Moab, UT: Real People Press.

Philo, G. (2002) 'Television news and audience understanding of war, conflict and disaster.' *Journalism Studies*, 3(2), 173–186.

Piaget, J. (1932) *The Moral Judgement of the Child*. London: Routledge & Kegan Paul.

Piff, P. K., Kraus, M. W., Côté, S., Cheng, B. H. and Keltner, D. (2010) 'Having less, giving more: The influence of social class on prosocial behavior.' *Journal of Personality and Social Psychology*, 99(5), November 2010, 771–784.

Piliavin, J. A., Dovidio, J. F., Gaertner, S. L. and Clark, R. D. III (1981) *Emergency intervention*. NY: Academic Press.

Pines, M. (1987) 'Shame – What psychoanalysis does and does not say.' *Group Analysis*, 20, 16–31.

Pogge, T. (2004) 'Assisting the Global Poor.' In Chatterjee, D. (ed.) *The Ethics of Assistance: Morality and the Distant Needy*. Cambridge: Cambridge University Press.

Polonsky, M. J., Shelley, L. and Voola, R. (2002) 'An examination of helping behaviour: Some evidence from Australia.' *Journal of Nonprofit & Public Sector Marketing*, 10(2), 67–82.

Potter, J. and Wetherell, M. (1995) 'Discourse Analysis.' In Smith, J.A., Harré, R. and van Langenhove, L. (eds) *Rethinking Methods in Psychology*. London: Sage.

———. (1987) *Discourse and Social Psychology*. London: Sage.

PPP (2005) Public Perceptions of Poverty – Qualitative Study Wave 2. Alice Fenyoe at Synovate for Comic Relief/DFID, October 2005.

PPP (2007a) Public Perceptions of Poverty – Quantitative Survey Wave 6. Andrew Darnton and TNS for Comic Relief/DFID, April 2007.

PPP (2007b) Public Perceptions of Poverty – Qualitative Study Wave 4. Alice Fenyoe at TW Research for Comic Relief/DFID, May 2007.

Prentice, D. A. and Miller, D. T. (1996) 'Pluralistic Ignorance and the Perpetuation of Social Norms by Unwitting Actors.' In Zanna, Mark, P. (ed.) *Advances in Experimental Social Psychology*. London: Academic Press.

Price, R. (2003) 'Transnational civil Society and advocacy in world politics.' *World Politics*, 55(4), 579–606.

Ramos, H., Ron, J. and Thoms, O. N. T. (2007) 'Shaping the Northern media's human rights coverage, 1986–2000.' *Journal of Peace Research*, 44(4), 385–406.

Rajagopal, B. (2003) *International Law from Below: Development, Social Movements and Third World Resistance*. New York: Cambridge University Press.

Rajaram, P. K. (2002) 'Humanitarianism and representations of the refugee.' *Journal of Refugee Studies,* 15(3), 247–264.

Rawls, J. (1971) *A Theory of Justice.* Cambridge, MA: Harvard University Press.

Reicher, S. and Haslam, S. A. (2010) 'A social psychology of collective solidarity and social cohesion.' In Stürmer and M.Snyder (eds) *The Psychology of Prosocial Behavior.* Oxford: Blackwell.

Reiff, D. (2002) *A Bed for the Night: Humanitarianism in Crisis.* London: Vintage.

Rheingold, H. (1993) *The Virtual Community: Homesteading on the Electronic Frontier.* Reading, MA: Addison-Wesley.

Richey, L. A. and Ponte, S. (2011) *Brand Aid: Shopping Well to Save the World.* Minneapolis, MN: University of Minnesota Press.

Risse, M. (2005) 'How does the global order harm the poor?' *Philosophy and Public Affairs,* 33(4), 349–376.

Ron, J., Ramos, H. and Rodgers, K. (2005) 'Transnational information politics: NGO human rights reporting, 1986–2000.' *International Studies Quarterly,* 49(3), 557–588.

Rorty, R. (1989) *Contingency, Irony, and Solidarity.* Cambridge: Cambridge University Press.

———. (1993) 'Human rights, rationality, and sentimentality.' In Shute, S. and S. Hurley (eds) *On Human Rights (Oxford Amnesty Lectures) 1993.* NY: Basic Books.

Rose, N. (1985) *The Psychological Complex: Psychology, Politics, and Society in England, 1869–1939.* London: Routledge & Kegan Paul.

———. (1999) *Powers of Freedom: Reframing Political Thought.* Cambridge: Cambridge University Press.

Roseneil, S. (2006) 'The ambivalence of Angel's "arrangement": A psychosocial lens on the contemporary condition of personal life.' *The Sociological Review,* 54(4), 847–869.

Ruse, M. (1991) 'The Significance of Evolution.' in Singer, P. (ed.) *A Companion to Ethics.* (pp. 500–510) Oxford: Blackwell.

Rusthon, J. P. (1982) 'Social Learning Theory and the Development of Prosocial Behavior.' in Eisenberg, N. (ed.) *The Development of Prosocial Behaviour.* NY: Academic Press.

Rustin, M. (1991) *The Good Society and the Inner World: Psychoanalysis, Politics and Culture.* London: Verso.

Sabat, S. R. (2001) *The Experience of Alzheimer's Disease: Life through a Tangled Veil.* Oxford: Blackwell.

———. (2003) 'Malignant Positioning.' In Harré, R. and Moghaddam, F. M. (eds) *The Self and Others.* (pp. 85–98) Westport CT: Praeger.

Salovey, P., Mayer, J. D. and Rosenham, D. L. (1991) 'Mood and Helping: Mood as a Motivator of Helping and as a Regulator of Mood.' in Clark, M. S. (ed.) *Review of Personality and Social Psychology: Vol.12. Prosocial behavir.* (pp. 215–237) London: Sage.

Sandler, J. (1985) 'Towards a reconsideration of the psychoanalytic theory of motivation.' *Bulletin of the Anna Freud Centre,* 8: 223–244.

———. (1986) 'Comments on the Self and Its Objects.' In Lax, R. F., Bach, S. and Burland, J. A. (eds) *Self and Object Constancy. Clinical and Theoretical Perspectives.* The Guildford Press: New York and London.

Sandler, J., Holder, A. and Meers, D. (1963) 'The Ego Ideal and the Ideal Self.' *The Psychoanalytic Study of the Child,* Vol XVIII, New York: International University Press.

Sandler, J. and Rosenblatt, B. (1962) 'The Concept of the Representational World.' In Sandler, J. and Rosenblatt, B. (eds) *The Psychoanalytic Study of the Child,* Vol XVII. New York: International University Press.

Schafer, R. (1960) 'The loving and beloved superego in Freud's structural theory.' *The Psychoanalytic Study of the Child,* 15:163–188.

Scheffler, S. (2010) 'Morality and Partiality.' In Cottingham, J. and Feltham, B. (eds) *Partiality and Impartiality: Morality, Special Relationships, and the Wider World.* Oxford: Oxford University Press.

Schroeder, D. A., Penner, L. A., Dovidio, J. F. and Piliavin, J. A. (1995) *The Psychology of Helping and altruism: problems and puzzles.* London: McGraw-Hill, Inc.

Schwartz, S. H. (1992) 'Universals in the Content and Structure of Values: Theoretical Advances and Empirical Tests in 20 countries.' In Zanna, M. (ed.) *Advances in Experimental Social Psychology.* (Vol. 25 pp. 1–65) Orlando, FL: Academic Press.

Schwartz, S. and Boehnke, K. (2004) 'Evaluating the structure of human values with confirmatory factor analysis.' *Journal of Research in Personality,* 38, 230–255.

Schwartz, S. H. and Gottlieb, A. (1976) 'Bystander reactions to a violent theft: Crime in Jerusalem.' *Journal of Personality and Social Psychology,* 34, 1188–1199.

Schwartz, S. H. and Howard, J. A. (1982) 'Helping and Cooperation: A Self-Based Motivational Model.' In Derlega, V. J. and Grzelak, J. (eds) *Cooperation and Helping Behavior: Theories and Research.* (pp. 327–353) New York: Academic Press.

Searle, J. (1969) *Speech Acts: An Essay in the Philosophy of Language.* Cambridge: Cambridge University Press.

Seaton, K. (2005) *Carnage and the Media: The Making of Breaking News about Violence.* London: Allen Lane.

Selznic, P. (1992) *The Moral Commonwealth: Social Theory and the Promise of Community.* Berkeley, CA: University of California Press.

Seu, I. B. (2003) 'Your stomach makes you feel that you don't want to know anything about it': Desensitization, defence mechanisms and rhetoric in response to and Human Rights abuses.' *Journal of Human Rights,* .2(2), 183–196.

———. (2010) ' "Doing Denial": Audiences' reactions to human rights appeals.' *Discourse and Society,* 21. (4): 438–457.

———. (2011a) ' "Shoot the messenger": Dynamics of positioning and denial in response to human rights appeals.' *Journal of Human Rights Practice,* 3(2), 139–161.

———. (2011b) 'Virtual Bystanders to Human Rights Abuses: A Psychosocial Analysis.' In Cushman, T. (ed.) *Handbook of Human Rights.* (pp. 533–547). London: Routledge.

———. (forthcoming) *Bystanders to Human Rights Abuses: The Psychology of Inaction.* Cambridge: Cambridge University Press

Shaw, L. L., Batson, C. D. and Todd, R. M. (1994) 'Empathy avoidance: Forestalling feeling for another in order to escape the motivational consequences.' *Journal of Personality and Social Psychology,* 67(5), 878–887.

Short, D. (2009) 'Sociological and Anthropological Approaches.' In Goodhart, M. (ed.) *Human Rights*. Oxford: Oxford University Press.

Sibley, D. (1995) *Geographies of Exclusion: Society and Difference in the West*. London: Routledge.

Silverstone, R. (2007) *Media and Morality: On the Rise of the Mediapolis*. Cambridge: Polity.

Singer, P. (1972) 'Famine, affluence and morality.' *Philosophy and Public Affairs*, 1(3), 229–243.

———. (2004) 'Outsiders: Our Obligations to Those Beyond Our Borders.' In Chatterjee, D. (ed.) *The Ethics of Assistance: Morality and the Distant Needy*. Cambridge: Cambridge University Press.

———. (2009) *The Life You Can Save: Acting Now to End World Poverty*. London: Picador.

Sliwinski, S. (2009) 'The aesthetics of human rights.' *Culture, Theory and Critique*, 50(1), 23–39.

Slovic, P. (2007a) ' "If I look at the mass I will never act" ': Psychic numbing and genocide.' *Judgement and Decision Making*, 2, 79–95.

Slovic, P. (2007b) 'Psychic numbing and genocide.' *Psychological Science Agenda*, 21, 1–19.

Slovic, S. and Slovic, P. (2004) 'Numbers and nerves: Toward an affective apprehension of environmental risk.' *Whole Terrain*, 13, 14–18.

Small, D. A. and Loewenstein, G. (2003) 'Helping a victim or helping the victim: Altruism and identifiability.' *Journal of Risk and Uncertainty*, 26(1), 5.

———. (2007) 'Sympathy and callousness: The impact of deliberative thought on donations to identifiable and statistical victims.' *Organizational Behavior and Human Decision Processes*, 102(2), 143–153.

Smart, B. (1985) *Michael Foucault*. London: Tavistock Publications.

Smiley, M. (1992) *Moral Responsibility and the Boundaries of Community: Power and Accountability from a Pragmatic Point of View*. Chicago: Chicago University Press.

Smith, A. (2002) *The Theory of the Moral Sentiment*. Cambridge: Cambridge University Press.

Smith, D. M. (1994) *Geography and Social Justice*. Oxford: Blackwell.

———. (1997a) 'Back to the good life: towards an enlarged conception of social justice.' *Environment and Planning D: Society and Space*, 15, 19–35.

———. (1997b) 'Geography and ethics: A moral turn?' *Progress in Human Geography*, 21, 596–603.

Solomon, R. C. (1995) 'Justice as Vengeance, Vengeance as Justice: A partial Defence of Polymarchus.' In Sterba, J. P., Machan, T. R., Jagger, A. M., Galston, W. A., Gould, C. C., Fisk, M. and Solomon, R. C. (eds) *Morality and Social Justice: Point/Counterpoint*. (pp. 251–300) London: Rowman & Littlefield.

Solomon, L. Z., Solomon, H. and Stone, R. (1978) 'Helping as a function of number of bystanders and ambiguity of emergency.' *Personality and Social Psychology Bulletin*, 4, 318–321.

Sontag, S. (2003) *Regarding the Pain of Others*. London: Penguin.

Sorokin, P. (1954) *The Ways of Power and Love*. Boston: Beacon Press.

Staszak, Jean-Francois. (2008) 'Other/Otherness.' In Thrift, N. and R. Kitchin (eds) *International Encyclopaedia of Human Geography*. Amsterdam: Elsevier.

Staub, E. (1989a) *The Roots of Evil. The Origins of Genocide and Other Group Violence*. Cambridge and New York: Cambridge University Press.

———. (1989b) 'The evolution of bystanders, German psychoanalysts and lessons for today.' *Political Psychology*, 10(1), 39–52.

———. (1990) 'Moral exclusion, personal goal theory, and extreme destructiveness.' *Journal of Social Issues*, 46(1), 47–64.

———. (1993) 'The Psychology of bystanders, perpetrators, and heroic helpers.' *International Journal of Intercultural Relations*, 17, 315–341.

———. (1996) 'Responsibility, helping, aggression, and evil.' *Psychological inquiry*, 7(3), 252–254.

———. (2003) *The Psychology of Good and Evil.* Cambridge: Cambridge University Press.

Sterba, J. P. (1981) 'The welfare rights of distant peoples and future generations: Moral sideconstraints on social policy.' *Social Theory and Practice*, 7, 99–119.

Sterba, J. P., Machan, T. R., Jagger, A. M., Galston, W. A., Gould, C. C., Fisk, M. and Solomon, R. C. (eds) (1995) *Morality and Social Justice: Point/Counterpoint.* London: Rowman & Littlefield.

Sturmer, S., Snyder, M. and Omoto, A. M. (2005) 'Prosocial emotions and helping: The moderating role of group membership.' *Journal of Personality and Social Psychology*, 88(3), 532–546.

Supphellen, M. and Nelson, M. R. (2001) 'Developing, exploring, and validating a typology of private philanthropic decision making.' *Journal of Economic Psychology*, 22(5), 573–603.

Swinyard, W. R. and Ray, M. L. (1979) 'Effects of praise and small requests on receptivity to direct mail appeals.' *Journal of Social Psychology*, 108, 177–184.

Sykes, G. M. and Matza, D. (1957) *Techniques of Neutralisation: A Theory of Delinquency.* Princeton, NJ: Princeton University Press.

Sypnowich, C. (1993) 'Justice, community, and antinomies of feminist theory.' *Political Theory*, 21, 484–506.

Tajfel, H., Billig, M., Bundy, R. P. and Flarnent, C. (1971) 'Social categorization and intergroup behaviour.' *European Journal of Social Psychology*, 1, 149–178.

Tajfel, H. and Turner, J. C. (1985) 'The Social Identity Theory of Intergroup Behavior.' In Worchel, S. and Austin, W. G. (eds) *Psychology of Intergroup Relations.* (pp. 6–24) Chicago: Nelson-Hall.

Taylor, J. (1998) *Body Horror: Photojournalism, Catastrophe and War.* New York: NYU Press.

Tester, K. (2001) *Compassion, Morality and the Media.* Buckingham: Open University Press.

Thomas, A. (1982) *Frank Terpil: Confessions of a Dangerous Man.* [Film] Available from New York: Studio Film & Tape, Inc.

Thomas, G. and Batson, C. D. (1981) 'Effect of helping under normative pressure on self-perceived altruism.' *Social Psychology Quarterly*, 44, 127–131.

Thomas, G. C., Batson, C. D. and Coke, J. S. (1981) 'Do Good Samaritans discourage helpfulness?: Self-perceived altruism after exposure to highly helpful others.' *Journal of Personality and Social Psychology*, 40, 194–200.

Thompson, J. (1990) *Ideology and Modern Culture: Social Theory of the Media.* Cambridge: Polity.

Tierney, K., Bevc, C. and Kuligowski, E. (2006) 'Metaphors matter: Disaster myths, media frames, and their consequences in Hurricane Katrina.' *Annals, AAPSS*, 604: 57–81.

Tileagă, C . (2005a) 'Accounting for extreme prejudice and legitimating blame in talk about the Romanies.' *Discourse and Society*, 16(5), 603–624.
———. (2005b) 'Talking about integration and discrimination.' *International Journal of Critical Psychology*, 14, 119–137.
———. (2006) 'Representing the "Other".' *Journal of Community and Applied Social Psychology*, 16(1), 19–41.
Titmus, R. (1971) *The Gift Relationship*. London: Pantheon Books.
TNS. (2010) 'UK general public attitudes to towards development 2010.' Presentation for DFID/COI.
Tronto, J. (1987) 'Beyond gender difference to a theory of care.' *Signs: Journal of Women in Culture and Society*, 12, 645–663.
———. (1993) *Moral Boundaries: A Political Argument for an Ethic of Care*. London: Routledge.
Tuan, Y. F. (1989) *Morality and Imagination: Paradoxes of Progress*. Madison, WI: University of Wisconsin Press.
Turner, B. (1993) 'Outline of a theory of human rights.' *Sociology* 27(3), 506.
Turner, J.C. (1982) 'Towards a Cognitive Redefinition of the Social Group.' In H. Tajfel (ed.) *Social Identity and Intergroup Relations*. Cambridge: Cambridge University Press pp.15–40.
Turner, J. C., Hogg, M. A., Oakes, P. J., Reicher, S. and Wetherell, M. S. (1987) *Rediscovering the Social Group: A Self-Categorization Theory*. Oxford: Basil Blackwell.
Van Der Valk, I. (2003) 'Right-wing parliamentary discourse on immigration in France.' *Discourse & Society*, 14(3), 309–348.
Van Dijk, T. A. (1988) *News as Discourse*. Hillsdale, NJ: Erlbaum.
———. (1992) 'Discourse and the denial of racism.' *Discourse and Society*, 3(1), 87–118.
———. (1993a) 'Editor's foreword.' *Discourse & Society*, 4, 131–132.
———. (1993b) 'Principles of critical discourse analysis.' *Discourse & Society*, 4, 249–283.
———. (1993c) *Elite Discourse and Racism*. London: Sage.
———. (2000a) 'New(s) Racism: A Discourse Analytical Approach.' In Cottle, S. (ed.) *Ethnic Minorities and the Media*. (pp. 33–49) Milton Keynes: UK Open University Press.
———. (2000b) 'The Reality of Racism.' In Guido Zurstiege (Hrsg.), On analyzing parliamentary debates on immigration. Festschrift. Für die Wirklichkeit (=Festschrift for Siegfried Schmidt). (pp. 211–226) Wiesbaden: Westdeutscher Verlag.
———. (2002) 'Discourse and Racism.' In Goldberg, D. and Solomos, J. (eds) *The Blackwell Companion to Racial and Ethnic Studies*. (pp. 145–159) Oxford: Blackwell, pp.
Vaughan, K. B. and Lanzetta, J. T. (1980) 'Vicarious instigation and conditioning of facial,expressive and autonomic responses to a model's expressive displays of pain.' *Journal of Personality and Social Psychology*, 38, 909–923.
Vestergaard, A. (2008) 'Branding the humanitarian: The case of Amnesty International.' *Journal of Language and Politics*, 7(3), 200–216.
Vetlesen, A. J. (1993) 'Why does proximity make a moral difference? Coming to terms with lessons learned from the holocaust.' *Praxis International*, 12, 371–386.

Walster, E., Walster, G. W. and Berscheid, E. (1978) *Equity Theory and Research*. Boston: Allyn and Bacon.

Walzer, M. (1983) *Spheres of Justice: A Defence of Pluralism and Equality*. Oxford: Blackwell.

Warren, P. E. and Walker, I. (1991) 'Empathy, effectiveness and donations to charity: Social psychology's contribution.' *British Journal of Social Psychology*, 30, 325–337.

Weintrobe, S. (ed.) (2013) *Engaging with Climate Change: Psychoanalytic and Interdisciplinary Perspectives*. London: Routledge.

Wenar, L. (2011) 'Poverty is No Pond: Challenges for the Affluent.' In Illingworth, P., Pogge, T. and Wenar, L. (eds) *Giving Well: The Ethics of Philanthropy*. Oxford: Oxford University Press.

Wetherell, M. (2012) *Affect and Emotion: A New Social Science Understanding*. London: Sage.

Wetherell, M. and Potter, J. (1992) *Mapping the Language of Racism: Discourse and the Legitimation of Exploitation*. Hemel Hempstead: Harvester Wheatsheaf.

——— (1988) 'Discourse Analysis and the Identification of Interpretative Repertoires.' In Antaki, C. (ed.) *Analysing Everyday Explanations*. London: Sage.

Wiggins, D. (1998) 'What Is the Force of the Claim that One Needs Something?' In Brock, G. (ed.) *Necessary Goods: Our Responsibility to Meet Others' Needs*. Lanham, MD: Rowman & Littlefield.

Williamson, G. M. and Clark, M.S. (1989) 'Providing help and desired relationship type as determinants of changes in mood and self-evaluations.' *Journal of Personality and Social Psychology*, 56, 722–734.

Wodak, R. (2004) 'Critical Discourse Analysis.' In Seale, C., Gobo, G., Gubrium, J. F. and Silverman, D. (eds) *Qualitative Research Practice*. London: Sage.

Wodak, R. and Meyer, M. (2001) *Methods of Critical Discourse Analysis*. London: Sage Publications.

Wolheilm, R. (1991) *Freud*. 2nd Ed. London: Fontana Press/Harper Collins.

Wood, L. A. and Kroger, R. O. (2000) *Doing Discourse Analysis: Methods for Studying Action in Talk and Text*. London: Sage.

Wright Mills, C. (1940) Situated actions and vocabularies of motives. *American Sociological Review*. 904–13.

Wumser, L. (1981) *The Mask of Shame*. London: The John Hopkins University Press.

Yinon, Y. and Landau, M. O. (1987) 'On the reinforcing value of helping behavior in a positive mood.' *Motivation and Emotion*, 11(1), 83–93.

Yuval-Davis, N. (2006) 'Belonging and the politics of belonging.' *Patterns of Prejudice*, 40(3), 197–214.

Zagefka, H. and R. Brown. (2008) 'Monetary donations following humanitarian disasters: Full research report.' ESRC End of Award Report. RES-000-22-1817. Swindon: ESRC.

Zizek, S. (2001) 'Njutning förbjuden.' *Dagens Nyheter*. 22 August.

Zolberg, A. and Woon, L. (1990) 'Why Islam is like Spanish: Cultural incorporation in Europe and the United States.' *Politics and Society*, 27(1), 5–38.

Index

Note: The letters 'f' and 't' following locators refer to figures and tables

Printed and bound in the United States of America